This book is dedicated to all who have served in the armed forces, as well as to those in higher education who have committed their lives to providing all students—including our student veterans—with the opportunity for an extraordinary education.

CONTENTS

ACKNOWLEDGMENTS

Special Thanks

The authors would like to thank the following colleagues, who contributed materially to this text:

Jason Dean, Veteran, U.S. Army (SGT). Mr. Dean was president of Northern State University's Veterans Club, where he received a BA in political science. Mr. Dean is currently serving as the associate registrar and veterans coordinator at the University of South Dakota (USD), where he is also pursuing an MS in administration.

LeighAnn Dunn, Veteran, U.S. Army (SPC). Ms. Dunn received a BS in communication disorders and an MA in multicategorical special education from the University of South Dakota. She served as president of the USD Veterans Club, which is a chapter of the Student Veterans of America. Ms. Dunn is currently pursuing an EdD in adult and higher education with a focus on veterans in postsecondary education at the University of South Dakota.

Casey Fideler, Veteran, U.S. Navy, HM3 (FMF). Mr. Fideler received a BS in business administration and accounting and a JD from the University of South Dakota. He cofounded the Veterans' Legal Education Group at the University of South Dakota. Mr. Fideler has also received an LLM in taxation from the University of Florida.

Eric Gage, U.S. Air Force (SSG). Mr. Gage received a BA in history and a BS in political science from the University of South Dakota. He served as president of the USD Veterans Club, which is a chapter of the Student Veterans of America. Mr. Gage remains very active in the South Dakota veterans' community.

Dusty Ginsbach, U.S. Army (SSG). Mr. Ginsbach received a BS in criminal justice from Chadron State College. He is currently pursuing a JD at the University of South Dakota and is president of the USD Veterans' Legal Education Group. Mr. Ginsbach serves as a graduate teaching assistant in USD's Center for Teaching and Learning, where he focuses on student veteran success.

Edward S. Hruska III, U.S. Marine Corps (Cpl). Mr. Hruska received a BS in sociology with minors in criminal justice and English from South Dakota State University. He served as the president of the South Dakota State Veterans' Club. Mr. Hruska served as a graduate teaching assistant in USD's Center for Teaching and Learning, where he focused on student veteran success. He is currently pursuing a JD from the University of South Dakota.

Thomas Martin, U.S. Army (LTC, Ret.). LTC Martin attended South Dakota State University on a Four Year Army Reserve Officers' Training Corps (ROTC) Scholarship and was a distinguished military graduate with a BS in history. He later earned an MS in logistics management from the Florida Institute of Technology. LTC Martin served more than twenty-one years on active duty in the Regular Army, and his final assignment was chair of the Military Science Department and commander of the ROTC Battalion at the University of South Dakota.

Lisa Schindele, Veteran, U.S. Marine Corps (Sgt). Ms. Schindele received a BS in human resource management from Park University while serving in the Marines and completed her MBA at the University of Phoenix. She also served as an instructional designer with USD's Center for Teaching and Learning, where she trained faculty to better understand and serve student veterans.

Larry Tentinger, U.S. Navy (CPO, Ret.). Dr. Tentinger received a BSEd in physical education and health, an MA in health education, and an EdD in adult and higher education from the University of South Dakota. He is an emeriti professor in the Division of Kinesiology and Sport Science at the University of South Dakota. He served in combat with the Army in Vietnam, the Navy in Desert Storm, and the Marines during three tours in Iraq. Dr. Tentinger is designated as a Fleet Marine Warfare Specialist and holds the distinction of being selected as the 2004 Navy Reserve Force Sailor of the Year.

Additional Acknowledgments

The photo on page 182 is provided courtesy of University of South Dakota (© 2010)

I am focused on a goal to get into graduate school. I don't have time to deal with the kid stuff. And I'm 20. I should be a kid. I'm told that all the time "you need to relax" but if I were to ask any professor or even you, you don't necessarily get to where you are by partying five days a week. It's not going to work. It won't happen. I have a goal.

—Martin, Air Force veteran (Wheeler, 2011, p. 117)

This book began in 2009 as a partnership between the Center for Teaching and Learning and the Office of Disabilities Services at the University of South Dakota (USD). The directors were searching for a way to obtain grant funding and were passionate about training faculty and staff to better serve student veterans with disabilities. Through their efforts, the Fides (pronounced "fee-days") program came into being.[1] The goal of this program was to phase in, over three years, high-quality, evidence-based development opportunities specifically designed to enable key university constituencies—the faculty, staff, and administration—to understand their role in providing extraordinary learning experiences for every veteran returning from Operations Enduring Freedom and Iraqi Freedom. The program was funded in 2010 through a congressionally directed Fund for the Improvement of Postsecondary Education (FIPSE) grant. Materials from Fides have been featured by prominent educational organizations and are being used by the National Center for Posttraumatic Stress Disorder (PTSD), colleges, universities, and boards of regents across this nation. This book represents one of the culminating outcomes from this grant and presents best practices for faculty, staff, and administration in serving student veterans.

Student veterans are returning to higher education in record numbers and with tremendous resources. They are financially independent, disciplined, and goal-oriented. Data on persistence and graduation rates show that they are also a student population at risk, and it is our hope that the material contained in this book will enable institutions to minimize this risk, to build on student veterans' strengths, and to help these students realize the tremendous potential that they possess.

This book could not have been written without the help of a great many people. We would like to thank our partners, spouses, and children, who allowed us to take the time necessary to complete this project. We would also like to thank the many members of our immediate families who have served in the military. We are proud of you and thankful for your service. We would like to thank the student veterans from two campuses, Monroe Community College (Rochester, New York) and the University of South Dakota, for being willing to share their lives with us. We offer a special thanks to Darin Jerke, USD Center for Teaching and Learning, and to Carol Kelley for providing editing assistance. Your thoughts were invaluable! Thanks to John von Knorring, president of Stylus, for his assistance and support, and thanks to Laura Jenski and the staff of USD's Office of Sponsored Programs and Research for all your assistance with the Fides grant.

Finally, a special thank you to all our student veterans. It is our goal that higher education will serve you as well as you have served this nation.

Bruce Kelley, Justin Smith, Ernetta Fox, and Holly Wheeler
December 15, 2012
Vermillion, South Dakota, and Rochester, New York

The material in this book was developed under a congressionally directed grant administered through the U.S. Department of Education. However, it does not necessarily represent the policy of the Department of Education and does not assume endorsement by the federal government.

Endnote

1. *Fides* is Latin for "promise."

Reference

Wheeler, H. A. (2011). *From soldier to student: A case study of veterans' transitions to first-time community college students* (Doctoral dissertation). Available from Pro-Quest Dissertations and Theses Database. (UMI No. 3465899)

PART ONE

THE STRENGTHS OF OUR STUDENT VETERANS AND THE CHALLENGES THEY FACE

I

SETTING THE STAGE

Student Veterans in Higher Education

I came home May 17th. I started classes May 27th.

—Wayne, former Marine (Wheeler, 2011, p. 108)[1]

The Servicemen's Readjustment Act of 1944 was passed on June 22, just sixteen days after the D-day invasion of the Normandy beaches. This act stipulated that "any person who served in the active military or naval forces . . . shall be entitled to vocational rehabilitation . . . or to education or training." Service members were paid "the customary cost of tuition, and such laboratory, library, health, infirmary and other similar fees as are customarily charged, and may pay for books, supplies, equipment, and other necessary expenses" (Servicemen's Readjustment Act of 1944). This act became known as the GI Bill, and by 1950 more than 6 million veterans had enrolled in college using these benefits, changing the face of higher education. Educational benefits have been provided to military veterans ever since through a succession of legislative acts. The Post-9/11 Veterans Educational Assistance Act (often called the Post-9/11 GI Bill) was passed in 2009 and is the newest legislative version of this benefit. A unique feature of the Post-9/11 GI Bill is that benefits can be transferred to a spouse or child under certain circumstances, and the U.S. Department of Veterans Affairs (VA) estimates that 594,000 student veterans or their dependents received federal aid from this program in 2012 (College Board Advocacy & Policy Center, 2012, p. 18). The Post-9/11 GI Bill generally increases the benefits for military veterans and their dependents compared to the previous (1984) Montgomery GI Bill (Radford, 2009, pp. 1–2), and as a result a new wave of student veterans is entering postsecondary education. Although not as numerically dominant as their 1944 predecessors, it seems likely that they too will leave their mark on higher education.

Students who are active-duty service members, reservists, members of the National Guard, and veterans (referred to throughout the rest of this book as

3

"student veterans" or "military students")[2] constituted 4.2% of the total undergraduate population in the United States during the 2007–2008 academic year—a total of 875,000 students enrolled nationwide (Radford & Wun, 2009). Recent drawdowns in the U.S. military, coupled with the Post-9/11 GI Bill, have more than doubled this number, and 88.2% of the institutions that participated in the most recent American Council on Education (ACE) survey indicated that they had experienced moderate or substantial gains in student veteran enrollment (McBain, Kim, Cook, & Snead, 2012, pp. 7–8, 49). ACE predicts that almost 2 million veterans returning from the Iraq and Afghanistan Wars have enrolled or will soon enroll in postsecondary education (American Council on Education, 2008, p. 1). Institutions that can leverage the strengths of student veterans and that can ease the challenges of their transition to higher education will find that they add immeasurably to the educational experiences of the entire academic community.

Student veterans enter higher education with many advantages, for the experience of serving in the armed forces provides "greater self-efficacy, enhanced identity and a sense of purposefulness, pride, camaraderie, etc." (Litz & Orsillo, 2004, p. 21). As one student veteran stated,

> I am much more driven than I would have been had I attended school right after high school. I see the value, not only monetarily, but [in terms of] time and effort, in putting forth the necessary effort to excel at my studies. (Doenges, 2011, p. 55)

Student veterans have financial independence from their parents and have had professional training and development opportunities that will benefit their experience in college (Dalton, 2010, p. 1). Enlistment in the armed forces results in higher levels of college enrollment and increases the likelihood of attaining a two-year degree—albeit after a time lapse of 16 years (Loughran, Martorell, Miller, & Klerman, 2011, pp. 40, 49).

Student veterans also face significant challenges. According to the National Center for Education Statistics (NCES), veterans are 21.2 percentage points less likely than nonveterans to attain a bachelor's degree and are 4.1 percentage points more likely to drop out of postsecondary institutions without attaining a degree of any sort. The number of veterans who have an average collegiate GPA below 1.75 is 59.5%, and only 26.5% expect to achieve a bachelor's degree or higher. Student veterans have typically been out of school for some time when they transition back to higher education and are more likely to have earned average grades while in high school (Kingsbury, 2007, p. 71). Six-year graduation rates tend to be lower for student veterans, but this measure may not be the most effective way of judging student veteran success. Any student who is deployed, for example, will miss at least

Figure 1.1 Risk Index for Student Success in Higher Education (U.S. Department of Education, 2011).

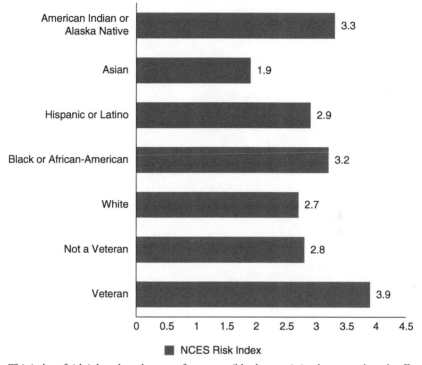

■ NCES Risk Index

This index of risk is based on the sum of seven possible characteristics that may adversely affect persistence and attainment: delayed enrollment, type of high school degree, attendance pattern, dependency status, single parent status, has dependents, and work intensity while enrolled.

one year of college, and enlistment clearly delays graduation (Loughran et al., 2011, p. 49). As a result of these and other factors, veterans have a higher risk index for success in postsecondary education than any racial or ethnic minority (see Figure 1.1).

In addition to these risk factors, student veterans may experience transitional challenges as they leave the military and enter higher education. The challenges associated with this transition are heightened when a student has a disability, for these students may need additional resources to succeed.

Veterans value education and believe that it is a priority despite the challenges they face. The military's educational benefits play a substantial role in a person's decision to enlist and provide potential students with high educational aspirations the means to attain their goals (Kleykamp, 2006, p. 286). As one currently enlisted student said, "I am taking classes. I don't see myself ever stopping. There is so much to learn out there. I want to go as far as I can" (Cook & Kim, 2009, p. 20). Student veterans have resources that many at-risk

Figure 1.2 Total Student Aid for Veterans Used to Finance Postsecondary Educa-tion Expenses in Constant 2011 Dollars (in Millions), 2000–2001 to 2011–2012 (College Board Advocacy & Policy Center, 2012, p. 10).

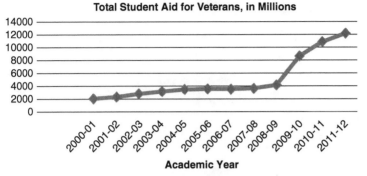

Note: Data from the VA indicates that 40% of student financial aid from the GI Bill goes to public institutions (both two-year and four-year), 24% goes to private nonprofit institutions, and 36% goes to for-profit institutions (College Board Advocacy & Policy Center, 2011, p. 16).

student populations do not have. As illustrated in Figure 1.2, federal student aid for veterans increased 424% from 2001 to 2012, even after adjusting for inflation. During the 2008–2009 academic year the federal government provided $4.1 billion in financial aid to veterans, but this amount jumped to more than $12.2 billion by 2011–2012 owing to the effects of the Post-9/11 GI Bill (College Board Advocacy & Policy Center, 2012, p. 10).

Given these resources, institutions that can successfully recruit and retain student veterans will find themselves at a competitive advantage, especially in an era of tight fiscal resources and increasing pressure to make ends meet.

Returning service members bring great strengths to higher education. They are mature, have had significant life experiences, and bring a cross-cultural awareness to the college campus. One of their greatest strengths is that they are highly motivated to serve others. The same NCES report that indicated that veterans are at high risk for academic failure also documents that they volunteer more hours per month (22.9) than any other demo-graphic and 7.6 hours more on average than nonveteran students. Colleges and universities can build on these strengths to develop academic programs that enrich both the institution and its community. Institutions that wish to enhance student veteran success in significant ways also need to develop holistic initiatives to mediate student veterans' transition into higher educa-tion. Colleges and universities can fulfill the educational promise of each student veteran only by recognizing both their strengths and their challenges. As one Army veteran noted, "A resilient service member and a truly military-supportive school is a powerful partnership!" (Zackal, 2012).

Who Are Our Student Veterans?

Veterans returning to school under the Post-9/11 GI Bill are demographically different from the typical incoming first-year student. A total of 84.5% of all military undergraduates in the classroom are older than the traditional college student, 47.3% are married, and 47.0% have children, including 14.5% who are single parents (Radford & Wun, 2009). Military members and veterans as a group seek associate's degree programs at two-year colleges at a higher rate than the traditional college population (see Tables 1.1 and 1.2). Combat and noncombat veterans are more racially diverse than nonveterans, more likely to be first-generation college students, and more likely to have attended public schools than the nonveteran population (National Survey of Student Engagement, 2010, p. 17). Almost 77% of student veterans attended school part-time during the 2007–2008 academic year, and only 37.7% of military undergraduates used veterans' education benefits (see Table 1.3). Combat veterans who are first-year students are five times more likely to be transfer students and eight times more likely to enroll in distance-learning courses than nonveteran first-year students (see Table 1.4).

Finally, student veterans are overwhelmingly male compared to the general student population: 73.1% of undergraduate student veterans are male, compared to 35.2% of nontraditional nonmilitary students and 47.1% of traditional nonmilitary students (Radford, 2009, p. 7). Student veterans, as these data show, differ in important ways from the "traditional" student

TABLE 1.1
Distribution of Undergraduates by Military Status and Institution of Enrollment (Radford & Wun, 2009, p. 6)

Institution Type	Percentage of Military Service Members and Veterans Who Attend	Percentage of Non-military, Dependent Undergraduates Who Attend
Public 2-Year	43.3%	32.2%
Public 4-Year	21.4%	38.2%
Private Not-for-Profit 4-Year	13.5%	16.3%
Private For-Profit	12.4%	4.1%
Other or Attended More than One Institution	9.4%	9.2%
TOTAL	**100%**	**100%**

Source of Data: 2007–2008 National Postsecondary Student Aid Study

TABLE 1.2
Distribution of Undergraduates by Military Status and Degree Program (Radford & Wun, 2009, p. 6)

Degree Program	Percentage of Military Service Members and Veterans Who Are Enrolled in the Following Degree Programs	Percentage of Nonmilitary, Dependent Undergraduates Who Are Enrolled in the Following Degree Programs
Certificate	5.4%	3.9%
Associate's Degree	46.9%	32.8%
Bachelor's Degree	41.9%	59.3%
Not in a Degree Program or Other	5.8%	4.0%
TOTAL	**100%**	**100%**

Source of Data: 2007–2008 National Postsecondary Student Aid Study

TABLE 1.3
Distribution of Undergraduates by Military Status and Attendance Status (Radford & Wun, 2009, p. 6)

Attendance Status	Military Service Members and Veterans	Nonmilitary, Dependent Undergraduates
Full-Time/Full Year	23.4%	56.2%
Full-Time/Part Year	16.4%	13.8%
Part-Time/Full Year	23.1%	16.5%
Part-Time/Part Year	37.1%	13.4%
TOTAL	**100%**	**99.9%**

Source of Data: 2007–2008 National Postsecondary Student Aid Study

body. Programs and services that are designed to assist first-time full-time students may not be ideal for reaching student veterans.

Student Veterans and Disabilities

Veterans returning from Operation Iraqi Freedom (OIF), Operation Enduring Freedom (OEF), and Operation New Dawn (OND) are unique from past generations of veterans. Advances in body armor, vehicle protection, medical procedures, and treatment mean that a greater number of these veterans will be enrolling in college with both visible and invisible disabilities. The percentage of OIF, OEF, and OND veterans who have disabilities is

TABLE 1.4
Student Characteristics by Veteran Status and Class Level, by Percentage (NSSE, 2010, p. 17)

Student Characteristic	Non-veteran First-Year Student	Non-veteran Senior Student	Veteran, Non-combat First-Year Student	Veteran, Non-combat Senior Student	Veteran, Combat First-Year Student	Veteran, Combat Senior Student
Percentage of Students with Transfer Credit	9%	41%	28%	71%	45%	80%
Percentage of Students Pursuing a Degree by Distance Education	2%	6%	11%	20%	16%	28%

Source of Data: 2007–2008 National Postsecondary Student Aid Study

uncertain, but estimates range as high as 40% (American Council on Education, 2010, p. 1; Grossman, 2009, p. 4). These disabilities can complicate a student's transition to college, and higher education must devise ways to proactively and respectfully address these challenges if we are to offer all our student veterans the greatest prospect for success.

Blasts are the most common cause of combat injuries (Gawande, 2004; Gondusky & Reiter, 2005; and Murray et al., 2005), but also prevalent are projectile injuries from "bullets and fragments, transportation accidents, and other environmental and combat hazards" (Kennedy et al., 2007, pp. 895–896). Many veterans have survived amputations; severe burns; hearing and vision loss; and head, spinal, and other serious injuries (Bilmes, 2008, p. 84; Lew, Jerger, Guillory, & Henry, 2007; Thatch et al., 2008). More than 250,000 troops discharged from the military by 2008 required treatment at medical facilities, including at least 100,000 with mental health conditions and 52,000 with posttraumatic stress disorder (PTSD) (Bilmes, 2008). Hoge, Auchterlonie, and Milliken (2006) found that

> the prevalence of reporting a mental health problem was 19.1% among service members returning from Iraq compared with 11.3% after returning from Afghanistan and 8.5% after returning from other locations. . . . Thirty-five percent of Iraq war veterans accessed mental health services in

the year after returning home; 12% per year were diagnosed with a mental health problem. (p. 1023)

In a later study, Hoge et al. (2008) discovered that

of 2525 soldiers, 124 (4.9%) reported injuries with loss of consciousness, 260 (10.3%) reported injuries with altered mental status, and 435 (17.2%) reported other injuries during deployment. Of those reporting loss of consciousness, 43.9% met criteria for post-traumatic stress disorder (PTSD), as compared with 27.3% of those reporting altered mental status, 16.2% with other injuries, and 9.1% with no injury. (p. 453)

Many of the soldiers who need mental health treatment do not report these problems or seek help owing to the stigma of seeking psychiatric assistance, especially in a volunteer army in which a disability designation may be seen as a hindrance to advancement and promotion (Hoge et al., 2004; Litz & Orsillo, 2004).

The studies mentioned here should not be used to stereotype student veterans, and it is important to remember that the majority of student veterans do not have any disability at all. It is clear, however, that a significant percentage of veterans are returning from OIF, OEF, and OND with varying types and degrees of disabilities. It is to the benefit of both these veterans and higher education to create supporting environments for these men and women if we wish to fulfill the promise this country makes to educate its veterans. As Duane (2007) succinctly writes, "Those who have sacrificed so much for our country deserve physical and mental health care, educational opportunities, and a real chance to live fulfilling lives" (p. 2123). It is our conviction that efforts that help the university community better serve returning veterans with disabilities will also have a positive influence on our ability to serve other populations with disabilities. For example, an estimated 5.3 million Americans are living with disabilities that resulted from traumatic brain injuries (TBIs) sustained in car accidents, sports injuries, and the like (Okie, 2005), and evidence suggests that wives of military veterans may be at elevated risk for PTSD (Al-Turkait & Ohaeri, 2008).

Book Overview

Chapters 1 through 3 of this book examine the strengths that student veterans bring to higher education and describe some of the challenges that they face as they pursue their academic dreams. This first chapter has described some of the ways in which military students differ from other student populations and has established why postsecondary institutions need to prepare for student veterans, including those with disabilities, both for the sake of the student and for the health of the institution. Chapter 2 examines the challenges that veterans face as they transition from being soldiers to students. Every branch of the service has a boot camp, at which civilians are trained to think and act like members of the military. Few veterans, however, are given any significant training when they leave the military and reenter civilian life in general, and higher education specifically. This transition is made even more difficult when a student has been deployed overseas, has been in combat, or has been deployed multiple times. Chapter 3 provides an introduction to student disabilities and contains hands-on activities that are designed to help the reader better understand what it means to have a variety of disabilities, especially those that tend to be common for persons with TBI or PTSD. It also examines differences in how the active military, the VA, and the Americans with Disabilities Act Amendments Act (ADAAA) define *disability*. These differences can unfortunately create confusion for student veterans.

Chapters 4 through 7 draw on the challenges underscored in the first three chapters and examine how institutions of higher education can assist their student veterans. Chapter 4 focuses on services and organizations that are often the point of first contact for our student veterans: student recruitment, enrollment management, admissions (and readmissions), orien- tation, and housing. Student veterans must navigate through a complex array of administrative information as they prepare to enter their academic careers, and this chapter examines how policies, procedures, and communication can be streamlined and reorganized to better serve these students. The chapter also explores the difficulties in adequately identifying student veterans. Simply using benefits as an indicator of veteran status, for example, is unreliable because a spouse or dependent can also access certain educational benefits under the Post-9/11 GI Bill. A more robust identification system can account for this and can also differentiate between veterans of current conflicts and those of the last century. Finally, chapter 4 examines a variety of strategies to make your campus "veteran friendly," such as establishing a student veterans club, connecting to extracampus veterans organizations, and creating a veterans' resource center.

Chapter 5 explores the services and organizations veterans are likely to use throughout their academic career, including the VA school certifying official (SCO), the Registrar's Office, Financial Aid, Academic Advising, Career Services, Student Health and Counseling, and Disability Services. This chapter underscores the importance of including veterans in policy-making decisions and explains how to establish an effective veterans task force. Chapter 6 describes innovative approaches to academic programs that can enhance student veterans' success. These programs include summer bridge programs, first-year seminars that focus on transition and resiliency, veterans-specific general education classes, veterans learning communities, and veterans studies programs. The chapter also explores how to connect to the broader veterans' community to improve the educational experience of both student veterans and nonmilitary students. Chapter 7, contributed by Holly Wheeler, associate professor in English from Monroe Community College (Rochester, New York), examines student veteran success specifically from the perspective of two-year institutions. Community colleges face different challenges and advantages when serving student veterans compared to four-year institutions, and this chapter considers the unique characteristics of that experience. This section of the book also highlights several successful two-year programs that have strong records of achievement in serving student veterans.

Chapters 8 through 10 describe the important role that faculty play in enhancing the success of student veterans. Chapter 8 focuses on course structure and design, using Fink's (2003) integrated model as a framework for exploring how to leverage the strengths of student veterans—their proclivity for service, for example—into the course structure. This chapter examines classroom policies ranging from attendance to grading procedures and also discusses the effect that new advances in classroom technology can have on course design and delivery. Finally, it describes how the principles of Universal Design (UD) can be harnessed to support student veteran success.

Chapter 9 looks at classroom management and specific learning activities that can enhance the success of student veterans, relying on the principles of adult learning, Fink's (2003) paradigm of significant learning, and research that has been developed by our center as part of a Fund for the Improvement of Postsecondary Education (FIPSE) grant. This chapter contains a number of concrete means for supporting student veteran success that faculty can specifically adapt for their courses.

Chapter 10 examines the classroom environment from three perspectives: the physical, the emotional, and the behavioral. The physical environment can be a significant barrier for students who have been recently deployed in combat zones and for whom large, unsecured spaces may be distracting. The behavioral environment is likewise important, for the typical classroom presentation differs markedly from the standard military briefing. One of the most interesting findings from our work with military students is how little patience they have for disruptive behaviors exhibited by their fellow students, such as talking, texting, and using their computers for activities not related to the course. Instructors need to understand this frustration, or they run the risk of having that frustration vented on teaching evaluations. Lastly, this chapter considers the emotional environment. What are questions that no veteran should have to answer? How do we identify student veterans, and draw on their expertise, without putting them on the spot? Are there ways that an instructor can structure the classroom to make student veterans feel safe from the discrimination and stereotypes that sometimes greet military students in academia?

The 2012 ACE report on campus programs for veterans and service members indicates that 70.1% of the responding institutions plan to provide professional development for staff within the next five years and that 63.3% plan to provide professional development for faculty (McBain et al., 2012, pp. 15–16). Chapter 11 describes how to create an effective development team and provides a framework for organizing faculty and staff training programs. Collaboration is necessary between Academic Affairs, Centers for Teaching and Learning, Academic Advising, the Registrar, and a host of other campus groups—including, most importantly, the student veterans themselves. The difficulties of navigating through the politics of veterans' issues (understanding, for example, the tensions that underlie regular army verses national guard and combat veterans verses noncombat veterans) are discussed, as are ways to build networks between diverse veterans' constituencies. Chapter 12 brings this book to a close with our concluding thoughts and a call for further action to better serve our student veterans.

Conclusion

There is a great need for faculty, staff, and administration to better understand the challenges that veterans returning from OIF, OEF, and OND face. As Cook and Kim (2009) write, "Veterans are not necessarily looking to be isolated or have special programs created on their behalf. More than anything, they are looking for an educational environment that provides the tools and resources that allow them to succeed" (p. 29). When we provide our student veterans with the opportunity for an extraordinary education, we also enhance the educational experiences of the entire academic community.

Chapter Summary

Veterans are returning to higher education with both unique advantages and challenges. The most significant challenges include transitioning from the military into higher education and overcoming existing and potential disabilities. Institutions that strategically build programs and services around the strengths and challenges of our student veterans fulfill a moral obligation owed these students—and at the same time will find themselves at a competitive advantage in student recruitment and retention. Most importantly, institutions that provide an extraordinary education for their student veterans will find that these students add immeasurably to the academic experiences of the institution as a whole.

Key Points

- There are large numbers of veterans returning from overseas conflicts, and they are enrolling in higher education in significant numbers because of the financial resources they have at their disposal.
- Student veterans have some advantages over other students, including a sense of identity, purposefulness, and pride. They are mature, have had significant life experiences, are motivated to serve others, and have a cross-cultural awareness and firsthand international experience that most students lack.
- Student veterans face significant challenges:
  - Veterans have a higher risk index for success in higher education than any racial or ethnic minority.
  - A significant number of student veterans may have disabilities, and these disabilities are often undiagnosed or unacknowledged owing to students' heightened sense of self-reliance and fear that a disability diagnosis could impede advancement and promotion in the military.
- Institutions that can successfully recruit and retain student veterans fulfill a moral obligation to these students—and will find themselves at a competitive advantage.

Notes

1. Unless indicated otherwise, the names of all veterans have been changed to preserve anonymity.
2. It is important for members of academia to understand that there are significant differences in each of these populations. Some of these men and women have completed their military service, whereas others may still be called into active duty at any time. Some may be participating in classes while in war zones thousands of miles away, whereas others are integral components of the local community. These students share far more similarities than differences as they transition to higher education, however, and in the interest of readability we have decided to refer to all of these populations under the general category of "student veterans" or "military students."

References

Al-Turkait, F. A., & Ohaeri, J. U. (2008). Post-traumatic stress disorder among wives of Kuwaiti veterans of the first Gulf War. *Journal of Anxiety Disorders, 22*(1), 18–31. doi:10.1016/j.janxdis.2007.01.011

American Council on Education. (2008). *Serving those who serve: Higher education and America's veterans* [Issue brief]. Washington DC: Author. Retrieved from http://www.acenet.edu/Content/NavigationMenu/ProgramsServices/Military Programs/serving/Veterans_Issue_Brief_1108.pdf

American Council on Education. (2010). *Accommodating student veterans with traumatic brain injury and post-traumatic stress disorder: Tips for campus faculty and staff.* Washington DC: Author. Retrieved from http://www.acenet.edu/news -room/Pages/Accommodating-Student-Veterans-with-Traumatic-Brain-Injury -and-Post-Traumatic-Stress-Disorder.aspx

Bilmes, L. J. (2008). Iraq's 100-year mortgage. *Foreign Policy, 165*, 84–85.

College Board Advocacy & Policy Center. (2011). *Trends in higher education series: Trends in student aid 2011.* New York: Author. Retrieved from http://trends .collegeboard.org/student-aid

College Board Advocacy & Policy Center. (2012). *Trends in higher education series: Trends in student aid 2012.* New York: Author. Retrieved from http://trends .collegeboard.org/student-aid

Cook, B. J., & Kim, Y. (2009). *From soldier to student: Easing the transition of service members on campus.* Washington DC: American Council on Education.

Dalton, K. S. (2010). *From combat to composition: Meeting the needs of military veterans through postsecondary writing pedagogy* (Master's thesis). Available from Pro-Quest Dissertations and Theses database. (UMI No. 1475346)

Doenges, T. (2011). *Calling and meaningful work among student military veterans: Impact on well-being and experiences on campus* (Doctoral dissertation). Available from ProQuest Dissertations and Theses database. (UMI No. 3468765)

Duane, J. F. (2007). True patriotism. *American Journal of Public Health, 97*(12), 2123.

Fink, L. D. (2003). *Creating significant learning experiences.* San Francisco: Jossey-Bass.

Gawande, A. (2004). Casualties of war—Military care for the wounded from Iraq and Afghanistan. *New England Journal of Medicine, 351*(24), 2471–2475.

Gondusky, J., & Reiter, M. (2005). Protecting military convoys in Iraq: An examination of battle injuries sustained by a mechanized battalion during Operation Iraqi Freedom II. *Military Medicine, 170*(6), 546–549.

Grossman, P. D. (2009). Foreword with a challenge: Leading our campuses away from the perfect storm. *Journal of Postsecondary Education and Disability, 22*(1), 4–9.

Hoge, C. W., Auchterlonie, J. L., & Milliken, C. S. (2006). Mental health problems, use of mental health services and attrition from military service after returning from deployment to Iraq or Afghanistan. *Journal of the American Medical Association, 295*(9), 1023–1032. doi:10.1001/jama.295.9.1023

Hoge, C. W., Castro, C. A., Messer, S. C., McGurk, D., Cotting, D. I., & Koffman, R. (2004). Combat duty in Iraq and Afghanistan, mental health problems, and barriers to care. *New England Journal of Medicine, 351*(1), 13–22. doi:10.1056/NEJMoa040603

Hoge, C. W., McGurk, D., Thomas, J. L., Cox, A. L., Engel, C. C., & Castro, C. A. (2008). Mild traumatic brain injury in U.S. soldiers returning from Iraq. *New England Journal of Medicine, 358*(5), 453–463. doi:10.1056/NEJMoa072972

Kennedy, J. E., Jaffee, M. S., Leskin, G. A., Stokes, J. W., Leal, F. O., & Fitzpatrick, P. J. (2007). Posttraumatic stress disorder and posttraumatic stress disorder-like symptoms and mild traumatic brain injury. *Journal of Rehabilitation Research & Development, 44*(7), 895–920.

Kingsbury, A. (2007, September 24). From combat to the campus. *U.S. News & World Report, 143*(10), 71.

Kleykamp, M. A. (2006). College, jobs or the military? Enlistment during a time of war. *Social Science Quarterly, 87*, 272–290. doi:10.1111/j.1540-6237.2006.00380.x

Lew, H. L., Jerger, J. F., Guillory, S. B., & Henry, J. A. (2007). Auditory dysfunction in traumatic brain injury. *Journal of Rehabilitation Research & Development, 44*(7), 921–928.

Litz, B., & Orsillo, S. M. (2004). The returning veteran of the Iraq War: Background issues and assessment guidelines. In *Iraq War Clinician Guide* (2nd ed.). Washington DC: Department of Veterans Affairs National Center for PTSD. Retrieved from http://www.ptsd.va.gov/professional/manuals/iraq-war-clinician-guide.asp

Loughran, D., Martorell, P., Miller, T., & Klerman, J. A. (2011). *The effect of military enlistment on earnings and education.* Santa Monica, CA: RAND Corporation.

McBain, L., Kim, Y., Cook, B., & Snead, K. (2012). *From soldier to student II: Assessing campus programs for veterans and service members.* Washington DC: American Council on Education. Retrieved from http://www.acenet.edu/news-room/Pages/From-Soldier-to-Student-II.aspx

Murray, C. K., Reynolds, J. C., Schroeder, J. M., Harrison, M. B., Evans, O. M., & Hospenthal, D. R. (2005). Spectrum of care provided at an Echelon II medical unit during Operation Iraqi Freedom. *Military Medicine, 170*(6), 516–520.

National Survey of Student Engagement. (2010). *Major differences: Examining student engagement by field of study—Annual results 2010.* Bloomington: Indiana University Center for Postsecondary Research.

Okie, S. (2005). Traumatic brain injury in the war zone. *New England Journal of Medicine, 352*(20), 2043–2047.

Radford, A. W. (2009). *Military service members and veterans in higher education: What the new GI Bill may mean for post-secondary institutions.* Washington DC: American Council on Education. Retrieved from http://www.acenet.edu/news-room/Pages/Military-Service-Members-and-Veterans-in-Higher-Education-What-the-New-GI-Bill-May-Mean-for-Postsecondary-Institutions-.aspx

Radford, A. W., & Wun, J. (2009). *Issue tables: A profile of military service members and veterans enrolled in postsecondary education in 2007–08* (Issue Tables NCES 2009182). Washington DC: National Center for Educational Statistics. Retrieved from nces.ed.gov/pubs2011/2011163.pdf

Servicemen's Readjustment Act of 1944, Public Law 78–346, 58 Stat. 284m. (1944).

Thatch, A. B., Johnson, A. J., Carroll, R. B., Huchun, A., Ainbinder, D. J., Stutzman, R. D., . . . Fannin, L. A. (2008). Severe eye injuries in the War in Iraq, 2003–2005. *Ophthalmology, 115*(2), 377–382.

U.S. Department of Education. (2011). *National Center for Education Statistics PowerStats* (PowerStats). Washington DC: Author. Retrieved from http://nces.ed.gov/datalab/

Wheeler, H. A. (2011). *From soldier to student: A case study of veterans' transitions to first-time community college students* (Doctoral dissertation). Available from ProQuest Dissertations and Theses database. (UMI No. 3465899)

Zackal, J. (2012). A student veteran's partnership for perseverance. *Higher Ed Jobs Career Articles.* Retrieved from http://www.higheredjobs.com/Articles/articleDisplay.cfm?ID=388&Title=A%20Student%20Veteran%27s%20Partnership%20for%20Perseverance

2

NAVIGATING THE LABYRINTH

The Transitional Experiences of Student Veterans

When I got home I was still driving in the center of the road so that the roadside bombs wouldn't get me. . . . Every time a door slammed a chill would run down my spine, a cold sweat, and [I took] a situational check of my environment; all in a split second. Most around me didn't even notice, unless they saw the first jump.

—Army veteran (personal correspondence, 2010)

T he student veteran's transition to higher education is unique compared to that of other student populations. Goodman, Schlossberg, and Anderson (2006) define a *transition* as "any event or nonevent that results in changed relationships, routines, assumptions, and roles" (p. 33). Military students face significant changes in all these areas as they mobilize for deployment, serve, and then return from deployment to enter higher education:

> Activated Guard and Reserve personnel may anticipate scheduled returns that do not occur . . . and scheduled returns that do occur . . . , but they cannot predict the timing or nature of their orders. . . . Additionally, colleges' and universities' fixed enrollment periods do not predictably coincide with the military's discharging of veterans at any given time. Student veterans must attend to asynchronous expectations and demands of both settings as well as their own personal transitions. (Rumann & Hamrick, 2010, p. 435)

The experience of deployment, return, and in many cases redeployment complicates students' transitions. Combat adds a layer of complexity to the process that is poorly understood. These events cause changes in relationships, disruption of routines, and a change in roles for student veterans returning to higher education.

Military training and immersion into the military culture establish patterns of behavior that can both help and hinder the transitional experience of student veterans. The military works very hard to develop unit cohesiveness, and veterans often speak of feeling isolated when they return to civilian life and leave behind this social support. The military is a purposeful enterprise, an entity in which roles and responsibilities are clearly defined on a 24/7 basis. This may be the antithesis of the stereotypical college student's life. Veterans sometimes report that they are unable to find the same sense of purpose in their classes and express frustration with their (nonveteran) classmates' own lack of purpose and discipline:

> Of course, I look at the other students like little kids who haven't been out in the real world yet. Most of them at 19–23 years of age are still pretty immature. I mean when I was 22 I was working in an Air Evac unit, working with patients usually other people my age coming back from Iraq with shrapnel wounds and other various injuries from war. These kids spend their days on YouTube and have no clue what's going on. I laugh to myself when they try to act like they "understand what's going on" and they don't. Or when they complain about how their life is so "stressful" it makes me want to throw up. (Doenges, 2011, p. 64)

Military students miss the camaraderie of their units and crews, and it is sometimes difficult for them to reestablish roles and relationships when they return to higher education. On the other hand, student veterans often have a profound appreciation for education that other students lack and have a disciplined, goal-oriented mind-set that enables them to mature into formidable scholars.

This chapter examines two profound transitions that student veterans experience. The first transition occurs when a civilian joins the armed forces and goes through the process of being transformed into a member of the military. The second transition occurs when military personnel leave the service and reenter the civilian world to become students in our colleges and universities. Higher education faculty, staff, and administrators must understand both of these transitions if we are to serve student veterans well.

Reader Reflection: Remembering Significant Transitions

Take a few moments and answer these questions for yourself as you consider recent transitions in your life:

1. What were the complicating factors?
2. How would you describe your state of mind?
3. What resources were the most helpful during the transition period?

Becoming Military

Civilians enter the military for a variety of reasons, including an increased sense of patriotism, significant educational benefits, and the desire to serve in an occupation that teaches life skills and discipline (Ackerman, DiRamio, & Mitchell, 2009, p. 6). The military effectively and efficiently changes its inductees from civilians to military personnel through a process called basic training, or "boot camp." This process has been finely honed over decades, and it effectively and efficiently breaks down individuals in order to rebuild them into a specific military mold. It is a process of changing one's mind-set and lifestyle: "A lot of people join because they need that lifestyle change. They were bad before, or hey, they were lonely and needed some sort of organization like to feel they mattered to somebody" (Bryan, former Marine, from Maurin, 2012, p. 59). Each branch of the service has a boot camp, which ranges from eight weeks for the Coast Guard to twelve weeks for the Marine Corps. Boot camp is followed in each branch by some version of advanced training, as outlined in Table 2.1.

TABLE 2.1 Training Cycle of the Military Branches (adapted from Military.com, n.d.)	
Army and Army National Guard	One-week indoctrination and nine weeks basic training, followed by advanced individual training (AIT).
Air Force and Air National Guard	Eight-and-a-half weeks Basic Military Training Program (BMT), followed by Tech School for certain specialties.
Coast Guard	Eight weeks basic training, normally followed by Class A-School training for certain specialties and "Striker" Schools (on-the-job training) for other specialties.
Marine Corps	Twelve weeks basic training, followed by infantry or combat training, followed by military occupational specialty (MOS) training for certain specialties.
Navy	Nine weeks basic training, including "Processing Week," followed by advanced training for certain specialties in "A" School.

The socialization of the military is second to none. The result is a unified force that is capable of executing complex missions in highly hazardous environments. The transformational effects of boot camp are remembered long past the initial training:

> "India! 3096!" I can still hear this chant in my mind. It was my company and platoon number, but it means so much more. The change that happens to a person during boot camp is severe, and it drives every person to heighten some hidden characteristics in themselves. The mean person becomes cruel, the somewhat religious become devout. The bland become bleach and are washed out. (Marine veteran, personal correspondence, 2012)

The initial goal of basic training is identity formation. An individual enters as a civilian and leaves as a soldier, Marine, sailor, coast guardsman, or airman. Graduation from boot camp is not the equivalent of an academic commencement, but rather the celebration of membership into a new family:

> It was a defining moment in my life. A time where the ultimate goal, the highest dream, was to become a Marine. During those months that dream seemed out of reach. It was a tunnel with the light at the end blocked by three Drill Instructors. Unrelenting Marines schooled in the obsession of minutia. But even they eventually gave their approval, and the title of Marine was bestowed. The Marine graduation was attended by most of my family, but I didn't even really mind if they were there. My new family surrounded me. My new brothers. (Marine veteran, personal correspondence, 2012)

This family, forged through the hardships and tribulations of boot camp, becomes one of the most important elements of a new soldier's life.

Military culture reinforces a soldier's new identity with tradition and ritual rooted in history:

> First and foremost, the Army is Soldiers. No matter how much the tools of warfare improve, it is Soldiers who use them to accomplish their mission. Soldiers committed to selfless service to the Nation are the centerpiece of Army organizations. Everything the Army does for the Nation is done by Soldiers supported by Army civilians and family members. Only with quality Soldiers answering the noble call to serve freedom can the Army ensure the victories required on battlefields of today and the future. (U.S. Department of the Army, 2005, p. 1-1)

This new identity requires strict discipline, a chain of command, and unhesitating execution of orders. Military training sets its men and women apart from the general population. Only about one half of one percent of the

U.S. population has been on active military duty at any given time during the past ten years, and it is not surprising that 84% of post-9/11 veterans report that the public does not understand the problems faced by those in the military or their families (Pew Research Center, 2011, p. 2).

The difference between military and civilian life is significant, but this becomes exacerbated by the experience of serving in war zones. A survey of more than 1,700 soldiers and Marines who had served in Iraq (Hoge et al., 2004, p. 18) revealed the following:

- 94.9% received small-arms fire
- 94.5% saw dead bodies or remains
- 92.0% were attacked or ambushed
- 89.2% received artillery, rocket, or mortar fire
- 86.2% knew an injured or killed service member
- 81.2% fired or directed fire at the enemy
- 75.4% saw injured women/children but were unable to help
- 69.8% saw a dead or seriously injured American

The following reflection, written by a student veteran, provides a glimpse of the personal cost that these data represent. As his platoon advanced on Baghdad,

> the bridges were secured, and a group of cars sat at the foot of the bridge riddled with 50-caliber machine gun fire. When I asked what had happened, the Marines responded that their orders were to allow no persons on or across the bridge, no exceptions. They were mostly [small cars] but their grisly contents suggested families fleeing as opposed to Iraqi fighters. No movement came from the cars, and I couldn't help.
>
> We continued north upon securing the bridges. Passing shelled village and fleeing populations. We were greeted as liberators; as butchers. We were greeted by smiling eyes; by eyes as cold as the darkest hate. Men threw fresh bread to us; men held up their maimed and injured children in pleas for help.
>
> We passed one village in the dead of night. All was quiet save for the grind of the armor heading north. To the front of the column, an explosion was triggered. I never saw who began the firing, but through my night-vision goggles, I could see every track, of the 14 tracks in the convoy, pumping rounds out into the village. After the melee of rounds stopped, a call came over the communications stating that the explosion had been a misfired 40mm grenade round. I don't know if any people were still in that village during our shooting spree, but I was betting that any people left were either dead or dying. (Marine veteran, personal correspondence, 2012)

Every veteran's story is unique, but many have experienced similar situations.

Combat veterans transitioning back into civilian life often struggle to reconcile their battlefield survival strategies with the roles and responsibilities of civilian life. Some skills that are essential and deeply ingrained on the battlefield may be counterproductive when transitioning back into civilian life (list adapted from Munroe, 2007):

1. **Unrelenting Vigilance.** Military personnel in combat zones must be on constant alert for danger—from the enemy, from the elements, from the use of heavy and dangerous equipment. When they return home, ordinary events such as a traffic jam or an unexpected crowd of people in a hallway can evoke a sense of danger and vulnerability. The service member may attempt to keep constant vigilance to remain in control, but that can be physically and mentally exhausting:

   > They call it combat stress disorder, but I think everybody gets it a little bit. Like for some you get used to the adrenal[ine] rush because you're always in the action or you're sometimes in the action. So you get used to having the rush of being scared. But for a lot of us, it was, like, we got the rush of there's always something pissing you off. (Rumann & Hamrick, 2010, p. 441)

   The experience can be fatiguing for friends and family who are accustomed to living in safety and who do not understand the ever-vigilant mentality. The inability to stand down can be a severe disadvantage for student veterans, for they may find that the noisy and crowded spaces typical in campus settings are highly distracting and emotionally tiring.

2. **Trust.** Military personnel in combat zones often learn to trust only other members of the U.S. military. Strangers are viewed with initial distrust, for it is safer to assume that everyone is the enemy until proven otherwise. Distrust and suspicion can severely damage important relationships at home, including marriage, and can build barriers between the service member and other family members. A veteran may perceive someone who is being friendly or helpful as manipulative. In the classroom it can result in a hesitation to engage with other students, instructors, and staff members. "It's not that I don't trust people, it's that I don't want to have to, you know?" (Rumann & Hamrick, 2010, p. 441).

3. **Focus on Mission.** On the battlefield "the mission" is the primary goal, and all attention and resources are directed to its completion. In the civilian world, "mission" is more diffuse, with job, family, and perhaps education all making claims on time and resources. It is

sometimes difficult for returning veterans to balance competing priorities and to decide how to effectively divide their attention and time.

4. **Decision Making.** Following orders is critical to personal safety, the safety of the unit, and the success of the mission. Officers and noncommissioned officers are often required to give and execute life-and-death orders, even when information is not fully available. Decisions are made quickly and communicated clearly, and orders are carried out with very little discussion. Hesitation may be dangerous or even deadly. Decision making with family members and classmates, in contrast, tends to be cooperative, with time taken to consider questions and options. Discussion plays a fundamental role in the process. It can be difficult and frustrating for combat veterans to shift their decision-making paradigm as they transition into academia, especially when they are asked to complete reflective assignments or to participate in team-based learning activities.

5. **Emotional Control.** Combat exposes military personnel to overwhelming events that elicit intense emotions. Soldiers learn to numb fear so that they may react quickly and decisively in stressful situations. "Pain is fear leaving the body" is a slogan used by all the services, especially during boot camp (Lorber & Garcia, 2010, p. 297). Anger is also useful, as it enhances the ability to use force effectively. It is difficult to selectively control emotions, however, and the range of acceptable feelings may narrow to anger and numbness. Drugs and alcohol help sustain emotional numbing, but these substances can be abused after the service member returns home. Relationships at home can be difficult because of this. Veterans often report having strongly defensive or aggressive emotional reactions to family situations and in their interactions with friends. It can be difficult for veterans to open up fully about the emotions they experienced while on the battlefield, and they may seem withdrawn. Universities need to have trained counseling staff on site to help student veterans who may be struggling to come to grips with what they have experienced. Finally, every university should develop collaborative ties with the closest VA [Veterans Affairs] center.

Servicemen and servicewomen who serve "on the ground" experience potentially traumatic events on a regular basis. There is a mental drain from working in an environment in which ambush or attack with an improvised explosive device (IED) is continually possible. Even if nothing happens, the stress remains. Heat, exhaustion, and sleep deprivation magnify the disruptive effects. The elements themselves seem at times to conspire against the soldiers (Hoge, 2010). This student veteran's experience is representative of many others:

While we started to settle in for a night of gunfire and explosions, the wind picked up. From a mile away, you could see the ground heave and rise, and whatever was coming was [a] more elemental enemy than I had ever faced. The sand whipped against everything, obscuring even the Marine 10 feet away. Rifles that were cleaned and oiled soon became inoperable. No barrier stood up to that silt in its penetrative fury, and soon we all were coated, looking ghost-like with the fine powder that clung to our skins. I never knew how long it lasted, but all movement was ceased for the time being. (Marine veteran, personal correspondence, 2012)

Not every combat veteran will struggle with the challenges we have identified, and not every veteran has served in combat. For those who have, however, it is important to recognize that the skills and habits that promote survival on the battlefield may make readjustment to civilian (and student) life difficult.

Simply coming off deployment and returning to the United States, even when one is not transitioning out of the armed forces, can be a difficult adjustment. One student veteran described his experience as follows:

I never knew what I was looking for. Yet I could tell upon my return that I wasn't the only one who felt that same sense of drifting along. My [unit] was in a state of unrest. Yes, the [unit's] training resumed, but the days were rowdy and the nights became unstable. The incidents began to pile up, and it wasn't long before the [unit] started to experience the collateral damage in the unrest we had all brought back.

When all the Marines had returned from leave, the commander issued a [unit]-wide urinalysis. This was a catalyst, as each of the 4 companies had multiple "drug-pops." Long-term Marines, career Marines, were caught with marijuana, cocaine, and other drugs in their system. As the USMC [U.S. Marine Corps] policy is zero tolerance, these combat veterans were promptly processed for discharge under "other than honorable" conditions. Try as you may, a discharge like that is a one-way ticket to bumsville, and we all knew it. But that wasn't the main problem, just an incidental that hurt the leadership core of our [unit].

What was the most drastic was the culture of binge drinking and violence that had been bred in the [unit]. Marines were racking up DUIs [driving under the influence citations] out in the town and on base. Drunken brawls were common on the weekends, and I was as much to blame as everyone else. Private First Class "Thompson" was one of the first assaults we experienced. He had felt disrespected by another Marine, and in a fit of rage, head-butted the Marine twice, breaking the Marine's nose and orbital bone. "Carter" was the next, but this time the deaths started.

Carter was living out with his girlfriend, who also had a young child. We never knew that his drinking had gotten out of control, but his actions spoke enough. During one of Carter's benders, the child began to cry in its crib, and the girlfriend was working. Carter, rather that consoling the child, shook it until it became quiet. But the quiet wasn't that the child had stopped, but that Carter had killed the infant. Last I knew he was still in Leavenworth's military prison.

"Menendez" was the next. "Farley" was driving, and Menendez was a passenger. Both Marines were drunk, fresh off a night in Myrtle Beach. Rounding a curve, Farley lost control of the jeep, and rolled into a ditch. Menendez was ejected, but the jeep crushed his skull.

There were others that [died], from time to time, and everyone blamed it on the drinking. But the truth is probably something else. The truth is that we had been unleashed in Iraq, and once off, no one realized how to reestablish control. Many are the nights I woke up on the floor, empty bottles of whiskey peppering the room, wondering what I had done. In my stupor, I would always gauge my behavior off of the other Marines that surrounded me, but they were as lost as I was. (Marine veteran, personal correspondence, 2012)

Every unit's postdeployment experience is their own—some go through easier adjustments, some even more difficult than that described. Higher education must address how to best serve those students who have had the most negative transitional experiences. These few students often require resources that are above and beyond those typically offered by colleges and universities.

The experience of reintegration into civilian life affects veterans in ways that we are still struggling to understand. A Pew Research Center study (2011) found that 44% of veterans who served after September 11, 2001, indicated that reentry was difficult. Table 2.2 lists factors that affect the ease of this transition, both positively and negatively.

One key finding from the Pew study was that military personnel who frequently attended religious services had an easier time readjusting to civilian life. The analysis showed that veterans who attended religious services at least once a week had a 67% easier reentry experience. Another finding was that marriage made the transition to civilian life more difficult for veterans. Post-9/11 veterans who were married while in the military were 15% less likely to have an easy military-to-civilian transition than single veterans. The counterproductive use of battlefield strategies in a civilian world, as noted previously, partially explains this finding, and the strain of multiple deployments over the last decade intensifies the separation experience. It is clear that more research in this area is needed to fully explain these results (Morin, 2011, p. 3, 6).

The military provides a variety of end-of-deployment debriefing opportunities as military members process out of the service. The Transition Assistance Program (TAP) provides transitional support for service members, which often includes career counseling, résumé assistance, and other job

	TABLE 2.2 Factors Related to the Difficulty or Ease of Transitioning From Service to Civilian Life (Morin, 2011)
Factors	*Percentage Point Change in the Likelihood That a Veteran With Characteristic Would Have an Easy Time Reentering Civilian Life (Negative Numbers Indicate a Harder Time, Positive Numbers an Easier Time)*
Experienced a Traumatic Event	–26
Seriously Injured	–19
Post-9/11 Veteran Who Was Married While Serving	–15
Post-9/11 Veteran	–15
Served in Combat	–7
Knew Someone Killed or Injured	–6
College Graduate	+5
Understood Missions	+10
Officer	+10
Religious Post-9/11 Veteran	+24

search resources. Interviews with veterans indicate that these training sessions vary in both their quality and their effectiveness. These programs provide good information but are often seen as the last checkpoint before reuniting with family and loved ones. The TAP services are not utilized to their fullest extent as a result. The VA also provides postdeployment debriefings on educational and medical benefits. The VA bureaucracy is difficult to understand, however, and problems plague the system. It is at times perceived as ineffective, and some service members believe that if they admit any medical or mental problems their return home will be delayed (Ackerman et al., 2009, p. 9). National Guard units have an educational officer who helps soldiers and airmen navigate the benefits process, but there is no analogous position for regular service members.

The cultural differences between military and civilian life are often difficult to bridge. Asking veterans to lay aside the uniform and return to civilian life is not as simple as a change of clothes. The path to reclaim a civilian identity is at times uncertain and contrasts with the well-designed and executed process that molded individuals into their military persona in the first place.

Transitions Into Higher Education

If the difference between military and civilian life is significant, then the disparity between military and academic cultures is conspicuous. Research indicates that student veterans face heightened difficulties when they adjust to civilian life and transition to college life concurrently (Holloway, 2009; Radford, 2009). This is caused in part by the difficulty of working through the twin bureaucracies of the military (including the VA) and higher education. Because the culture and behavioral norms of the military and higher education can be radically different, members of the military must navigate through a series of cultural incongruities when they transition into higher education (see Table 2.3).

These cultural incongruities tend to be the greatest for those who experienced deployment on the ground in the Middle East. The incongruities may be less conspicuous for student veterans returning from other theaters

TABLE 2.3 Incongruities Between Military and Academic Cultures		
Cultural Reference	*Military*	*Higher Education*
Structure	Strict chain of command	Loose, collegial
Authority	Absolute	Relative
Response to Authority	Oriented toward obedience to superiors	Oriented toward critical assessment of leadership
Teaching and Learning	Transfer of information through briefings	Knowledge is constructed through experience and discussion
Gender Stratification	Heavily weighted toward the masculine	More egalitarian —gender-neutral values espoused
Community Cohesion	Based on group loyalty and conformity	Based on varied interests and individuality
Sense of Purpose	Mission is given, mission is accomplished	Discover your own path
Social Norms	Conservative	Liberal
Institutional Norms	Rooted in history and tradition	Rooted in history and tradition

or from bases supporting the war on terrorism (WOT) from relatively safe locations, such as Turkey. U.S. armed forces are stationed in many locations across the world, and as a result the deployment experiences of student veterans vary widely (Maurin, 2012, pp. 62–63). Survey tools, such as the cultural congruity scale shown in Figure 2.1, can help faculty, staff, and student veterans themselves understand how they feel about their ability to navigate and fit into the culture of higher education.

Institutions have become increasingly aware of the challenges veterans face as they acculturate to civilian campuses, and 55% of responding institutions in a survey by McBain et al. (2012) listed transitioning as a priority issue on campus, a 22 percentage-point increase from 2009:

> Given not only the very different social structures of the military and academe but also the complicated historical context influencing the two worlds' interactions and stereotypes of both service members and college students still present in American society, the increase is unsurprising. The encouraging news is that campus respondents have identified the issue of social acculturation as a priority to address on behalf of their military/veteran students. (p. 24)

Figure 2.1 Cultural Congruity Scale for Military Students.

Instructions: On a scale of 1 (not at all) to 5 (a great deal), indicate the extent to which you have experienced the following feeling or situation at school.

- I feel as though I have to change myself to fit in at school.
- I try not to show the parts of me that are "military."
- I often feel like a chameleon, having to change myself depending on the military history of the person I am with.
- I feel that my military background is incompatible with other students.
- I can talk to my classmates at school about my military experiences.
- I feel I am leaving my military values behind by going to college.
- My military values are in conflict with what is expected at school.
- I feel that my language and/or appearance make it hard for me to fit in with other students.
- I feel that instructors are supportive of me as a veteran.
- I feel accepted at school as a veteran or service member.

Source: adapted from Weber (2012)

Although the increase is indeed encouraging, it is still a concern that 45% of the institutions that responded do not identify this as a priority issue.

Maurin (2012, p. 58) has identified four main themes that characterize the transition from military to campus life. These include identity-change negotiation, postservice privilege and entitlement, on-campus isolation, and enhanced academic maturity. These themes reflect the shared experiences of Maurin's subjects. Each can play a significant role in the academic success of our student veterans.

The theme of "identity-change negotiation" recognizes that military training and deployment instills a deeply ingrained set of beliefs and a renewed sense of one's purpose. Student veterans must renegotiate their identity when they return to higher education. The military creates a certain mind-set, which can be even more deeply imprinted by the experiences of deployment and combat. In the Army and Marines, particularly, personnel are trained to "suppress their emotions and push forward even under emotionally or physically taxing conditions" (Maurin, 2012, p. 61). As noted previously, this mind-set takes a toll when these men and women return to campus. When student veterans talk of being listless, drifting, and feeling a loss of purpose, they are often referring to this change in identity:

> [The military] changed my views on life, but it seems that I am right back where I started. I am back where I grew up, and I feel like I did a full circle in my life and now I am back right where I started. I joined the Army to try and help me figure out what I wanted to do with my life and gain some direction. But now that I am out I am right back to where I started, in the same town with no life goals and no direction. (Doenges, 2011, p. 59)

Student veterans have moved from a world where everything they did—everything that they were—was purpose-driven. As a result, they struggle to find a similar purposefulness in higher education. This experience appears to be significantly different for women than it is for men, so much so that we discuss women's experiences separately at the end of this chapter.

"Postservice privilege and entitlement" refers to those benefits and honors that veterans are legitimately due and how difficult it is at times to access those benefits. It also refers to a widespread discomfort with overt displays of gratitude: "It's what we are supposed to do. It is really nice to be thanked but no Marine, or military personnel for that matter, wants to be singled out" (Maurin, 2012, p. 63). The combined bureaucracies of higher education and the VA make receiving benefits a challenge at times, which can be devastating for veterans who have just come off active duty and who are relearning how to live on a budget. Delays in benefits cause unnecessary stress. Student veterans are sometimes required to fund their tuition for several months until they are reimbursed. These expenses are often put on a credit card, which can create an additional financial burden with accumulated interest.

An additional frustration faced by many student veterans is discovering that only limited academic credit is given for military training and experience. Guidelines for transferring military training into academic credit have been established by the American Council on Education (ACE). The decision as to how many credits to accept, however, is still left up to individual institutions. Well-informed and qualified personnel in an institution's financial aid office are singularly important to a smooth transition for student veterans, and best practices for this office are described in chapter 5.

Many student veterans report a sense of on-campus isolation, Maurin's third theme. Veterans have support from their families and their communities but feel alone and set apart in academic environments. Even veterans who have been on campus prior to their military experience feel that they have changed beyond the understanding of their classmates. Bryan, a former Marine, felt so different from the members of his former fraternity upon returning to college that he opted to maintain alumni status and did not interact socially with his fraternity brothers (Maurin, 2012, p. 66). James, another Marine, felt similarly: "I don't feel like I can truly relate to a lot of these people around here because I see things so differently. And you know, I feel like an alien" (Maurin, 2012, p. 67). Another student veteran put it this way:

> At first I don't talk to any students at school. I really don't. When I sit in class I'll probably say hey to somebody but I won't start up a conversation. Somebody can be sitting next to me the entire time and I won't talk to them unless they talk to me first. (Maurin, 2012, p. 68)

Military students also indicate that they feel isolated from faculty and staff. The National Survey of Student Engagement (NSSE) reports that first-year combat veterans were less engaged with faculty and perceived less campus support. Veterans who were seniors also scored significantly lower on student-faculty interaction and perceived less campus support than nonveteran seniors (National Survey of Student Engagement, 2010, p. 18). Social support in the military can easily be taken for granted because its omnipresent and personal relationships are often forged through extreme circumstances. Many student veterans state that "being there for a buddy" is the primary reason they persist in their military service. If higher education could help student veterans re-establish camaraderie at college around a new mission of graduation, then they would be more likely to persist in college as well, for it is clear that student veterans value education and have developed key disciplines that enable them to succeed. This leads to Maurin's last theme, "enhanced academic maturity."

Military students transition to education with an enhanced academic maturity, regardless of whether they are first-time students or have had prior college experience. "[Thinking about my deployment experiences] helps me get out of bed in the morning. I'll be like, 'This sucks, but Iraq was worse. Shut up and get out of bed'" (Rumann & Hamrick, 2010, p. 443). While certain elements of military training do not translate well into higher education, the general discipline and focus of the military is seen as an asset by student veterans:

> You're so much more focused about life and what you want to do and what you need to do to get to that point. You see college as such a stepping stone to get to what you want to do. You know you just have to get it done. You're so much more focused. When you come back, you have more direct focus. (Maurin, 2012, p. 72)

Jacob, a Navy veteran, agreed:

> If you're in the military and you don't work hard, people look down on you. And if you have too many people looking down on you it's a really bad feeling. And it's just kind of followed me. I want to prove myself to the professors that I'm going to do the work that they assign and I am going to do it to the best of my ability. It's all about proving yourself. (Maurin, 2012, p. 73)

For many veterans, education has become a new mission, one with positive long-term outcomes: "I don't think college has changed all that much, just me. . . . I think more about what I want to do for the rest of my life" (Rumann & Hamrick, 2010, p. 442).

Academic maturity is counterbalanced at times by the amount of time student veterans have been away from high school or previous college experience:

> I'm so rusty. Like that's, I get frustrated I guess 'cause I'm sitting in class and our teacher is like well y'all should already know how to do this, this, this, and this. And all the kids are like, "oh yeah, I remember how to do that. I can do it with my eyes closed, no problem." And I'm still struggling, like two plus two is five? (Maurin, 2012, p. 73)

Military students can also feel frustration because nonmilitary peers are several years ahead of them in school:

> All of my friends are settling down with jobs and women they've known for awhile. Everyone else's lives are falling together, and it kind of looks like yours is falling apart. I've got a lot of work to do. That really bugs me. It makes me feel unsuccessful in spite of [my veteran status]. I'm a couple of

years back. I want this stuff to be taken care of. . . . The measure of success at college is really graduating, getting a job. . . . When you look at what I've done [military service], it's a good thing, but on that scale [i.e., academic progress] it's useless. (Rumann & Hamrick, 2010, p. 444)

Despite these frustrations, student veterans believe that the military has taught them a mental agility and intellectual discipline that will allow them to prevail.

The Difficulty of Transitioning With a Disability

War exacts a toll from those who go through it. Exposure to traumatic events, serious injury, and the loss and removal of friends and comrades owing to injury and death significantly affect the ability of veterans to reenter civilian life (Morin, 2011, p. 2). Disabilities can make reentry into education even more challenging. Diagnosing disabilities is sometimes difficult, and screening for "invisible" disabilities,—such as posttraumatic stress disorder (PTSD), depression, and traumatic brain injury (TBI)—is imperfect. Veterans filing for disability benefits often face long waiting times—sometimes as long as a year—because the system is bogged down and overburdened with claims. The bottom line is that "soldiers aren't adequately screened, diagnosis and treatment of traumatic brain injury are still haphazard, and there hasn't been nearly enough change in the warrior culture so that getting help is smart rather than sissy" (Kristof, 2012). The difficult challenges that student veterans with disabilities face are discussed in much greater depth in chapter 3.

Transitional Challenges for Women Veterans

Women are becoming a larger proportion of the veteran population, and as such they are also returning to higher education in larger numbers. Only 2.5% of the armed forces were women in 1973, but by 2005 women made up almost 14% of the active-duty armed forces (U.S. Department of Veterans Affairs, 2007). More than 182,000 women have deployed to Iraq or Afghanistan (Baechtold & DeSawal, 2009, p. 35). Between October 7, 2001, and March 5, 2012, 110 women had been killed in Operation Iraqi Freedom (OIF) and 34 in Operation Enduring Freedom (OEF) (U.S. Department of Defense, 2012).

Women serve in roles that are vital to the success of our armed forces. Although women were technically excluded from ground combat operations until recently, the lack of a defined front line and the guerrilla nature of the current conflicts have meant that women service members have had to counter the enemy in the same manner as their male counterparts: by engaging in firefights, taking prisoners, and occasionally becoming casualties. In June 2005 Sergeant Leigh Ann Hester of the 617th Military Police Company (Kentucky National Guard) became the first woman to be awarded the Silver Star, the nation's third-highest medal for valor, since World War II. Her citation noted actions against the enemy, including the killing of at least three insurgents (Department of Defense Task Force on Mental Health, 2007, p. 58). The absence of clearly defined combat lines and the insurgent nature of warfare against terrorists have put female veterans at risk for exposure to combat-related trauma and subsequent mental health issues such as PTSD. Twelve percent of the veterans who sought VA care from 2002 to 2006 were women (Department of Defense Task Force on Mental Health, 2007, p. 58), and female veterans of OEF and OIF have sought VA care at a higher rate than male veterans (17% versus 11%) (Department of Defense Task Force on Mental Health, 2007, p 59). In addition, military sexual trauma (MST) can contribute to mental health problems for women: 55% of female VA outpatients indicated that they were sexually harassed while in the military and 23% reported that they were sexually assaulted in a study by Skinner at al. (2000, p. 291).

Women veterans face unique challenges when transitioning back into higher education. The military promotes a hierarchical structure that emphasizes power, independence, self-reliance, and emotional control (Lorber & Garcia, 2010, pp. 296–298). These characteristics are typically considered to be masculine, and women veterans report that they often have to "redefine their feminine identities in order to work within a male-dominated system" (Wheeler, 2011, p. 40). Women who are entering higher education from the military often feel as if they are being asked to shift identities again:

> When the structured military community is removed, the individual is forced to again redefine who she is as a civilian, a veteran, a female, and a student. . . . Therefore, when women veterans re-enter civilian life, they are often unsure of how to fulfill not only their specific role as a student but also their role as a woman. The gender issue is distinctly different for men because they are often rewarded by society for displaying strong male characteristics. (Baechtold & DeSawal, 2009, p. 40)

Women veterans often have more difficulty finding other women veterans on campus and had few same-sex role models while serving in the military (Baechtold & DeSawal, 2009, p. 40).

In the end, women veterans may hesitate to participate in programs designed to facilitate the transition of other veterans—having spent three or more years in the male-dominated armed forces, they may feel a distinct desire to separate themselves from these programs. Institutions may want to consider facilitating events that are restricted to women veterans only and identifying ways to help these veterans find each other. Student affairs personnel and counseling staff need to be aware of the unique needs of women veterans. In the classroom, faculty need to understand that women student veterans may at times wish to distance themselves from other (especially male) veterans and may be even more reluctant to openly identify themselves as a veteran.

Conclusion: Athena's Labyrinth

If postsecondary institutions can begin to understand the many types of transitional challenges that student veterans face as they return to college, higher education can then begin to provide relevant signposts to help them navigate the bureaucratic labyrinth. In the military, transitions come with specific labels, training, and support called standard operating procedures (SOP). The transition to higher education is far less directed. Student veterans must negotiate the complexities of their benefits, apply and be accepted to the institution of their choice, and register for courses in an environment that is highly unstandardized. Student veterans, facing all the challenges listed previously, often feel as though they are in a bureaucratic maze and have difficulty understanding the unspoken (or hard-to-find) rules and regulations governing college life. As newcomers, they have trouble fitting in—they have lost the role clarity that they experienced in the military, they may have lost their social support, and they keenly feel the cultural differences of traditionally aged students and higher education in general. Mental health issues, PTSD, learning disabilities, and the adjustment of living with an acquired physical disability all add to the difficulty some veterans experience as they reenter higher education.

Weber (2012) examined the emotional and mental health issues related to student departure in one of the first studies of factors that affect retention of veterans. Her sample included 490 student veterans and service members, including 323 who had been deployed at least once following 9/11. She found that social support and cultural congruity were primary factors contributing to student veteran retention and recommended comprehensive training programs for faculty and staff to help them understand military/veteran readjustment issues (Weber, 2012). Higher education can best support student veterans through their transitions by understanding their world and acting as a competent and gracious host.

Chapter Summary

Veterans go through a significant enculturation process when they join the military and develop an identity that shapes them for the rest of their life. It is sometimes difficult for men and women to transition out of the military, and the difficulty can be intensified by the experience of ground combat.

Veterans who move from the military into higher education face additional challenges in terms of isolation and cultural incongruity. Men and women, however, experience these incongruities in significantly different ways. Veterans returning to college must negotiate an identity change, figure out how to identify and access appropriate VA resources, and overcome feelings of alienation on campus. Student veterans also transition into higher education with enhanced academic maturity, discipline, and a goal-oriented mind-set that can turn them into formidable scholars. The presence of disabilities can further hinder a student's transition. In the end, institutions of higher education must meet the transitional needs of our incoming military students if colleges and universities wish to create an environment in which these students have the best opportunity for success.

Key Points

- Student veterans' transition into higher education is unique compared to that of other student populations.
- Military students have experienced a life-changing enculturation process that transformed them from civilians into highly capable members of our armed forces.
- Veterans have developed skills that are essential and deeply ingrained on the battlefield but that may be counterproductive when transitioning back into civilian life.
- The military provides a variety of end-of-deployment debriefing opportunities for members of the services, but these training sessions are perceived as highly variable in both their quality and effectiveness.
- Members of the military must navigate through a series of cultural incongruities when they transition into higher education.
- Student veterans often struggle to receive the benefits they are due because of the combined bureaucratic inefficiencies of both higher education and the VA.
- Many student veterans report that they feel isolated from other students and the faculty, which can put them at academic risk.
- Student veterans transition into higher education with an enhanced academic maturity that includes a profound respect for the value of education, discipline and focus, and a goal-oriented approach to education that gives them the tools to be formidable scholars.
- Disabilities, especially invisible ones (e.g., TBI, depression, and PTSD) make the transition process much more difficult.

- The transitional experience appears to be very different for women than it is for men, but more research is needed in this area.
- Higher education can best support student veterans through their transitions by understanding their world and acting as a competent and gracious host.

References

Ackerman, R., DiRamio, D., & Mitchell, R. L. G. (2009). Transitions: Combat veterans as college students. *New Directions for Student Services, 2009*(126), 5–14. doi:10.1002/ss.311

Baechtold, M., & DeSawal, D. M. (2009). Meeting the needs of women veterans. In R. Ackerman & D. DiRamio (Eds.), *Creating a veteran-friendly campus: Strategies for transition and success* (pp. 35–43). San Francisco: Jossey-Bass. doi:10.1002/ss.314

Department of Defense Task Force on Mental Health. (2007). *An achievable vision: Report of the Department of Defense Task Force on Mental Health.* Falls Church, VA: Defense Health Board. Retrieved from www.health.mil/dhb/mhtf/mhtf-report-final.pdf

Doenges, T. (2011). *Calling and meaningful work among student military veterans: Impact on well-being and experiences on campus* (Doctoral dissertation). Available from ProQuest Dissertations and Theses database. (UMI No. 3468765)

Goodman, J., Schlossberg, N. K., & Anderson, J. L. (2006). *Counseling adults in transition: Linking practice with theory* (3rd ed.). New York: Springer.

Hoge, C. W. (2010). *Once a warrior—Always a warrior: Navigating the transition from combat to home—Including combat stress, PTSD, and mTBI.* Guilford, CT: GPP Life.

Hoge, C. W., Castro, C. A., Messer, S. C., McGurk, D., Cotting, D. I., & Koffman, R. (2004). Combat duty in Iraq and Afghanistan, mental health problems, and barriers to care. *New England Journal of Medicine, 351*(1), 13–22. doi:10.1056/NEJMoa040603

Holloway, K. M. (2009). Understanding reentry of the modern-day student veteran through Vietnam-era theory. *Journal of Student Affairs, 28,* 11–17.

Kristof, N. D. (2012, August 10). War wounds. *New York Times.* Retrieved from http://www.nytimes.com/2012/08/12/opinion/sunday/war-wounds.html

Lorber, W., & Garcia, H. A. (2010). Not supposed to feel this: Traditional masculinity in psychotherapy with male veterans returning from Afghanistan and Iraq. *Psychotherapy: Theory, Research & Practice, 47*(3), 296–305.

Maurin, K. H. (2012). *Negotiating cultural transitions: Contemporary student veterans and Louisiana institutions of higher education* (Doctoral dissertation). Retrieved from http://etd.lsu.edu/docs/available/etd-01032012–155853/unrestricted/kayharrisonmaurin_diss.pdf

McBain, L., Kim, Y., Cook, B., & Snead, K. (2012). *From soldier to student II: Assessing campus programs for veterans and service members.* Washington DC: American Council on Education. Retrieved from http://www.acenet.edu/news-room/ Pages/From-Soldier-to-Student-II.aspx

Military.com. (n.d.). *Compare training programs* [website]. Retrieved from http://www .military.com/Recruiting/Content/0,13898,rec_step09_compare_training,,00.html

Morin, R. (2011). *The difficult transition from military to civilian life.* Pew Social & Demographic Trends. Retrieved from http://www.pewsocialtrends.org/2011/12/08/ the-difficult-transition-from-military-to-civilian-life/

Munroe, J. (2007, May 19). Working with veterans and their families: Post-traumatic stress disorder (PTSD), other key issues, and clinical dilemmas [Power-Point]. Presentation for the Greater Boston Physicians for Social Responsibility Conference, Boston, MA. Retrieved from http://www.psr.org/chapters/boston/ peace-and-security/medical-consequences-of-iraq-war.html

National Survey of Student Engagement. (2010). *Major differences: Examining student engagement by field of study—Annual results 2010.* Bloomington: Indiana University Center for Postsecondary Research.

Pew Research Center. (2011). *War and sacrifice in the post-9/11 era.* Washington DC: Author. Retrieved from http://www.pewsocialtrends.org/files/2011/10/veterans -report.pdf

Radford, A. W. (2009). *Military service members and veterans in higher education: What the new GI Bill may mean for post-secondary institutions.* Washington DC: American Council on Education. Retrieved from http://www.acenet.edu/news -room/Pages/Military-Service-Members-and-Veterans-in-Higher-Education -What-the-New-GI-Bill-May-Mean-for-Postsecondary-Institutions-.aspx

Rumann, C. B., & Hamrick, F. A. (2010). Student veterans in transition: Re-enrolling after war zone deployments. *Journal of Higher Education, 81*(4), 431–458. doi:10.1353/jhe.0.0103

Skinner, K. M., Kressin, N., Frayne, S., Tripp, T. J., Hankin, C. S., & Millder, D. R. (2000). The prevalence of military sexual assault among female veterans' administration outpatients. *Journal of Interpersonal Violence, 15*(3), 291–310.

U.S. Department of Defense. (2012, March 19). Military casualty information. Retrieved from http://siadapp.dmdc.osd.mil/personnel/CASUALTY/castop.htm

U.S. Department of the Army. (2005). *The Army.* Field Manual 1. Washington DC: Headquarters, Department of the Army.

U.S. Department of Veterans Affairs. (2007). *Women veterans: Past, present and future.* Washington DC: Author.

Weber, D. (2012). *Academic success and well-being following OEF/OIF deployment* (Doctoral dissertation). Available from ProQuest Dissertations & Theses database. (UMI No. 3495315)

Wheeler, H. A. (2011). *From soldier to student: A case study of veterans' transitions to first-time community college students* (Doctoral dissertation). Available from Pro-Quest Dissertations & Theses database. (UMI No. 3465899)

3

STUDENT VETERANS AND DISABILITIES

The bomb blasted thru the windshield right to my face, vehicle flipped three times, and an M-16 rifle smashed right into my skull. It was lights out. My brain, my mind . . . right away I noticed things weren't the same. The simplest things like putting on a seat belt is frustrating. Short term memory is gone. The Army was my life, it's all I ever wanted to do. I'm not gonna quit, for my kids, for my wife. It's been seven years since the IED [improvised explosive device] blasted my vehicle, my brain. The only thing I can do is take it one day at a time for the rest of my life.

—Specialist who sustained a severe brain injury in an IED explosion
(U.S. Department of the Army, 2012, p. 20)

Combat operations in the Middle East have produced a new generation of military personnel with injuries and wounds—both visible and invisible—received in service to their country. The war on terrorism (WOT), which encompasses Operation Iraqi Freedom (OIF), Operation Enduring Freedom (OEF), and Operation New Dawn (OND), is the longest sustained conflict in U.S. history, and current advances in body armor and medical treatment have meant that more service members are surviving wounds to return home. Two new laws, the American with Disabilities Act Amendment Act (ADAAA) and the Post-9/11 GI Bill, have created the opportunity for a perfect storm in higher education through "a series of crises resulting from a failure to recognize what is unique to the needs of veterans with disabilities" (Grossman, 2009, p. 4).

The number of veterans from all conflicts with disabilities increased by 25% between 2001 and 2009 and totaled more than 2.9 million by the end of 2009. The U.S. Department of Veterans Affairs (VA) has been overwhelmed at times by the number of new claims. As of 2009, 181,000 veterans from the WOT were collecting disability payments, 915,000 cases were backlogged, and disability benefits took an average of six months to process. From 2000 to 2004, doctor-patient ratios in the VA rose from 335:1 to 531:1, and the average time needed to resolve disputed benefit claims rose to 5.5 years (Church, 2009, pp. 11, 14, 25–26). The increasing backlog of disability claims at the VA has even resulted in a class-action lawsuit by veterans against the government (Chong, 2008). Higher education also faces the prospect of being inundated if it does not recognize the specialized challenges that confront this subsection of the student veteran population. As Grossman (2009) writes,

> The presence and legitimate expectations of veterans with disabilities can wake up colleges and universities that have too long practiced benign neglect when it comes to facilities' access and have responded to auxiliary aid responsibilities on an *ad hoc* basis. . . . Some colleges, universities and systems are already on the path of opportunity, while others seem destined to be in the center of the storm. (p. 6)

Higher education must take a proactive stance toward student veterans with disabilities by understanding their unique needs and finding solutions that provide them with the resources and services to which they are legally entitled.

Veterans often have difficultly speaking about their disabilities. Service members may feel that noncombat injuries are not "real" wounds. They sometimes ignore their invisible wounds, such as posttraumatic stress disorder (PTSD), depression, and traumatic brain injury (TBI), and many are concerned about what peers and leaders will think if they seek help or treatment. A veteran who suffered a concussion and later developed headaches, short-term memory loss, insomnia, balance problems, and dizziness said, "If you [were] not bleeding or losing a limb or eyesight, you were not medically evacuated" (Arenofsky, 2009, p. 9). One study of soldiers and Marines who had served in Iraq showed that while 81.6% of the respondents acknowledged that they had a need for mental health services, only 43.9% were interested in receiving help, and only 24.4% had received professional help (including help from mental health professionals, general medical doctors, and chaplains and other members of clergy) in the past year. The top three reasons that these personnel chose not to seek help were "I would be seen as weak," "My unit leadership might treat me differently," and "Members of my unit might have less confidence in me" (Hoge et al., 2004, pp. 20–21). Although 60–70% of our veterans do not have disabilities, the 30–40% who have sustained physical, psychological, or cognitive injuries face additional challenges when they join our college and university communities. It is often said that "no one comes home from war unchanged." This is especially true for student veterans with disabilities. The men and women of our military who return home as "wounded warriors" have been changed the most.

What is the definition of a *wounded warrior*? According to the House of Representatives Wounded Warrior Program, he or she is

[A] disabled veteran who has served on active duty since September 11, 2001, has fewer than 20 years of military service, and has received either a Memorandum Rating of 30 percent or greater from their service Physical Evaluation Board or a VA service-connected disability rating of 30 percent or greater. . . . (Chief Administrative Officer of the House, n.d.)

According to the NCO Promotion Board (n.d.), "wounded warrior" refers to the entire population of wounded, ill, and injured service members or veterans. This broader description merges well with the definition of *disability* in the ADAAA, which states that disability with respect to an individual includes the following:

- A physical or mental impairment that substantially limits one or more major life activities of such individual;
- A record of such an impairment; or
- Being regarded as having such an impairment. (Americans with Disabilities Act Amendments Act of 2008)

One of the challenges that student veterans with disabilities face is that the military, the VA, and the ADAAA all have slightly different definitions of *disability*. The military defines *disability* as a "service-connected physical (or mental) impairment which renders a member unfit to perform duties of the assigned military specialty." The VA defines it as a "mental or physical disease or injury resulting from or aggravated by military service" (Smith & Miller, 2011). This means that service members who are classified as having a disability by the military because they are no longer able to perform their duties may not automatically qualify for accommodation under the ADAAA or (more commonly) that military personnel who do not qualify for a disability rating through either the military or the VA may qualify for accommodation under the ADAAA. Student veterans with disabilities—wounded warriors—are protected under the ADAAA from discrimination, and institutions must determine how to best provide these students with full and equal access to all the programs, services, and activities they are due.

Understanding the Differences Between the War on Terrorism and Past Conflicts

The United States became involved in two major conflicts in response to the terrorist attacks on September 11, 2001: OEF, the war in Afghanistan; and OIF, the war in Iraq. The OIF campaign was renamed OND in September

2010 to signify the reduced role of the U.S. military in Iraq. For the purposes of this chapter, OND will be considered part of OIF.

Since October 2001, about 2.4 million U.S. troops have been deployed to Afghanistan and Iraq in 3 million tours of duty lasting more than 30 days (Institute of Medicine, 2010, p. 13; U.S. Department of Veterans Affairs, 2012a, p. 3). There are many differences between previous U.S. military conflicts and the current WOT that have bearing on the mental and physical health of our returning personnel. These include the following:

- Duration of conflict: OEF became the longest military operation in U.S. history on June 7, 2010, when it exceeded the Vietnam War's 103 months (Hampson, 2010).
- Personnel: OEF and OIF are the first extended conflicts to rely on an all-volunteer military with heavy dependence on the National Guard and reserves (Institute of Medicine, 2010, p. 17).
- Length of deployment: The length of deployments for the Army at the start of OEF was twelve months, but in 2007 the Army extended deployments to seventeen months, and in some instances deployments are as long as two years (Lafferty, Alford, Davis, & O'Connor, 2008, p. 5; Tice, 2010).
- Repeated deployments: Forty percent of military service members have been deployed more than once, and 263,150 service members have been deployed more than two times (Institute of Medicine, 2010, p. 25).
- Shortened dwell time: Dwell time, which is the time between deployments, has been shorter than the previously established policies of two years for members of the active military and five years for National Guard and reserve units (Institute of Medicine, 2010, p. 26). Almost two-thirds of military service members have had less than 24 months dwell time at home to reset, retrain, and recuperate prior to redeployment (U.S. Department of the Army, 2012, pp. 3–4).

The nature of the combat and the type of injuries sustained in the WOT directly affect the types of disabilities of student veterans returning to campus. Past wars and military actions, with the exception of Vietnam, have been largely conventional, with several days of intense combat followed by lengthy periods of inactivity, with easily identifiable combatants, and with clear distinctions between battle zones and safe zones (Lafferty et al., 2008, p. 5; U.S. Department of the Army, 2012, pp. 3–4). The pace of operations has remained persistently high in Afghanistan and Iraq, however. Soldiers remain under constant threat from unidentifiable combatants using insurgency warfare, guerrilla attacks, and increasingly sophisticated and effective explosive mechanisms. There are few safe zones, and soldiers are provided very few opportunities for mental or physical rest (Lafferty et al., 2008, p. 5; U.S. Department of the Army, 2012, pp. 3–4). Despite the tempo of violence, fatality rates have been low. There have been dramatic improvements in personal and vehicle armor. Advancements in battlefield medicine, such as rapid evacuation to a trauma center, have also significantly improved survival. The combination of improved protection and medical care has meant that soldiers who would have died in previous wars are now surviving (Lafferty et al., 2008, pp. 5–6; Institute of Medicine, 2010, p. 29; U.S. Department of the Army, 2012, p. 11). The fatality to wounded ratio as of July 2009 was 1:4.4 for OEF and 1:7.3 for OIF. These ratios are much more favorable than those for the Vietnam War (1:2.6) and World War II (1:1.7) (Leland & Oboroceanu, 2010, p. 9). The military's ability to save the lives of those who have been wounded is extraordinary, but one of the outcomes has been that more soldiers now survive to return home with severe physical, psychological, and cognitive injuries.

The Human Impact of the War on Terrorism

As of September 14, 2012, the Defense Manpower Data Center (DMDC) officially placed total fatalities for the WOT at 6,515 and the total number of personnel wounded in action for OEF and OIF at 49,531 (Defense Casualty Analysis System, 2012). The actual number of soldiers whose health has been affected by the war is substantially larger, however, because wounded-in-action numbers do not account for a large population of soldiers returning from combat with undiagnosed combat-related, noncombat, or deployment-related injuries and illnesses (U.S. Department of the Army, 2012, p. 11). More than 804,700 WOT veterans who were discharged from the military between October 1, 2002, and March 31, 2012, obtained health care from the VA (U.S. Department of Veterans Affairs, 2012a). An analysis of VA data shows the following:

- 56.1% were active duty, while 43.9% were members of the reserves and National Guard.
- 56.7% were diagnosed with diseases of the musculoskeletal system and connective tissue.
- 52.8% were diagnosed with mental disorders, including
  - 228,361 diagnosed with PTSD and
  - 174,700 diagnosed with depressive disorder.
- 44.8% were diagnosed with diseases of the nervous system or sense organs. (U.S. Department of Veterans Affairs, 2012a)

It is important to interpret these statistics from military and VA sources with caution because they apply only to those OEF and OIF veterans who have accessed military or VA health care. The statistics do not account for veterans who are using other health care sources.

PTSD, depression, and TBI deserve special mention, for they are this conflict's "signature" injuries. The 2008 RAND report, *Invisible Wounds: Mental Health and Cognitive Care Needs of America's Returning Veterans*, estimates that 31% of veterans returning from OEF and OIF have PTSD, depression, or TBI (Tanielian et al., 2008, p. 12). This means that as many as 744,000 veterans returning from OEF and OIF may have one or more of these three disabilities.

Posttraumatic Stress Disorder, Depression, and Traumatic Brain Injury

What's the difference between going into a combat zone and being injured physically versus being injured mentally? One gives you a visible scar and the other doesn't. Imagine how you would feel to be completely whole and not have the mind to function—just locked inside a hell you can't escape. (Eliscu, 2008)

PTSD, previously referred to in the military as shell shock, battle fatigue, war neurosis, or exhaustion, was formally recognized in 1980, when it was added to the third edition of the *Diagnostic and Statistical Manual of Mental Disorders* (Lafferty et al., 2008, p. 6). PTSD is an anxiety disorder that can develop in response to exposure to an extreme traumatic or dangerous event (National Institute of Mental Health, 2009). These traumatic events may include military combat, terrorist attacks, violent personal assaults, or serious accidents that a person responds to with fear or helplessness (American Council on Education, 2010, p. 3). The criteria for a diagnosis of PTSD include the following:

- A history of exposure to a traumatic event, that is, any event that involves actual or threatened death or injury and an initial response of fear, helplessness, or horror.
- Recurrent and intrusive recollections or memories of the event, including nightmares; distraction caused by intrusive images, thoughts, or perceptions of the event; and reexperiencing the event through hallucinations or flashbacks.
- Avoidant or numbing behavior, including avoidance of things that were previously enjoyable because they remind the person of the

traumatic event; avoidance of thoughts, feelings, or conversations associated with the traumatic event; inability to recall aspects of the traumatic event; and a sense of foreshortened future.

- Hyper-arousal, including feeling constantly on edge or hyper-alert, difficulty sleeping, difficulty concentrating, and anger. (U.S. Department of the Army, 2012, p. 22; U.S. Department of Veterans Affairs, 2011)

It is normal for most people to experience some psychological symptoms following a traumatic event. A diagnosis of PTSD, however, is based on the intensity and duration of symptoms. Symptoms typically emerge within a few months of the traumatic event but may appear many months or even years later (American Council on Education, 2010, p. 3).

PTSD may affect student veterans in a variety of ways. It may inhibit interaction with peers during discussion and group work because students with PTSD are often reluctant to share their own thoughts and opinions. Some course topics might cause extreme anxiety for the student. Students may feel discomfort in classes when seating is not the same from week to week or in classes that are exceptionally large. PTSD affects a student's ability to focus during timed activities when there are distractions in the room, such as shuffling noises or people in the hallway. The disorder may also cause difficulty in concentrating and reading for extended periods of time and has been linked to substance abuse, acute stress disorder, somatoform disorders, depression, and other mood and anxiety disorders (Cozza et al., 2004). One of the most difficult challenges of PTSD is that it sometimes has a delayed onset (Hoge et al., 2008), and symptoms of the disorder can begin to manifest themselves after the student veteran has already transitioned into higher education.

Depression is the most prevalent mood disorder affecting the U.S. population today, but it is often not considered a combat-related injury (Tanielian et al., 2008, p. 30; U.S. Department of the Army, 2012, p. 27). Depression is often linked to grief and loss, however, which can be significant for service members who lose their comrades (Tanielian et al., 2008, p. 3). Depression is diagnosed as a persistent feeling of sadness or hopelessness that lasts for at least two weeks. Symptoms include a loss of interest in activities, limited energy, inability to concentrate or pay attention, difficulty in making decisions, and changes in appetite or sleeping patterns (Institute of Medicine, 2010, p. 67). People with depression may feel hopeless about the future and may harbor thoughts of suicide (U.S. Department of Veterans Affairs, 2012b).

TBI has been defined as an alteration in brain function, or other evidence of brain pathology, caused by an external force (Brain Injury Association of

America, 2011). TBI may be caused by bullets or shrapnel hitting the head or neck but also by blasts from mortar attacks, IEDs, grenades, or roadside bombs:

> Physical injuries from concussive events can affect both the brain, as a phys-ical injury, and the mind, as a psychological injury. Physical injuries to the brain can be more readily identifiable with more obvious implications on health and well-being, while injuries to the mind (or invisible wounds) can be harder to detect and diagnose. (U.S. Department of the Army, 2012)

Although penetrating brain injuries are easy to identify, closed head wounds from blasts, which may damage the brain without leaving an exter-nal mark, are difficult to identify (Williamson & Mulhall, 2009, p. 3). TBI appears to account for a higher percentage of casualties in the WOT than it has in other recent U.S. wars (Okie, 2005, p. 2044). Warden (2006, p. 400) found that 28% of all individuals medically evacuated to the Walter Reed Army Medical Center had TBI, and Kennedy et al. (2007, p. 896) found that between January 2003 and February 2007, 29% of the patients medically evacuated to Walter Reed Army Medical Center had evidence of both TBI and PTSD. Twenty-two percent of the soldiers wounded in the current con-flicts have had head injuries, compared to 12–14% of the soldiers wounded in the Vietnam War (Okie, 2005). Modern body armor, which in general pro-tects its wearer from more serious injury, has increased the proportion of TBIs:

> By effectively shielding the wearer from bullets and shrapnel, the protective gear has improved overall survival rates, and Kevlar helmets have reduced the frequency of penetrating head injuries. However, the helmets cannot completely protect the face, head, and neck, nor do they prevent the kind of closed brain injuries often produced by blasts. (Okie, 2005, p. 2045)

The U.S. Department of Defense Military Health System (2012) reported that 253,330 soldiers had been diagnosed with TBI as of August 20, 2012. In some cases TBI can go undetected until service members return home and find they can no longer function as they did before deployment (Institute of Medicine, 2010, p. 63).

TBIs are classified as focal or diffuse; open or closed; and mild, moder-ate, or severe. A focal injury is localized to a small area of the brain, whereas a diffuse injury occurs over a large area of the brain. An open injury (also called a penetrating injury) occurs when the brain's protective coverings are penetrated by an object; otherwise the injury is closed (Bagalman, 2011, p. 2). TBI diagnoses range in severity. In a Department of Defense survey of medical diagnoses of TBI for all military personnel from 2000 to 2012, 76.8% were classified as mild, 16.6% were classified as moderate, 1.0% were classified as severe, and 1.6% were classified as penetrating (U.S. Department of Defense Military Health System, 2012).

A mild TBI may be temporary, and the majority of people who suffer this injury will recover, although the timetable for recovery can vary widely from person to person. Symptoms of a mild TBI may include headaches, fatigue, irritability, dizziness, balance problems, decreased concentration and attention span, decreased speed of thinking, memory problems, and mood swings. A moderate TBI occurs when the person loses consciousness for a few minutes to a few hours and experiences confusion lasting from days to weeks. Physical, cognitive, or behavioral impairments last for months or may become permanent. A person with a moderate TBI usually has a good recovery and successfully learns to compensate for any deficits resulting from the injury. A severe TBI occurs when a prolonged unconscious state or coma lasts days, weeks, or months (Brain Injury Association of America, n.d.).

TBI is the most common injury among those wounded in OEF and OIF. TBIs can accumulate for troops exposed to multiple blasts, leading to serious neurological problems that are not immediately apparent after the injury (Institute of Medicine, 2010, p. 62; Williamson & Mulhall, 2009, p. 3).

TBI produces a number of symptoms, including the following:

- Cognitive problems involving judgment, concentration, information processing, distraction, language use, sequencing, and short-term memory.
- Perceptual problems involving hearing, vision, orientation to space and time, touch, balance, and pain sensitivity.
- Physical problems involving motor skills, endurance, fatigue, speech, headaches, and seizures.
- Behavioral and emotional problems, including irritability, impatience, problems with impulse control, stress, problems with self-awareness, mood swings, personality changes, difficulty reading social cues, and problems with dependence/independence.
- Psychiatric problems, including depression, hallucinations, paranoia, and suicidal thoughts. (Church, 2009, p. 46)

PTSD, depression, and TBI are the signature wounds of the WOT, but it is often difficult to distinguish each from the other because they share symptoms and may, in fact, compound the others' effects. Hoge et al. (2008) found that

mild traumatic brain injury (i.e., concussion) occurring among soldiers deployed in Iraq is strongly associated with PTSD and physical health problems 3 to 4 months after the soldiers return home. PTSD and depression are important mediators of the relationship between mild traumatic brain injury and physical health problems. (p.453)

Although the relationship between TBI and related disorders, such as acute stress disorder (ASD) and PTSD, has not been definitively proven, many clinicians and medical authorities believe a relationship exists (Kennedy et al., 2007; Murray et al., 2005).

Soldiers who lost consciousness as a result of a TBI are nearly three times as likely to meet criteria for PTSD, and depression is also often associated with TBI (Williamson & Mulhall, 2009, pp. 4–5). The overlapping symptoms and comorbidity of PTSD, depression, TBI, and other physical or psychological health issues is complex. In response, the VA has put into place a comprehensive system of rehabilitation services for polytrauma. In 2005 the VA defined *polytrauma* as "injury to the brain in addition to other body parts or systems resulting in physical, cognitive, psychological, or psychosocial impairments and functional disability." This definition was expanded in 2009 to include concurrent injury to two or more body parts or systems that resulted in cognitive, physical, psychological, or other psychosocial impairments (Institute of Medicine, 2010, pp. 62, 66).

PTSD, depression, and TBI qualify as disabilities when they substantially limit one or more major life activities as defined in the ADAAA: "Major life activities include, but are not limited to, caring for oneself, performing manual tasks, seeing, hearing, eating, sleeping, walking, standing, lifting, bending, speaking, breathing, learning, reading, concentrating, thinking, communicating, and working." PTSD, depression, and TBI may affect any or all of the major life activities listed in the legislation. But major life activities related to education—learning, reading, concentrating, thinking, and communicating—are greatly affected by the cognitive deficits or impairments resulting from these injuries. Most student veterans with these diagnoses, therefore, will qualify for a variety of services at their institution under the ADAAA.

Impact on Education

John is medically retired from the Air Force, having served in both OIF and OEF. He has major depression and social phobia. Despite these challenges, he has decided to work toward a bachelor's degree in alcohol and drug studies:

> I do pretty well but the depression hits me every so often and it makes it difficult for me to study. I'm also so highly medicated at times that I can't really function. I may spend most of the week in bed and my attention and

focus aren't that well. I was a 3.8 grade point average student but because of my depression I've fallen to a 2.5 grade point average. I've gotten a couple of Fs since I fell so far behind that I couldn't catch up. I've also failed most of my correspondence courses since I really lack the motivation and since I don't have deadlines I put everything off and just focus on my online classes so I don't fall behind. I really struggle between the depression or maybe I'm just not motivated. I know with having Social Phobia I'll never use my degree but it's a goal in life and it gives me something to keep me going. . . . I've never used the Disability Services. I've always felt like I wouldn't qualify. (Kelley, Fox, Smith, & Wittenhagen, 2011, pp.173–174)

Faculty and disability services providers must be prepared to provide reasonable and appropriate academic accommodations as wounded warriors transition to campus. They must recognize that student veterans may not be aware that their newly acquired disability, either visible or invisible, will affect them in the classroom, and they may not understand that the effects of the disability may develop over time (Shackleford, 2009, p. 36). Student veterans with disabilities, faculty, and disability service providers must collaborate to ensure that the academic accommodations provided in the classroom are effective in meeting current needs and are flexible enough to accommodate future needs.

Student veterans returning to campus with visible or sensory disabilities, including amputations, injuries of the musculoskeletal system, burns, visual impairments, and hearing impairments will generally be able to identify needed resources. Disability service providers and faculty can limit the impact of these disabilities through a variety of accommodations, including the following:

- A student veteran who is an amputee learning to use a prosthetic arm may need a note taker in class, a scribe for exams, or access to a one-handed keyboard or a trackball mouse.
- A student veteran who has a hearing impairment may need preferential seating at the front of the class, the use of a frequency modulation (FM) system to hear lectures, or transcriptions from live online chat sessions.
- A student veteran who has a visual impairment may need printed materials in a larger font size, books in an alternate format, or screen reader software.
- A student veteran who uses a wheelchair may need classrooms moved to accessible buildings or a lower table in science labs.

It is more difficult for faculty and disability service providers to recognize the impact of PTSD, depression, and TBI in the classroom because they primarily affect cognitive ability and behavioral health (U.S. Department of the Army, 2012, p. 66). Many student veterans with these disabilities are entering postsecondary education with the full expectation that colleges and universities will be prepared to meet their needs. Student veterans with invisible disabilities must be provided with appropriate academic accommodations to ensure their full and equal access to education. This requires an understanding of the possible cognitive deficits relating to such disabilities, including their impact on a student's ability to learn and to demonstrate the knowledge that he or she has gained.

Impact on Learning

Postsecondary institutions may be better prepared to provide services to student veterans with cognitive deficits related to PTSD, depression, or TBI than they realize. This is because the academic accommodations that are currently being provided to students with learning disabilities—which are cognitive deficits—to ensure their full and equal access to education may be applicable, with some adaptions, for student veterans with cognitive deficits. To understand the cognitive deficits that may affect student veterans with PTSD, depression, or TBI and their ability to learn, it is important to first look at cognition. *Cognition* is defined as

> the intellectual or mental processes through which information is acquired and processed. It includes the ability to attend to and process information (attention), acquire new information (memory), and use information strategically in planning, problem-solving, and self-monitoring (executive functions). (U.S. Department of Veterans Affairs, 2010, p. 57)

Cognition may also be understood through an information processing model:

- Input—the acquisition of information through one of the five senses
- Integration—organizing and synthesizing new information with information already in the memory system
- Storage—storing information for later use
- Output—expressing information through speech, writing, or movement (MacCluskie & Weifel, 2002, pp. 90–91)

Cognitive deficits may be defined as a wide variety of impaired brain tasks and brain functions related to cognition. They include learning disabilities, which are generally diagnosed when a person is young. Injuries such as TBI and stroke may also lead to cognitive deficits. Cognitive deficits associated with PTSD, depression, and TBI affect at least one and possibly all areas of cognition and may negatively affect academic performance. In addition to cognitive deficits, student veterans with these injuries often have behavioral symptoms that include mood changes, anxiety, impulsiveness, emotional outbursts, and inappropriate laughter (Okie, 2005, p. 2045). Student veterans with cognitive deficits have more frequent and more severe headaches than student veterans without, which may also affect their academic performance (Institute of Medicine, 2010, p. 36).

Cognitive deficits associated with PTSD, depression, and TBI create many of the same challenges related to the input, integration, storage, and output of information as other learning disabilities. Tasks that the veteran easily accomplished prior to deployment, for example, may suddenly require concentrated attention—a distinction in focus that is often described as associative or cognitive. Associative tasks are two or more tasks that the brain can perform at the same time, that is, multitasking. Cognitive tasks, in contrast, are tasks that the brain can perform only one at a time (Rosen, Lavoie, & Rosen, 2004). A student who is first learning to play the piano must focus on the instrument solely—it is a cognitive task. A student who is able to sing while playing the piano, however, has learned both activities so well that they have become associative tasks. The typical college classroom often requires students to perform associative tasks, such as simultaneously listening to a lecture, reading a PowerPoint presentation, and writing notes. Students with learning disabilities or student veterans with cognitive deficits may find any one of the tasks (listening, reading, or writing) to be a cognitive task. Students with learning disabilities have often had years to practice strategies and learn techniques to convert a cognitive task into an associative task, but student veterans with cognitive deficits have generally not had time to develop those strategies (Davies, Matthews, Stammers, & Westerman, 2000, p. 258).

Understanding Invisible Disabilities

Academic accommodations allow students with disabilities to learn and demonstrate knowledge by ameliorating the impact of their disability. Accommodations do not give students with a disability an advantage over their classmates without disabilities but rather ensure the same access to education. It is important to remember that academic accommodations must be tailored to the unique needs of each individual student. An academic accommodation that works for one student veteran may not work for another, even if they share the same cognitive deficit. Instructors generally understand why extended time for an exam is an appropriate academic accommodation for a student veteran who is first learning to use a prosthetic hand, but they may struggle to understand why extended time for an exam is an appropriate accommodation for a student veteran with a cognitive deficit. The following activities can help faculty and staff better understand the challenges that student veterans with these invisible disabilities face. These activities are organized around cognitive deficits that are common to PTSD, depression, and TBI. The suggested accommodations may not be appropriate for every student.

Amnesic aphasia, a "loss of memory for words due to a brain dysfunction," is a cognitive deficit (Thomas, 1993, p. 133). **Dysnomia** is a learning disability in which students are "forgetting words or having difficulty finding words for written or oral expression" (Thomas, 1993, p. 592).

Reader Reflection: Understanding Amnesic Aphasia and Dysnomia

Tell someone about your last vacation, but don't use any words with the letter *N*. Next, type a paragraph about your experience eating at a new restaurant, but don't use any words with the letters *T* or *S*.

Most people who complete this Reader Reflection activity find that it takes them much longer to describe the situation than would normally be the case. The activity demonstrates the difficulty a student with amnesic aphasia or dysnomia experiences when recalling words from memory to speak or write. Each word has to be internally double-checked, causing a significant delay when speaking or writing.

Academic accommodations: Extend time for exams; provide extra time for the student to respond to questions in class; provide access to a dictionary and thesaurus for essay exams; and provide additional lead time for papers and other written assignments. Other accommodations may be necessary depending on the individual needs of the student.

Auditory processing disorders affect how the brain perceives and processes what it hears and may occur with or without a hearing loss. Students may have difficulty remembering spoken directions and people's names, may require that words or sentences be repeated, and may have difficulty hearing in noisy environments (National Center for Learning Disabilities, n.d.).

Reader Reflection: Understanding Auditory Processing Disorders

A *mondegreen* is a word or phrase that results from a mishearing of something said or sung. Varicose veins, for example, might be heard or understood as "very close veins" (Merriam-Webster.com). While monde-greens cannot exactly replicate the experience of a student with an auditory processing disorder, they do force one to listen more intently to understand what is being said. Read the following nursery rhyme aloud:

> *Marry hatter ladle limb*
> *Itch fleas worse widest snore.*
> *An ever-wear debt Marry win*
> *Door limb worse shorter gore.*

Most readers recognize the poem in this Reader Reflection as a monde-green version of "Mary Had a Little Lamb" but are still required to slow down and listen carefully as they read it. A student with an auditory processing disorder finds that listening is a cognitive rather than an associative task, making it difficult to concentrate on other activities (such as taking notes) when listening is required.

Academic accommodations: Provide a note taker; record lectures digitally; allow students to utilize an FM hearing system in class to eliminate background noise; provide closed captioning on videos; provide transcription of online audio components; and transcribe verbal instructions into a written format. Other accommodations may be necessary depending on the individual needs of the student.

Dysgraphia is a cognitive deficit, an "inability to write properly, usually the result of a brain lesion" (Thomas, 1993, p. 590). **Disorders of written expression** is a learning disability that results in a student having poor handwriting, poor spelling, and frequent errors in grammar and punctuation (U.S. National Library of Medicine PubMed Health, 2010).

Reader Reflection: Understanding Dysgraphia and Disorders of Written Expression

Copy the following equations with your nondominant hand. If you are right-handed, use your left hand; if you are left-handed, use your right hand:

$$(x+a)^n = \sum_{k=0}^{n} \binom{n}{k} x^k a^{n-k}, f(x) = a_0 + \sum_{n=1}^{\infty} \left(a_n \cos\frac{n\pi x}{L} + b_n \sin\frac{n\pi x}{L}\right)$$

It generally takes longer to write out the equations in the Reader Reflection with the nondominant hand, and this activity focuses your concentration on the writing process. The exercise demonstrates the difficulty that students with dysgraphia or a disorder of written expression have in producing information in a written format. For them, writing is a cognitive task. It is not just the formation of the actual letters and symbols, but the focus required to do so, that creates academic challenges for the students.

Academic accommodations: Allow a student to use a computer for essay exams; extend time for exams; provide a note taker; provide a scribe for exams; record lectures digitally; provide the student with additional lead time for papers and other written assignments; allow the student to use speech-to-text software for essay exams and papers; and use alternative feedback strategies to assess spelling and grammar for in-class writing assignments for which the student does not have access to a spell checker. Other accommodations may be necessary depending on the individual needs of the student.

Reading disorders are a group of conditions that interfere with or prevent comprehension of written or printed material (Thomas, 1993, pp. 1678–1679). Students in higher education often experience reading disorders as a difficulty in either decoding or comprehending the written word.

Decoding is the process of breaking a word into individual phonemes and recognizing the word based on those phonemes. A phoneme is a single distinctive sound, for example the \g\ and \t\ in *dog* and *dot* are different phonemes; there are 44 phonemes in the English language. Students with decoding difficulty have trouble pronouncing words and recognizing the words out of context, confuse letters and the sounds they represent, read word by word, and ignore punctuation while reading (WGBH Educational Foundation, 2002).

Reader Reflection: Understanding Decoding Reading Disorders

Read the following quickly:

Inqiviquals wirh qyslexia, a teaqing qisotqet, srtuggle ro qecoqe anq sedatare the sounqs rhar make ud worqs anq may have qifficulry thyming. Teaqing skills ate paseq on worq tecognirion anq marching sounqs ro lerrets or a gtoud of lerrets. Rhis leaqs ro qifficulry unqetsranqing rhe meaning of senrences.

The time and concentration required to decode the paragraph in this Reader Reflection has made reading a cognitive task. To decode the paragraph, pronounce *d* as \p\; pronounce *p* as \b\; pronounce *q* as \d\; pronounce *r* as \t\; and pronounce *t* as \r\. This is the sort of challenge that all students with dyslexia face. Translated, the paragraph reads,

> Individuals with dyslexia, a reading disorder, struggle to decode and separate the sounds that make up words and may have difficulty rhyming.

Reading skills are based on word recognition and matching sounds to letters or a group of letters. This leads to difficulty understanding the meaning of sentences.

Comprehension is the ability to comprehend, give meaning to, and remember what is being read. Students with comprehension difficulty confuse the meaning of words and sentences, are unable to connect ideas in a passage, gloss over or omit details, have difficulty distinguishing significant information from minor details, lack concentration when reading, and must put their effort into reading individual words.

Reader Reflection: Understanding Comprehension Reading Disorders, Part 1

Read the following list of words. Do you know the meaning of each word?

dissonances	can	string	produced	comparing
lengths	numbers	after	from	tone
difference	fourth	divisions	reveals	left

Faculty and staff never have difficulty understanding the meaning of the words in this Reader Reflection. But in the right context, they can be quite confusing:

Reader Reflection: Understanding Comprehension Reading Disorders, Part 2

Read the following passage, and explain what it means to a friend:

"Dissonances can be derived from the same divisions of the string that produced consonances, by comparing together the lengths, taken to the left, which remain after each number. This also reveals the difference between two consecutive consonances. For example the lengths taken to the left after the numbers 3 and 4 will give the tone, which differentiates the fifth from the fourth." (Rameau, 1971, p. 27)

A student may be able to comprehend individual words, but that does not guarantee that he or she can understand the larger context of the sentence or paragraph. This particular example may be understandable if you have a background in music, but for many instructors this paragraph makes little sense. The time and concentration required to read the paragraph and comprehend its meaning have again transformed the reading process into a cognitive task.

Academic accommodations: Print materials in alternate formats; provide text-to-audio software; extend time for exams; provide a reader for exams; allow access to a dictionary or spell checker for essay exams; record lectures digitally; provide the student with additional lead time for papers and other written assignments; and translate written instructions into a verbal or audio format. Other accommodations may be necessary depending on the individual needs of the student.

The preceding Reader Reflection activities provide a glimpse of some of the challenges that student veterans with cognitive deficits resulting from PTSD, depression, and TBI face in the classroom. Other cognitive challenges may include short- and long-term memory loss, difficulty maintaining attention and focus, difficulty with organizing assignments and meeting deadlines, and difficulty moving quickly from one concept or task to another. It is important to remember that student veterans with disabilities—either visible or invisible—should not be treated as a group by faculty and disability service providers. Each student is an individual and academic accommodation must be provided on an individual basis. The application of Universal Design (UD) can mitigate many of these challenges for students, as discussed in chapters 8, 9, and 10.

Chapter Summary

Accommodating student veterans with disabilities can be a unique challenge for faculty and disability services providers. PTSD, depression, and TBI present new and personal challenges for the student veterans as they return to the classroom. By understanding the impact of these signature wounds, faculty and disability services providers can work in collaboration with the student veterans to provide them with the services and support that they need and are legally due.

Key Points

- PTSD, depression, and TBI are the signature wounds of OEF and OIF.
- Student veterans with PTSD, depression, or TBI may qualify as students with disabilities under the ADAAA.
- Student veterans with PTSD, depression, or TBI may experience cognitive deficits.
- Learning disabilities and cognitive deficits both affect brain tasks and brain function relating to cognition.

- Academic accommodations that are typically used for students with learning disabilities may be adjusted to assist student veterans with cognitive deficits.
- Academic accommodations must be individualized to the unique needs of each student veteran with a disability.

References

American Council on Education. (2010). *Accommodating student veterans with traumatic brain injury and post-traumatic stress disorder: Tips for campus faculty and staff.* Washington DC: Author. Retrieved from http://www.acenet.edu/news-room/Pages/Accommodating-Student-Veterans-with-Traumatic-Brain-Injury-and-Post-Traumatic-Stress-Disorder.aspx

Americans with Disabilities Act Amendments Act of 2008, Public Law No. 110–325, §3 (2008).

Arenofsky, J. (2009). Traumatic brain injury: An exploding problem. In K. Von Lunen (Ed.), *To war and back: Afghanistan and Iraq: A new generation of veterans* (pp. 8–12). Kansas City, MO: Veterans of Foreign Wars of the United States.

Bagalman, E. (2011). *Traumatic brain injury among veterans.* UNT Digital Library. Washington DC: Congressional Research Service. Retrieved from http://digital.library.unt.edu/ark:/67531/metadc40083/

Brain Injury Association of America. (2011, February 6). *BIAA adopts new TBI definition* [website]. Retrieved from http://www.biausa.org/announcements/biaa-adopts-new-tbi-definition

Brain Injury Association of America. (n.d.). *About brain injury* [website]. Retrieved from http://biausa.fyrian.com/about-brain-injury.htm#types

Chief Administrative Officer of the House. (n.d.). *Wounded Warrior Program: Frequently asked questions* [website]. Retrieved from http://cao.house .gov/wounded-warrior/frequently-asked-questions

Chong, J. (2008, April 22). Class-action suit against VA opens. *Los Angeles Times.* Retrieved from http://articles.latimes.com/2008/apr/22/local/me-veterans22

Church, T. E. (2009). *Veterans with disabilities: Promoting success in higher education.* Huntersville, NC: Association on Higher Education and Disability.

Cozza, S. J., Benedek, D. M., Bradley, J. C., Grieger, T. A., Nam, T. S., & Waldrep, D. A. (2004). Topics specific to the psychiatric treatment of military personnel. In *Iraq War clinician guide* (2nd ed.). Washington DC: Department of Veterans Affairs National Center for PTSD. Retrieved from http://www.ptsd.va.gov/professional/manuals/iraq-war-clinician-guide.asp

Davies, D. R., Matthews, G., Stammers, R. B., & Westerman, S. J. (2000). *Human performance: Cognition, stress, and individual differences.* New York: Psychology Press.

Defense Casualty Analysis System. (2012, September 14). *U.S. military casualties— Operation Iraqi Freedom (OIF) casualty summary by casualty category.* Defense Manpower Data Center. Retrieved from https://www.dmdc.osd.mil/dcas/pages/report_oif_namesalp.xhtml

Eliscu, J. (2008, April 3). The troubled homecoming of the Marlboro Marine. *Rolling Stone, 1049*: 56—61.

Grossman, P. D. (2009). Foreword with a challenge: Leading our campuses away from the perfect storm. *Journal of Postsecondary Education and Disability 22*(1), 4–9.

Hampson, R. (2010, May 28). Afghanistan: America's longest war. *USA Today*. Retrieved from http://www.usatoday.com/news/military/2010-05-27-longest -war-afghanistan_N.htm

Hoge, C. W., Castro, C. A., Messer, S. C., McGurk, D., Cotting, D. I., & Koffman, R. (2004). Combat duty in Iraq and Afghanistan, mental health problems, and barriers to care. *New England Journal of Medicine, 351*(1), 13–22. doi:10.1056/ NEJMoa040603

Hoge, C. W., McGurk, D., Thomas, J. L., Cox, A. L., Engel, C. C., & Castro, C. A. (2008). Mild traumatic brain injury in U.S. soldiers returning from Iraq. *The New England Journal of Medicine, 358*(5), 453–463. doi:10.1056/NEJMoa072972

Institute of Medicine. (2010). *Returning home from Iraq and Afghanistan: Preliminary assessment of readjustment needs of veterans, service members, and their families.* Washington DC: National Academies Press.

Kelley, B. C., Fox, E. L., Smith, J. M., & Wittenhagen, L. (2011). Forty percent of 2 million: Preparing to serve our veterans with disabilities. *To Improve the Academy, 30*, 173–185.

Kennedy, J. E., Jaffee, M. S., Leskin, G. A., Stokes, J. W., Leal, F. O., & Fitzpatrick, P. J. (2007). Posttraumatic stress disorder and posttraumatic stress disorder–like symptoms and mild traumatic brain injury. *Journal of Rehabilitation Research & Development, 44*(7), 895–920.

Lafferty, C. L., Alford, K. L., Davis, M. K., & O'Connor, R. (2008, Autumn). Did you shoot anyone? A practitioner's guide to combat veteran workplace and classroom reintegration. *Advanced Management Journal*, 4–18.

Leland, A., & Oboroceanu, M. J. (2010). *American war and military operations casualties: Lists and statistics.* Washington DC: Congressional Research Service.

MacCluskie, K. C., & Weifel, E. R. (2002). *Using test data in clinical practice: A handbook for mental health professionals.* Thousand Oaks, CA: Sage Publications, Inc.

Mondegreen. (n.d.). In *Merriam-Webster.com*. Retrieved from http://www.merriam -webster.com/dictionary/mondegreen

Murray, C. K., Reynolds, J. C., Schroeder, J. M., Harrison, M. B., Evans, O. M., & Hospenthal, D. R. (2005). Spectrum of care provided at an Echelon II medical unit during Operation Iraqi Freedom. *Military Medicine, 170*(6), 516–520.

National Center for Learning Disabilities. (n.d.). *Auditory processing disorders: By age group.* Retrieved from http://www.ncld.org/types-learning-disabilities/adhd-related -issues/auditory-processing-disorders/auditory-processing-disorder-by-age-group

National Institute of Mental Health. (2009). *What is post-traumatic stress disorder, or PTSD?* Retrieved from http://www.nimh.nih.gov/health/publications/post -traumatic-stress-disorder-ptsd/what-is-post-traumatic-stress-disorder-or-ptsd.shtml

NCO Promotion Board. (n.d.). *DoD approved wounded, ill and injured-related definitions.* Retrieved from http://www.ncopromotionboard.com/army-promotion -questions/wounded-definition.html

Okie, S. (2005). Traumatic brain injury in the war zone. *New England Journal of Medicine, 352*(20), 2043–2047.

Rameau, J. (1971). *Treatise on harmony* (P. Gossett, Trans.). New York: Dover Publications, Inc.

Rosen, P. (Producer), Lavoie, R. (Writer), & Rosen, P. (Director). (2004). *How difficult can this be? The F.A.T. city workshop: Understanding learning disabilties* [Motion picture]. Washington DC: WETA-PBS Video.

Shackleford, A. L. (2009). Documenting the needs of student veterans with disabilities: Intersection roadblocks, solutions, and legal realities. *Journal of Postsecondary Education and Disability, 22*(1), 36–42.

Smith, J. M., & Miller, W. K. (2011, January 10). Students veterans with disabilities: Transition to higher education [PowerPoint]. Fides: Developing the Academic Promise for Our Student Veterans Conference, Vermillion, SD.

Tanielian, T., Jaycox, L. H., Schell, T. L., Marshall, G. N., Burnam, M. A., Eibner, C., Karney, B. R., Meredith, L. S., Ringel, J. S., & Vaiana, M. E. (2008). *Invisible wounds of war: Summary and recommendations for addressing psychological and cognitive injuries.* Santa Monica, CA: RAND Corporation. Retrieved from http://www.rand.org/pubs/monographs/MG720z1.html

Thomas, C. L. (1993). *Taber's cyclopedic medical dictionary.* Philadelphia: F. A. Davis Company.

Tice, J. (2010, June 21). Army considers shorter deployments. *USA Today.* Retrieved from http://www.usatoday.com/news/military/2010-06-21-army-modifying -deployments_N.htm

U.S. Department of Defense Military Health System. (2012). *DoD worldwide numbers of traumatic brain injury.* Retrieved from http://www.health.mil/ Libraries/TBI-Numbers-Current-Reports/dod-tbi-worldwide-2000-2012Q2-as -of-120820.pdf

U.S. Department of the Army. (2012). *Army 2020: Generating health & discipline in the force ahead of the strategic reset.* Retrieved from http://usarmy.vo.llnwd.net/ e2/c/downloads/235822.pdf

U.S. Department of Veterans Affairs. (2010). *Traumatic brain injury: Independent study course.* Washington, DC: Author. Retrieved from http://www.publichealth .va.gov/docs/vhi/traumatic-brain-injury-vhi.pdf

U.S. Department of Veterans Affairs. (2011). *DSM criteria for PTSD* [website]. Retrieved from http://www.ptsd.va.gov/professional/pages/dsm-iv-tr-ptsd.asp

U.S. Department of Veterans Affairs. (2012a). *Analysis of VA health care utilization among Operation Enduring Freedom (OEF), Operation Iraqi Freedome (OIF), and Operation New Dawn (OND) veterans.* Washington DC: Epidemiology Program, Post Development Health Group, Office of Public Health, Veterans Health Administration, Department of Veterans Affairs. Retrieved from http://www .publichealth.va.gov/epidemiology/reports/oefoifond/health-care-utilization/ index.asp

U.S. Department of Veterans Affairs. (2012b). *Depression* [website]. Retrieved from https://www.healthwise.net/myhealthevet/Content/StdDocument .aspx?DOCHWID=hw30709#hw30711

U.S. National Library of Medicine PubMed Health. (2010, November 15). *Disorder of written expression.* Retrieved from A.D.A.M. Medical Encyclopedia: http://www.ncbi.nlm.nih.gov/pubmedhealth/PMH0002510/

Warden, D. (2006). Military TBI during the Iraq and Afghanistan Wars. *Journal of Head Trauma Rehabilitation, 21*(5), 398–402.

WGBH Educational Foundation. (2002). *Difficulties with reading* [website]. Retrieved from http://www .pbs.org/wgbh/misunderstoodminds/readingdiffs.html

Williamson, V., & Mulhall, E. (2009). *Invisible wounds: Psychological and neurological injuries confront our newest veterans.* New York: Iraq and Afghanistan Veterans of America. Retrieved from http://iava.org/content/invisible-wounds -psychological-and-neurological-injuries-confront-new-generation-veterans-0

PART TWO

INNOVATIVE APPROACHES
TO SERVING VETERANS
ON CAMPUS

4

RECRUITMENT TO
ORIENTATION

What veteran-friendly colleges don't do is coddle veterans. Instead, they create environments in
which vets have the tools to engage in debate and make use of resources.

—Army veteran (American Council on Education, 2008, p. 8)

The first three chapters of this book have highlighted many of the challenges military personnel face as they enter into higher education, as well as the strengths that sustain them through the process. The rest of this book examines ways to prepare our campuses for veterans' success. As indicated in this book's title, the approach must be integrated. From broad policies regarding recruitment, admissions, and orientation to specific types of learning activities in the classroom, the following chapters examine how to remove obstacles and build on strengths to enhance the academic success of student veterans. The goal of higher education should be to provide all students—including student veterans—with the opportunity for an extraordinary education. This goal will be achieved only if institutions accept the responsibility to confront "inflexible ways of thinking, removing impediments to institutional innovation, and underwriting the risks associated with bold change" (U.S. Department of the Army, 2005, pp. 4–10).

The next two chapters examine best practices related to the most common student and administrative services. This chapter focuses on the recruitment, admissions, and orientation process, and the following chapter explores resources that are typically accessed by students after they have been enrolled, including services related to health and counseling. This delineation is by no means clear, so the following provides an outline of what each chapter covers:

Chapter 4

- Identifying and tracking student veterans
- Clarifying structure and communication
- Student veteran recruitment
- Admissions and readmissions
- Orientation
- Housing policies
- Student veteran organizations (SVOs)
- Student veterans' support and resource centers

Chapter 5

- The veteran's voice
- VA school certifying official
- Registrar's Office
- Financial Aid
- Academic Advising
- Career Services
- Student Health and Counseling
- Disability Services

Each of these areas plays an important role in serving our student veterans and can enhance or detract from the overall academic success of these students. Barr and Tagg (1995) declared that the mission of higher education was "not instruction but rather that of producing learning with every student by whatever means work best" (p. 13). This emphasis on learning does not solely apply to the classroom: "Roles under the Learning Paradigm, then, begin to blur. Architects of campus buildings and payroll clerks alike will contribute to and shape the environments that empower student learning" (p. 24). In addition, "a college's purpose is not to transfer knowledge but to create environments and experiences that bring students to discover and construct knowledge for themselves, to make students members of communities of learners that make discoveries and solve problems" (p. 15). Student veterans engage in learning whether they are in the classroom, talking with the Veterans Affairs school certifying official (VA SCO), accessing disability services, or filing for GI benefits. It is every institution's responsibility to ensure that each of these learning experiences reflects an understanding of the unique strengths and needs of student veterans.

One of the greatest challenges in higher education is that its disparate, often compartmentalized units tend to remain isolated. Institutions can provide student veterans with a quality educational experience only when these units collaborate. Working together, the various elements of student and administrative services can create an environment in which the beliefs, behaviors, and values of our student veterans can be expressed and respected. Together, they can provide the support military students need to help them leverage their strengths into academic success. Colleges and universities have increasingly understood the need for this support. Sixty-two percent of the responding institutions in the latest national survey by the American Council on Education (ACE) (McBain, Kim, Cook, & Snead, 2012) currently provide programs and services that are specifically designed for student veterans, an increase of five percentage points from the 2009 survey (Cook & Kim, 2009). Seventy-one percent of these institutions indicated that developing programs and services for student veterans was part of their long-term strategic plan, an increase of 14 percentage points since 2009 (McBain et al., 2012, p. 3).

Identifying and Tracking Student Veterans

One of the challenges that higher education faces is a lack of information about military students. According to a recent study, just 32% of institutions collect retention and completion rates specifically for undergraduate student veterans, 25% report having a detailed understanding of why military students withdraw, and only 10% of colleges and universities know the first-year retention rate of their student veterans (Fain, 2012). Institutional researchers face a significant challenge in simply identifying student veteran populations. Data can be collected on the number of students using military benefits, but this provides an incomplete depiction of the number of actual military students on campus. Student veterans may have exhausted their educational benefits or may have chosen not to use them. In addition, some students who use VA benefits are dependents of military personnel, and not veterans themselves. Institutions should ideally develop ways to identify student veterans early in their enrollment process through admissions websites and printed forms. This is difficult in and of itself, for as we noted in chapter 1, there are differences between military students, Reserves, National Guard personnel, and veterans.

A form that simply asks whether or not a student is a veteran is likely to miss students who have not yet ended their military careers. Service members who have not actually experienced combat may likewise be hesitant to identify themselves as veterans, even if they technically qualify. It is better to ask more generically, "Have you ever served in the U.S. armed forces?" Follow-up questions may be needed if the institution wishes to collect data on students' branch of service or their status as a member of either the National Guard or the Reserve. Institutions may also want to collect data regarding dependency status and chapter of benefits. Forms that ask questions related to military service should provide a short explanation of why this information is being collected. Students should understand that data will be used only to improve resources and services for student veterans. Contact information will be used to develop communications networks that will alert student veterans to changes in their benefits and inform them of veterans-related campus activities. Identification of and clear communication with student veterans is an essential first step for institutions that wish to better serve military students (American Council on Education, 2010, p. 7).

Reader Reflection: Identify Next Steps

How well does your institution monitor the retention and degree completion rates of student veterans?
Is the number of student veterans on campus shared with all applicable administrative offices?

Clarifying Structure and Communication

Chapter 2 examined the challenges that student veterans face when they transition from the military to higher education. Some of these challenges are cultural and societal, but some are structural, and those are easier (but not necessarily easy) to address. The military is structured so that it is immediately clear where you need to go and who you need to see to resolve any particular issue. The same is not true in higher education. Who does one see to put money on a copier card? Is it the library? The business office? Student affairs? The university copy center? Where is the SCO located—the Registrar's Office, Financial Aid, or the Business Office? O'Herrin (2011) notes,

> One of the biggest frustrations voiced by veterans is the daunting and unfamiliar bureaucracy of higher education. While the military is also an enormously complex bureaucracy, information about how to navigate it is ingrained in troops through specific training from the beginning of their military careers. Many veterans have spoken to the sense of alienation they feel upon beginning class and often allude to feeling confused and overwhelmed during their first terms because they aren't sure where to turn for assistance. (p. 16)

As one veteran lamented,

> [During deployment], the tasks are set up. You know what to do. Within the first month or so everything becomes routine. It is the same every day.

It gets really old, but you know exactly what is going to happen. . . . In the Marine Corps someone will tell you outright what they want. There is no guesswork involved. . . . For college [on the other hand], there is no clear "Do this, go home, you're done." (Rumann & Hamrick, 2010, p. 441)

Student veterans can become very frustrated with the lack of direction when it comes to accomplishing certain administrative processes within academic institutions.

To make matters worse, there is little uniformity between institutions of higher education. When a member of the military transfers from one unit to another, the structure remains the same. This is emphatically not the case when military students transfer from one college to another. Military students, who have often received academic credit from a number of institutions, are disproportionally affected by the lack of consistency among institutions of higher education. When soldiers go from one command to the next, they receive an "outprocessing" packet that indicates what they need to do to "clear" their current assignment and move on to the next. This packet contains checklists of everything that they need to do, the contacts involved, and a map of the new installation. Schools that mimic this process in their own procedures will help veterans (as well as other students) ease into their new academic assignments. One example of such a resource is the registration/course preparation checklist developed at the University of South Dakota. This checklist, illustrated in Figure 4.1, prepares student veterans to enroll in courses, file for benefits, and sign up for housing.

A checklist such as this is one way that higher education institutions can communicate clearly to student veterans where appropriate resources are located. Structures and processes should be clarified as an essential step in preparing an institution for student veterans' success. Colleges and universities should also strive to clarify whom student veterans should contact regarding most common services—identifying resources by name, and not just by job title, if at all possible.

Example of Best Practices: University of California–Los Angeles Veterans Resource Team

The University of California–Los Angeles's Veterans Resource Office maintains a Veterans Resource Team that lists the points of contact for offices that tend to be important for student veterans. The website gives names, positions, office locations, and pictures for each member of the team and provides student veterans with a quick and easy way to contact staff who are familiar with their situations and needs. See www.veterans.ucla.edu/currentstudents/staffhelp.htm

Figure 4.1 Registration/Course Preparation Checklist.

Military Student Checklist to assist you in preparation for the **fall 2012 semester**.

- File your FAFSA by the priority deadline March 15. List USD's code of **003474** on your FAFSA **(www.fafsa.ed.gov)**. All military students are encouraged to file the FAFSA. Submitting the FAFSA will determine your eligibility for federal financial aid, including grants, work study, and federal loans.
- Submit your $100 university deposit at **www.usd.edu/apps/deposits/**
- Apply to use GI Bill benefits using VONAPP at **www.ebenefits.va .gov/ebenefitsportal/ebenefits.portal?_nfpb=true&_nfxr=false&_ pageLabel=Vonapp**

Note: Financial aid and/or GI Bill benefits may not be immediately available. Please plan accordingly for collateral expenses such as relocation, housing, and other living costs.

To register for classes, you will need to complete the following steps:

- **Submit your immunization records to USD.**
- **http://admissions.usd.edu/accepted-students/upload/610 -12400-0371-USD-Student-Health-Immunization-Form.pdf**
  - You may submit **DD Form 214** in lieu of the immunization form.
  - Fax to 605-624-6636 or mail to USD Student Health, 20 S. Plum, Vermillion, SD 57069.
- **Set up your USD account and WebAdvisor.**
  - USD account set up: **www.usd.edu/accounts/pickup**
  - WebAdvisor set up: **https://boris.sdbor.edu/idm/retrieve-email .cfm**
    - View the WebAdvisor Tutorial at **http://admissions.usd.edu/ accepted-students/webadvisor-tutorial.cfm**
- **Fill out and submit your online Housing Application or Housing Exemption Request.**
  - **http://admissions.usd.edu/accepted-students/housing-application.cfm** *ALL** students must complete either the housing application or housing exemption form prior to enrolling in classes.
- **Select a registration option.**
  - Call the Admissions Office at 605-677-5434 and sign up for one of our Registration Events:
    - Monday, April 16
    - Wednesday, May 23

- Tuesday, June 12
- Tuesday, June 19
- Monday, July 23
- Friday, August 17
- Monday, August 27
- USD offers a service member/veteran-only transition course (A&S-100-U 931-N). Consult your advisor when registering for your classes.
- **After you register,**
  - Receive your ID card (2nd floor, Munster University Center) on registration day.
  - Bring your military documents (e.g., NOBE, DD 214) to the Veteran Services Office, 212 Belbas Center (605-677-8833).
  - Request an official service transcript be sent electronically to USD at **www.usd.edu/registrar/veterans-services/order-military -documents.cfm**
  - Check to make sure all required USD Admissions material is received:
    - Official high school transcripts and any final official college transcripts.
  - If you are eligible, apply for tuition assistance through your service (**www.gibill.va.gov/** or **http://mva.sd.gov/**)
- Beginning **mid-April**, financial aid award letters will be mailed to your permanent address. Read all information enclosed with the award letter before accepting your financial aid package. Please contact the Financial Aid Office at 605-677-5446 with any questions or if you have any unusual circumstances such as loss of income or employment—including separation from active duty—that you may have incurred following your original financial aid application.
- Reserve your books online **http://usd.bncollege.com/** Parking passes may be purchased at **www.usd.edu/financial-affairs/ business-office/parking.cfm**
- **Military families requiring day care**: Vermillion area childcare programs—including USD's Children's Center (**www.usd.edu/campus -life/childcare/**)—may require waiting lists. Please plan appropriately.
- After you register for classes, your bill will be available online at your SDePay account: **http://admissions.usd.edu/accepted -students/billing-and-payment.cfm**
- You will NOT receive a paper copy of your bill.

Classes commence August 27 at 4 p.m. Contact us at admissions@usd .edu or 605 677-5434

Student Veteran Recruitment

Veterans and military personnel represent a significant pool of potential students for postsecondary institutions. ACE reports that 64% of colleges and universities in its survey engaged in specific recruiting strategies to attract military students to their programs (McBain et al., 2012, p. 56). There is a fine line to walk when it comes to recruiting any specific student population, and Congress has recently investigated several for-profit universities for dishonest recruiting practices aimed at student veterans. These practices often target veterans in an attempt to subvert the Department of Education's 90/10 rule. This rule states that educational institutions cannot receive more than 90% of their funds from the federal government, but VA and Department of Defense benefits are not counted as "federal aid." An enterprising school can therefore receive more than 90% of its funds from the federal government if it enrolls students with VA benefits. If institutions are dedicated to educating student veterans and provide the resources they need to succeed, then this type of recruiting is simply good business. Institutions that recruit students with VA benefits without regard for their academic success are engaging in predatory enrollment practices. They have crossed the line from aggressive to dishonest recruiting.

Institutions are strongly urged to act ethically as they recruit military personnel. The Servicemembers Opportunity Colleges (SOC) Consortium is dedicated to facilitating the ethical enrollment of qualified student veterans and has set forth a number of recruiting guidelines that they expect their members to follow:

- Outreach to service members through advertising, college recruiting, and admissions information should adequately and accurately represent the programs, requirements, and services that the institution has available.
- Advertisements, promotional literature, and recruiting activities should primarily emphasize educational programs and services.
- Institutions should develop and use promotional and recruitment materials and practices that are ethical in every respect toward military members, and promotional materials should not have the capacity to mislead or coerce students into enrolling.
- Institutions should establish legitimate enrollment deadlines and bona fide scholarships and grants based on published criteria. They should refrain from promotional tuition discounts that do not serve the best interests of the military or its members.

- Institutions should refrain from marketing and recruiting practices in which ancillary technology devices (such as laptops, printers, and electronic readers) are offered as inducements to enroll in an educational program. If inducements are offered, any conditions for receiving such an inducement must be readily achievable by the military student and must not pose significant financial hardship or undue burden for receipt.
- Telemarketing should be performed in accordance with Federal Trade Commission and other state and federal regulations.
- Institutions should follow Department of Defense and military service guidance governing installation access and the use of retiree and dependent ID cards; such ID cards should not be used to gain base access for business purposes.
- All education-related activities on an installation or at an armory should be routed through the education center or education services officer for authorization.
- Military students should be given adequate time to make informed decisions about course enrollment. High-pressure promotional activities or "limited time only" enrollment discounts are inappropriate recruiting activities, and institutions should refrain from exerting undue pressure to enroll through follow-up calls or other forms of personal contact.
- Institutions should provide adequate access to the range of services appropriate to enrollment, including access to admissions and academic advisers, financial aid, delivery of course materials, competency testing, course placement, and counseling.
- Students who are admitted into a college program should possess the requisite knowledge and academic preparation to succeed. (SOC Consortium, 2012b)

These guidelines should be followed by all postsecondary institutions and by the faculty, staff, and third-party partners who constitute their recruitment teams.

Student veterans represent an unusual demographic for recruiting staffs. Even institutions that specialize in reaching nontraditional students will find important differences between veterans and their typical students. Student veterans can be hard to reach, for often they take classes while on deployment around the globe. The recruiting process must have a worldwide reach to be fully effective. For-profit online schools may have an advantage in this respect, as these institutions tend to be less place-bound than the traditional college or university. Student veterans have also experienced one significant recruiting event in their life already—their enlistment in the armed forces. Military students may view the college recruiting process through the lens of that experience.

Institutions should build on their individual strengths as they recruit veterans. Physical campuses should reach out first to their community and then explore how to expand their circle of influence into the area and states beyond. Reserve centers, base education centers, and National Guard armories are natural locations to place recruitment materials, as are job fairs, county fairs, and welcome-home events. Colleges and universities may wish to seek out educational partnerships with bases that are located in their geographical areas. This may even extend to developing specific programs or certifications that will be used solely by that base. Military personnel can be invited to campus for special "military only" campus tours. Institutions that develop veteran-friendly policies, such as exemption from mandatory housing policies, can market these policies to potential students. Colleges and universities can also sponsor and support special events for potential military students, such as a "military appreciation day" during a major sports event.

It is important to have someone in the Office of Admissions who fully understands the military's educational process and how end-of-deployment affects the reenrollment of students in the National Guard, Reserve, and Regular military units. Some institutions have established veteran recruiters to reach out to potential military students. These recruiters, who could be VA work-study candidates, can help veterans navigate financial aid benefits, application processes and more. A well-designed web presence is a necessity and should fully exploit the principles of Universal Design (UD) (see chapter 8). Web materials should also be readily accessible on mobile devices. Veterans' online resources should be easy to find and should come up as the first or second entry under any web search for "your institution, veterans resources." The website should clearly delineate contact information for important resources such as the SCO. Transcript evaluation policies and processes are important to most student veterans, and providing these policies in an easy-to-find location can make your institution more attractive to potential students. Universities may wish to adopt the SOC Consortium's Military Student Bill of Rights and prominently display this document on the admissions website. The Bill of Rights states that military students have certain rights regarding marketing, admissions, and student services practices, including the following:

- Accurate information about a school's programs, requirements, accreditation, and its potential impact on course transferability
- Access to basic college/university information and fees without disclosure of student personal information

- Educational planning and career guidance without high-pressure registration and enrollment efforts from institutions
- A clear and complete explanation of course/program enrollment procedures and all resulting financial obligations
- The ability to explore, without coercion, all financial aid options before signing up for student loans or other financial assistance
- Accurate scholarship information, free of misleading "scholarship" offers based on military tuition assistance
- Appropriate academic screening and course placement based on student readiness
- Appropriate, accessible academic and student support services
- Clearly defined drop/add and withdrawal policies
- Detailed information about how a military withdrawal will affect a student's academic standing and financial responsibilities
- Clearly defined grievance and appeals processes (SOC Consortium, 2012a)

In the end, each institution's website should provide clear and direct information regarding the most common questions and needs of newly enrolling military students.

Distance learning can play an important role in a veteran's transition back to college. Institutions should use their online resources to reach out to students who may not otherwise wish to return to higher education, such as those who are struggling with posttraumatic stress disorder (PTSD), depression, or traumatic brain injury (TBI) or who are adjusting to prosthetics. Online education provides time for veterans who need additional healing and recuperation. It also provides a flexible schedule to enable military personnel to search for employment, take care of family responsibilities, and attend counseling and doctor appointments (Helping Veterans Transition, 2009, p. 4).

Example of Best Practices: University of Wisconsin–Madison Office of Admissions and Recruitment Website

The University of Wisconsin's Office of Admissions and Recruitment website has a direct link to information for veterans. The website further explains what student veterans must do to apply (both as a first-year student and as a transfer) and provides links to Student Veterans Services. Other links provide information about military credit, financial aid, and campus resources. This is a strong example of an institution demonstrating ethical recruiting by emphasizing its commitment to the overall academic success of student veterans. See www.admissions.wisc.edu/veterans.php

Admissions and Readmissions

Student veterans often pursue their educational goals from a different time and place in life compared to traditional students. They may not have current college entrance exam scores, and past scores may not adequately reflect their current academic potential, especially after they have received military training. Previous experience in college, especially if it occurred before they entered in the military, may also provide a misleading indicator of how ready a student may be to reenter college. James, for example, was a former Marine who had earned a 0.9 grade point average (GPA) his first two semesters in college, before he enlisted. When he returned from deployment, he had earned a Purple Heart but still found it difficult to enroll at any institution:

> I wanted to get into college, you know, I wanted to get into college and then everybody was pumping me up. You know, yeah you're a Purple Heart veteran and you're this, and this, and that, and you know you're going to have no problem getting into school. Well I applied for [a specific institution] and it was just like almost impossible for them to accept me into school. I wrote them a personal letter. Stuff which I don't think even got read. (Maurin, 2012, pp. 63–64)

It is incumbent on each institution to consider the entire application portfolio when reviewing veterans' information for admission or readmission. Veterans have developed great strengths through their military experience, strengths that can specifically help them to succeed in the classroom. Prior learning assessments (specifically military transcripts) or portfolio models can be used to review veterans' applications (American Council on Education, 2010, p. 9). Institutions should determine whether enrolling veterans with only military transcripts should be admitted as new students or transfer students. Colleges and universities may also want to consider a policy of immediate admission for military students and veterans, even if conditional.

The admissions office must work closely with the registrar and academic departments to determine whether student veterans should receive credit for certain classes or at the very least have prerequisites waived for advanced courses. Veterans often have academic transfer credits from military transcripts and College-Level Examination Program (CLEP) tests that can affect admissions decisions, housing eligibility, or class status. It is common for veterans to have transfer credit from a number of institutions, as they pick up courses from base educational programs, online courses, and various other certification programs. They therefore present a more complex portfolio for determining course equivalencies. Where possible, student veterans should be given the benefit of the doubt when determining transfer credit. When credit is not granted, the reason should be clearly communicated in writing to the incoming student veteran. An excellent resource in making these judgments is ACE's online Guide to the Evaluation of Educational Experiences in the Armed Service (www.militaryguides.acenet.edu/index.htm). This guide is continually updated and evaluated by college and university faculty members.

Registration can be an extremely frustrating experience for student veterans because of uncertainty about how courses will transfer. Institutions that can find ways to expedite this process will generate a significant amount of goodwill among their military students. Institutions may also want to consider registration priority for student veterans. Many VA education benefits are time-bound, and veterans may become discouraged if the courses they need to graduate are closed. Well-informed faculty and staff are essential to making the first registration experience successful.

Institutions need to develop fully coherent policies related to the withdrawal and subsequent return of military students. Deployment can be a highly disruptive event in a student's life. Some colleges and universities impose academic penalties or additional costs for students who drop out and then return after a specified amount of time. Eliminating these policies for military students recognizes that they have no control over the timing of their deployment and facilitates their return to higher education. The withdrawal process itself should be clearly explained for students who are being deployed, and timelines should be explicit. A single point of contact should be established to help military students withdraw with minimal difficulties.

Best practices for admissions include the following:

- Evaluate military students through a holistic process that considers military transcripts and portfolios. Less emphasis should be placed on college grades or ACT/SAT scores received prior to military service.
- Consider implementing a policy of immediate admission for military students, even if conditional.
- Work closely with the registrar and academic units to quickly assess transfer credits and credit for military service.
- Develop policies related to the withdrawal and reenrollment of military students that do not unduly penalize those who are being deployed.
- Explain the withdrawal and readmissions processes clearly, and create checklists to help students account for the various steps that need to be taken.
- Consider offering student veterans registration priority.

Military students enter, leave, and reenter higher education at the Department of Defense's convenience, rather than at their or their college's convenience. Institutions that can streamline the application and reenrollment process will facilitate student veterans' continued pursuit of academic goals.

Orientation

Student veterans often have mixed feelings about college orientations. In a study by Wheeler (2011), not one veteran who experienced a full-day regular orientation found it useful: "It was really stupid. I thought it was a waste of time. I just wanted my school ID. I didn't need to be escorted around school. I can look at a map and find my way around" (p. 103). Not all veterans share this attitude. The concerns of 18-year-old students (and their parents), however, are generally far different from those of returning veterans. A veteran-specific breakout session during general orientation or a veteran-only orientation program can convey a higher level of support to incoming military students and can begin to address their specific concerns (American Council on Education, 2010, p. 7).

One of the primary goals of a veteran-specific orientation is to put military students in touch with the people who can help them solve problems related to their educational benefits. The SCO and informed members from the Financial Aid, Admissions, Business, and Registrar's Offices should therefore be included in the program. VA benefits are so complex that institutions may want to provide each student with a short one-on-one benefits counseling session with a qualified member of the Financial Aid Office. A short welcome by a high-profile university administrator can be a sign of strong support for student veterans, especially if that official can demonstrate an understanding of and concern for veteran-specific issues. Given the potential number of student veterans with disabilities, every orientation should introduce students to personnel from the Disabilities Services and Student Counseling Offices. Representatives from the VA, including the Vet Center and Vocational Rehabilitation Programs, should also be included if practicable. These professionals are an especially important resource for small institutions that may have a limited ability to provide veteran-specific counseling.

A strong veteran orientation connects incoming military students to other veterans, both on campus and in the broader community. Reserve Officers' Training Corps (ROTC) and other formal campus military organizations can be used to provide assistance. The SVO, if one exists, should give incoming students information on how to join. Orientations can connect incoming students with faculty and staff who have military backgrounds and can highlight future programs and events that will be of interest to student veterans, including any VA work-study programs. Food and beverages should be made available to secure both attendance and a positive first impression.

Online orientations can be an effective strategy for providing information to veterans, especially if they are in the midst of end-of-deployment debriefing activities. Incoming student veterans can take advantage of the flexibility and anytime accessibility of the online format. This strategy makes a great deal of sense for students who will be attending an institution primarily online. The disadvantage of this particular type of orientation is the loss of personal contact with staff members who will be the most instrumental in helping students with their course enrollment and benefits.

Best practices for orientations include the following:

- Develop veteran-specific orientations or include veteran-specific segments in traditional orientation programs.
- Connect student veterans with the people and resources that they need most, including the SCO, financial aid personnel, and representatives from Student Counseling and the Office of Disabilities Services.
- Connect incoming military students with current student veterans. Have student veterans conduct campus tours. Provide information on how to join on-campus veterans' groups.
- Connect incoming military students with faculty and staff who are veterans.

Orientation programs allow institutions to introduce themselves to new student veterans and to set the tone for how well (or poorly) they support the veterans' community. It is therefore an essential element in establishing the student veterans' overall academic experience.

Example of Best Practices: Cal Poly Pomona Online Orientation for Veterans

Cal Poly Pomona mandates that all new and transfer students go through either an in-person or an online orientation. An online orientation program for veterans has been implemented, with significant input from current student veterans. The program builds off the current orientation program but includes veteran-specific material and a focus on adult learners. The online orientation contains self-paced modules, a welcome from the president, and information about veteran-related resources. See www.csupomona.edu/~veterans/

Housing Policies

Many institutions have housing policies related to new students. Student veterans, however, may feel uncomfortable having to share a room with a nonveteran, especially if there is any appreciable difference in age between the roommates. Military students may have family situations, special medical needs, or life experience that makes staying in a residence hall unacceptable. Institutions should look for ways to exempt all student veterans from onerous housing policies and may want to consider developing family-friendly and veteran-only housing options. Housing personnel should clearly understand GI Bill housing allowances to best determine the options that are most attractive to incoming student veterans. For example, institutions with multiple campuses in one state should apply for individual facility codes for each campus so that military students receive the proper housing stipends (American Council on Education, 2010, p. 15). Colleges and universities should also examine residency requirements and how they affect student veterans. Many institutions (as well as state systems) have extended in-state tuition to all student veterans, regardless of their official residency status. Campuses have implemented a variety of housing accommodations for student veterans ranging from roommate selection to full-scale learning and living communities.

> *Example of Best Practices: University of California–Irvine Housing Guarantee for Veterans, Reservists (including National Guard), and Active-Duty Service Members*
>
> *University of California–Irvine guarantees an offer for on-campus housing for four years or until the normal degree completion date (whichever is longer). The housing benefit applies to both single veterans and veterans with families. Moreover, the housing guarantee extends through deployments, and students or their significant others may remain in the housing until the lease ends, even if their partner has been deployed. See www.veteran.uci.edu/campusbenefits/housing.php*

Student Veteran Organizations

Student Veteran Organizations (SVOs) can be a critical component of creating an educational environment in which student veterans feel comfortable. It provides visibility for student veterans, promotes their causes, and offers a place where student veterans can take a break from the civilian "clutter" and relax with their peers. A healthy SVO reaches out to all members of the armed forces and their dependents:

> Veterans are interested in connecting with fellow students who have similar experiences. Student organizations provide a vehicle through which veterans can express a collective voice of advocacy while also supplying a setting for learning, reflection, and participation beyond the traditional classroom. (Summerlot, Green, & Parker, 2009, p. 74)

The SVO functions as a combination social club, orientation group, and information exchange (Summerlot et al., 2009, p. 74). Darren, an Army sergeant who is active in his school's veterans club, explains the benefits:

We do things like go to basketball games and fun things. Things where a vet can feel welcome and have a social opportunity with other vets to get back into the swing of things. It is social support more than anything, but not counseling. (Maurin, 2012, p. 71)

The SVO allows student veterans to spend time with peers who have had similar experiences and speak a similar language.

Groups typically hold regular meetings to promote veterans issues, organize service activities, and provide academic and social resources to enhance the success of veterans and their dependents. It is not uncommon for SVOs to develop influence with university administrators and local politicians, and in some cases they have advocated strongly and successfully for changes in policies that hindered student veteran success (Summerlot et al., 2009, p. 77). The SVO serves as the focal point for veterans' activities on campus and may also be linked to national student groups such as the Student Veterans of America (SVA). The SVA is a coalition of SVOs that is dedicated to student veteran success. The organization was founded in 2008 and currently consists of more than 500 campus chapters. SVA's focus is to "provide programs and resources that enable student veterans to overcome administrative, integration, and academic barriers to graduation" (Military Family Research Institute, 2012, p. 17).

SVOs generally take on the organizational structure of other formally recognized student groups within the institution. They should be provided with the same funding, space, and marketing resources as these groups as well. Unlike most other student groups, SVOs often receive gifts of money and materials from alumni and local businesses. Institutions should develop policies to process and recognize these donations, and SVOs should be connected with the institutional foundation if one exists. Students and academic personnel who are interested in forming an SVO are encouraged to refer to *Success in 3-D for Student Veterans: How to Design, Develop and Deliver a Thriving SVO*. This manual was collaboratively produced by the SVA and Purdue University's Military Family Research Institute and is available at www.studentveterans.org/images/Documents/Success In3-D_MFRI-SVA_2012.pdf.

Student Veterans' Support and Resource Center

The presence of a dedicated office for student veterans is a strong indicator of an institution's commitment to serving veterans and military students. McBain et al. (2012) found that institutions with such a center were more likely to create new programs and services to support student veterans; establish recruiting strategies to attract these students; tailor common services, such as financial aid and tuition assistance counseling, to student veterans; increase staff to serve student veterans; offer specialized counseling services; offer faculty and staff training; and sponsor student organizations for veterans (pp. 9–10). Student Veterans' Support and Resource Centers focus institutional efforts to serve military students:

> An office exclusively serving veterans and service members centralizes the initial point of contact for this subpopulation. This centralized provision of student service promotes the development of a depth of veteran-related knowledge and campus resources that are accessible through a one-stop office. When individualized support or assistance is needed—whether academic, financial, or personal—a relationship built on trust can facilitate access to campus services. (McBain et al., 2012, p. 34)

The number of institutions that have such offices has increased significantly, from 49% in 2009 to 71% in 2012 (McBain et al., 2012, p. 9).

Funding Student Veterans' Support and Resource Centers can be a challenge. This space typically contains a study area with computers and wireless access, desks, tables, and bookcases. It often incorporates comfortable chairs and couches and may include a TV, refrigerator, or microwave. As with an SVO, alumni and local businesses may provide donations to the center to help offset the institutional costs. The space should facilitate the programs and services mentioned previously and should create an environment that welcomes and honors the service of student veterans. Some centers, for example, display patches or other mementos that honor units, ranks, and deployments; others have put up clocks that show local time in places such as Baghdad, Kabul, and Muskogee, Oklahoma—where GI Bills are processed (Abramson, 2012). In doing this, the centers set a tone for inclusiveness and understanding.

The creation of a Veterans' Resource Center is one of the most important steps an institution can take to indicate its willingness to serve students veterans. Other steps could be considered, however. Student veterans generally appreciate a gesture of thankfulness from those in higher education, particularly the institution's president. A dinner for student veterans that is hosted by the president, for example, might be feasible for small or midsize institutions. Reserved parking spaces (or simply providing student veterans with access to the "best" parking pass) can quietly indicate an institution's support. Complimentary athletics or fine arts passes—either for single events or entire seasons—can also express institutional appreciation for these students. Institutions should develop appropriate ways to express their gratitude, for student veterans will rarely seek out such treatment and may feel uncomfortable if too much is made of it. The best display of support, however, is to simply provide student veterans with the resources they need to successfully pursue their academic goals.

Conclusion

The services and resources examined in this chapter are among the first to reach out to student veterans. Through them, colleges and universities have the opportunity to demonstrate that they are proactive and understanding in their support for military students. Veteran-specific student groups and resource centers are an important component of that support and can enhance the early recruitment and admissions process. Once on campus, however, student veterans may need continued support and resources. Financial Aid, the Registrar's Office, Disabilities Services, Academic Advising, and many other offices come into repeated contact with student veterans. These offices can either enhance or detract from their academic experience and are the subject of this book's next chapter.

Chapter Summary

Veterans and military personnel represent a significant pool of potential students for postsecondary institutions. Recruitment should be conducted in an ethical manner. Enrollment decisions should be based on a student's current military accomplishments as well as his or her past academic record. It is vital to have someone in the Office of Admissions who fully understands the military's educational process and how end-of-deployment impacts the reenrollment of students in the National Guard, Reserve, and Regular military. Orientation and housing policies should be evaluated in terms of their usefulness for student veterans. Finally, institutions should intentionally use current student veterans, as well as faculty and staff with military experience, to reach out to incoming military students.

Key Points

- Higher education has a less formal and standardized organizational structure than does the military.
- Universities should develop checklists that define where students go for specific services and that step them through complicated processes such as enrollment.
- It is a challenge for institutions to identify exactly who their student veterans are and to determine how many are enrolled in their courses.
- Institutions should ideally develop ways to identify student veterans early in their enrollment process through campus admissions websites and forms.
- Institutions should act ethically as they recruit military personnel.

- It is vital to have someone in the Office of Admissions who fully understands the military's educational process, and how end-of-deployment cycles impact National Guard, Reserve, and Regular military units.
- Past educational experiences may not be authentic indicators of a veteran's academic potential. This is especially true if significant time has passed since the veteran has been in college or if prior educational experiences occurred before the student enlisted.
- Prior learning assessments or portfolio models can be used to review veterans' applications and are considered a best practice in admissions.
- Registration can be an extremely frustrating experience for student veterans because of uncertainty about how courses will transfer.
- A veteran-specific orientation (or orientation segment, at the very least) can convey a higher level of support to incoming military students and can begin to address concerns that are specific to them.
- Veterans' resources should be easy to find on an institution's website.
- Distance learning plays an important role in helping veterans transition back to college, and institutions should use their online resources to reach out to students who may not otherwise wish to return to higher education.
- Institutions should look for ways to exempt all student veterans from burdensome housing policies and may want to consider developing family-friendly and veteran-only housing options.
- SVOs can reach out to military students and their dependents. They provide academic and social resources to enhance the success of these students.
- The presence of a dedicated Student Veterans' Support and Resource Center is a strong indicator of an institution's commitment to serving military students.

References

Abramson, L. (2012, December 5). Vets flock to colleges . . . but how are they doing? National Public Radio. Retrieved from http://www.npr.org/2012/12/05/166501 611/vets-flock-to-colleges-but-how-are-they-doing

American Council on Education. (2008). *Serving those who serve: Higher education and America's veterans* [Issue brief]. Washington DC: Author. Retrieved from http://www.acenet.edu/Content/NavigationMenu/ProgramsServices/Military Programs/serving/Veterans_Issue_Brief_1108.pdf

American Council on Education. (2010). *Veteran Success Jam: Ensuring success for returning veterans.* Washington DC: Author. Retrieved from http://www.acenet.edu/news-room/Pages/Veterans-Jam-2010.aspx

Barr, R. B., & Tagg, J. (1995). From teaching to learning: A new paradigm for undergraduate education. *Change, 27*(6), 12–25.

Cook, B. J., & Kim, Y. (2009). *From soldier to student: Easing the transition of service members on campus.* Washington DC: American Council on Education.

Fain, P. (2012, December 4). Scrambling to understand veterans. *Inside Higher Ed.* Retrieved from http://www.insidehighered.com/news/2012/12/04/colleges-fail-track-performance-student-veterans-survey-finds

Helping Veterans Transition Into Your Programs. (2009). *Distance Education Report, 13*(20), 4–5.

Maurin, K. H. (2012). *Negotiating cultural transitions: Contemporary student veterans and Louisiana institutions of higher education* (Doctoral dissertation). Retrieved from http://etd.lsu.edu/docs/available/etd-01032012–155853/unrestricted/kayharrisonmaurin_diss.pdf

McBain, L., Kim, Y., Cook, B., & Snead K. (2012). *From soldier to student II: Assessing campus programs for veterans and service members.* Washington DC: American Council on Education. Retrieved from http://www.acenet.edu/news-room/Pages/From-Soldier-to-Student-II.aspx

Military Family Research Institute. (2012). *Success in 3-D for student veterans: How to design, develop and deliver a thriving SVO.* Retrieved from http://www.studentveterans.org/?page=Success_in_3D

O'Herrin, E. (2011, Winter). Enhancing veteran success in higher education. *Peer Review, 13*(1), 15–18. Retrieved from http://www.aacu.org/peerreview/pr-wi11/prwi11_oherrin.cfm

Rumann, C. B., & Hamrick, F. A. (2010). Student veterans in transition: Re-enrolling after war zone deployments. *Journal of Higher Education, 81*(4), 431–458. doi:10.1353/jhe.0.0103

SOC Consortium. (2012a). Military student bill of rights [website]. Retrieved from http://www.soc.aascu.org/socconsortium/BillOfRights.html

SOC Consortium. (2012b). Principles and criteria [website]. Retrieved from http://www.soc.aascu.org/socconsortium/SOCPrinCriteria.html

Summerlot, J., Green, S., & Parker, D. (2009). Student veteran organizations. In R. Ackerman & D. DiRamio (Eds.), *Creating a veteran-friendly campus: Strategies for transition and success* (pp. 71–79). San Francisco: Jossey-Bass. doi:10.1002/ss.311

U.S. Department of the Army. (2005). *The Army.* Field Manual 1. Washington DC: Headquarters, Department of the Army.

Wheeler, H. A. (2011). *From soldier to student: A case study of veterans' transitions to first-time community college students* (Doctoral dissertation). Available from ProQuest Dissertations & Theses database. (UMI No. 3465899)

5

STUDENT AND
ADMINISTRATIVE SERVICES

If you're going to sin, sin against God, not the bureaucracy; God will forgive you but the bureaucracy won't.

—Hyman Rickover, naval officer who developed the first nuclear-powered submarine (Greenhouse, 1986)

S tudent veterans who transition into higher education must navigate through a complex array of administrative processes and procedures. These processes are often related to their federal education benefits but can range from applying for disability accommodations to resolving credit from transferred courses. This chapter examines the student and administrative services that are typically accessed by students after they have been recruited and admitted and explores how they may be streamlined and reorganized to benefit student veterans. There is a challenge in presenting these "best practices": Few institutions have developed comprehensive assessment methods to track the effectiveness of their programs. As O'Herrin (2011) states, "Most measures of success for veteran-specific programs and services are anecdotal and qualitative." It is imperative that institutions begin to systematically assess their services for student veterans with outcomes-based measures. These results should then be published so that the broader educational community can develop a greater understanding of how to best help military students.

The American Council on Education (ACE) has conducted two national surveys on the programs and services that institutions of higher education provide for student veterans (Cook & Kim, 2009; McBain, Kim, Cook, & Snead, 2012). These surveys offer a national perspective on how well higher education is serving student veterans and measure how programs and services have changed between 2009 and 2012. These surveys found the following:

- Eighty-nine percent of the colleges and universities that currently offer services to veterans and military personnel have increased their emphasis on serving this student population since September 11, 2001. Institutions that have increased their emphasis include
  - 93% of public four-year institutions (up from 70% in 2009);
  - 85% of public community colleges (up from 65% in 2009); and
  - 89% of private not-for-profit four-year colleges and universities (up from 57% in 2009).

  The top two areas of increased emphasis, regardless of sector, have been the establishment of new programs and services for military students and the establishment of marketing and outreach strategies to attract veterans and military personnel (Cook & Kim, 2009, p. viii; McBain et al., 2012, p. 8).
- As of 2012, 33% of the responding institutions provided scholarships for veterans, and 24% offered scholarships for military students (McBain et al., 2012, p. 8). Other forms of financial assistance at public colleges and universities included eligibility for in-state tuition rates for both veterans and their family members. Discounted tuition rates for veterans and their family members were the most frequently cited type of financial assistance for private institutions (Cook & Kim, 2009, p. viii).
- Nearly 82% of all colleges and universities have established policies regarding tuition refunds for military activations and deployments, but only 28% of institutions with programs and services for military personnel have developed an expedited reenrollment process to help students restart their academic efforts (McBain et al., 2012, p. 8, 20). Forty-eight percent of the reporting institutions in 2012 required students returning from deployment to reenroll through standard processes, a decrease of 14 percentage points from the 2009 survey (Cook & Kim, 2009, p. viii; McBain et al., 2012, p. 20). Seventeen percent of the institutions required returning military students to reapply in order to enroll in courses (McBain et al., 2012, p. 20).
- The most common veteran-specific services reported in 2012 were financial aid and tuition assistance counseling (67%, up from 57% in 2009) and special campus social or cultural events (66%, not included in 2009). Other services included career planning (44.0% of the reporting colleges), the creation of a veteran student lounge (47.0%), veteran-specific orientation (49.3%), academic advising (50.2%), employment assistance (60.5%), and Veterans Affairs (VA) education benefits counseling (87.0%) (McBain et al., 2012, p. 21).

- Eighty-four percent of all institutions that offer services for student veterans have counseling centers that offer assistance with posttraumatic stress disorder (PTSD), and 95% of these colleges and universities offered counseling services for students with depression-related problems. Eighty-seven percent of the institutions that offer services for student veterans, 71% of which offer specific coordination with VA support systems, have established collaborative ties and referrals to off-campus support services (McBain et al., 2012, pp. 21–22).

Institutions "are becoming more consistently aware of and concerned with how best to meet the complex needs of veterans and military personnel who are pursuing postsecondary education" (McBain et al., 2012, p. 38). It is clear that a majority of colleges and universities have decided to support their military students with veteran-specific programs and services. In the end, each institution must use its own strengths, traditions, and fiscal resources to determine how these services are provided.

The Veteran's Voice

The best way for institutions to determine the needs of student veterans is to ask them. As one student veteran has noted, "The more you listen, the more we speak" (American Council on Education, 2008b, p. 3). Clear, direct communication links should be formed between the student veteran population and the administrative teams that make decisions about student services. Institutions can establish these links through, for example, surveys, electronic suggestion boxes, meetings with student veteran organizations, military student focus groups, and collaboration with student veterans in student government positions. Institutions should implement a review process to regularly update and revise all policies related to student veterans, and this review process should include input from student veterans. One way to do this is to create a veterans task force (Student Veterans of America, 2010, p. 7). This group should include members from across the institution, including staff from Academic Affairs, Student Affairs, and Financial Aid; members of the faculty; the VA school certifying official (SCO); and student veterans themselves. The task force can serve as a central communications point between student veterans and the institution and should be given the authority to recommend changes to current policies and processes to better support veterans' academic pursuits.

Example of Best Practices: University of Iowa Veterans Task Force
The University of Iowa formed its Veterans Task Force in 2009 to "assess the current University of Iowa veteran services, recommend strategies to enhance

veteran support services and increase veteran enrollment" (University of Iowa, 2009, p. 3). The task force comprised senior academic officials; student veterans; and representatives from the Iowa Workforce Development Program, Vocational Rehabilitation, the VA Medical Center, Disability Services, the Registrar, Air Force Reserve Officers' Training Corps (ROTC), and Academic Advising. After evaluating the strengths and weaknesses of current services, the group published a report detailing recommendations for immediate, intermediate, and long-term changes to policies and procedures that the university can use as a strategic guide for improving student veteran services.

On the Academic Front Line: The Veterans Affairs School Certifying Official

All VA students must file an application when they first start school. Students who haven't received VA benefits before must file an original application (Veterans VA Form 22-1990; dependents VA Form 22-5490; ToE students VA Form 22-1990e). Students who have received VA benefits before must file a Request for Change of Program or Place of Training (Veterans and ToE students VA Form 22-1995; dependents VA Form 22-5495). Students applying for CH 33 in lieu of (or relinquishing) another benefit should complete a VA Form 22-1990. (U.S. Department of Veterans Affairs, 2012, p. 19)

The SCO is perhaps the most important staff member for student veterans to know. This person keeps the VA informed of the enrollment status of military students and dependents, keeps current on VA rules and benefits, and maintains the records of all students using VA benefits. Student records must include transcripts, grade reports, drop slips, registration slips, tuition and fee charges, transfer transcripts, the school application, and records of disciplinary action. SCOs must report probations, suspensions, and graduations to the VA each semester. Certifying officials are encouraged (but not required) to assist students in applying for educational benefits, educate students about their responsibilities, keep various internal departments aware of developments that could affect a student's financial package, and help resolve payment problems (U.S. Department of Veterans Affairs, 2012, pp. 16–17). This official is the key to obtaining VA education benefits, and as the previous quoted passage shows, the requirements for students are at times less than transparent.

Institutions should make sure that student veterans and dependents using VA educational benefits know exactly where the SCO is located. Most institutions house this position in the Financial Aid or Registrar's Office, but sometimes this person is housed in the Business or even the Admissions

Office. University websites and admissions materials should clearly identify the location and contact information for this resource. SCOs can introduce themselves to veterans during orientations and at meetings of the student veteran organization. Personnel in Academic Advising, the Business Office, and the Financial Aid Office should know who this person is and how to reach him or her. It may be helpful to post the contact information on bulletin boards or on social media sites that are related to student veterans. In short, colleges and universities should do everything they can to make sure that student veterans know how to access this resource.

The SCO juggles information from three central offices: Business, Financial Aid, and the Registrar. Best practices for the SCO include the following:

- Establish clear lines of communication with the offices that support the position.
- Develop a system to track and communicate with your institution's student veterans and dependents. The system should be robust enough to differentiate between GI benefit chapters, branches of service, and military statuses (active duty, Reserve, veteran, National Guard, ROTC, dependent, etc.).
- Reach out to student veterans proactively through listservs, e-mail lists, and social media.
- Communicate with students frequently so that they are aware of changes in their benefits status, academic standing, and financial aid options.
- Know your students. Know their academic programs, their catalogs, and the status of their academic progress. Degree audits may be needed, for example, to be in compliance with certain VA guidelines.

The SCO often sets the tone for a student veteran's educational experience outside the classroom. A highly qualified, personable, and proactive SCO can quickly address issues that arise with VA benefits and can generate a positive sense of goodwill between the institution and its student veterans. A less-than-qualified or unmotivated SCO can alienate student veterans and create rifts that no other veteran support service—no matter how well led or well funded—can overcome.

Registrar's Office

The Registrar's Office plays a pivotal role for student veterans. Transfer credit, credit for prior life or educational experiences, residency status, and more are often decided through processes initiated in this office. McBain et al. (2012, p. 52) found that 83.0% of the institutions that responded to their survey awarded credit for military training, whereas 63.4% awarded credit for military occupational experience. The process is not uniform, however, and students may not receive credits in areas that count toward their graduation requirements:

> The main thing is just having the information so that once we do come to the university, we [know] what transfers over. I had credits from when I was in the Marine Corps. The registrar looked at me like I was stupid, trying to get credits for these classes. I just started over. (American Council on Education, 2008a, p. 6)

Institutions of higher education are aided in evaluating military credit through the Army/American Council on Education Registry Transcript System (AARTS) and Sailor/Marine American Council on Education Registry Transcript (SMART) system. ACE sends faculty members to military installations to evaluate military education, training, and experience and then recommends credit equivalencies. The Army, for example, offers areas of advanced individual training (AIT) that can range from finance and accounting to armored warfare (see appendix C for a complete list). These equivalencies are recorded in an official transcript (AARTS or SMART) that military students can submit to the Registrar's Office for credit evaluation. Private for-profit institutions are more likely to accept credit from these transcripts (91.7%) than private (78.6%) or public (80.8%) four-year institutions (McBain et al., 2012, p. 52).

The Registrar's Office serves as an important distributor of information. Staff in this office must recognize that student veterans who drop a course, withdraw from school, or change residency status may be putting their benefits at risk. Web-based registration systems should alert students to potential problems when they are engaged in actions that may risk their benefits, such as course drops. Institutions may want to consider eliminating *W*s on transcripts when a student is deployed or developing a code of "military withdrawal" to help protect the academic records of military students.

Registrar's best practices make complicated procedures transparent and establish clear lines of communication with other offices:

- Coordinate with Admissions to develop a way to definitively track student veterans and other students using VA benefits.
- Provide student veterans with contact information for the SCO, including office location and phone numbers.
- Distribute information that clearly describes VA benefits, defines how to access them, and proactively addresses common questions about the process of obtaining needed resources. Websites should be regularly checked to make sure that information is current.

- Ensure that the Registrar's website includes links to VA, military, and other federal forms that the student is likely to need to access his or her benefits.
- Stipulate clearly how transfer credits are evaluated and who to contact to receive credits based on professional experience.
- Put policies in place to accommodate students who are activated during an academic term.
- Consider eliminating *W*s on transcripts that are caused by military deployment or develop a special code for "military withdrawal" to protect the academic records of student veterans.

Institutions may also wish to consider priority registration, flexible enrollment deadlines, and a simplified readmissions process for student veterans (Ryan, Carlstrom, Hughey, & Harris, 2011, p. 61).

Example of Best Practices: University of Kansas Office of Veterans Services Website
        The University of Kansas Office of Veterans Services website, which is housed within the Registrar's Office, models a number of the preceding best practices. The SCO is clearly identified, by name, on the home page and an easy-to-navigate series of tabs provides links to information about the following:

- *Deployment in the middle of the academic term*
- *Information specific to each chapter of benefits*
- *Commonly used state and federal forms*
- *Scholarship information for veterans, spouses, and dependents*

        Links to other offices, including Admissions, Financial Aid, and Career Services are also easy to find. See http://veterans.ku.edu/index.shtml

Financial Aid

Individuals respect my service to my country, both in the sense of the sacrifice I made, and in the honor such service connotes. Systems, however, do not show such respect. They extend the bureaucratic quagmire beyond the military (as if that was not bad enough). Because of the systematic ineptitude of the financial aid department at my school, I have spent what amounts to a part-time job's worth of time dealing with financial aid issues. No wonder I am stressed beyond all limits. I am going to school, working part-time, and on top of it, I have to do someone else's job for them, because they cannot take the time to figure out my special situation. It is not as if this school is particularly horrible. It is the nature of a bureaucracy, of any system: if you don't fit into the prefabricated holes, good luck cutting your own in which to fit. (Doenges, 2011, p. 67)

Financial Aid Offices across this nation strive to make sure that this student's experience is singular, but still these offices often bear the brunt of student veterans' frustration. The Post-9/11 Veterans Educational Assistance Act has had a significant impact on veterans' opportunities for higher education, but it has also added significantly to the VA's workload. According to the U.S. Department of Veterans Affairs (2010), more than 518,000 students applied for a certificate of eligibility in the year following passage of the Chapter 33 Post-9/11 GI Bill. Processing increased from about 1,800 enrollments per day in August 2009 to 7,000 per day in February 2010 (U.S. Department of Veterans Affairs, 2010). The total amount of financial aid awarded to student veterans increased 408% between 2002 and 2012 (College Board Advocacy & Policy Center, 2012, p. 10), yet at least one study found that 65.9% of student veterans felt that financial concerns were their greatest challenge (Doenges, 2011, p. 52). A survey commissioned by the Iraq and Afghanistan Veterans of America (2012, p. 28) showed that 42% of the respondents felt that VA processing was slow, and 34% of respondents indicated that they had financial problems because of delays. Student veterans are justifiably concerned about the availability and timing of their financial benefits. Financial Aid Offices are often caught in the middle between the student and the VA bureaucracy.

Institutions have attempted to respond to veterans concerns about financial aid. McBain et al. (2012) found that just more than 67% of the institutions surveyed provided financial aid and tuition assistance counseling and 87% provided veterans' education benefits counseling (p. 52). Other best practices for staff members in the Financial Aid Office include the following:

- Maintain a thorough knowledge of the various chapters of the GI Bill, including amendments to the Post-9/11 GI Bill and Presidential Executive Order 13607 ("Establishing Principles of Excellence for Educational Institutions Serving Service Members, Veterans, Spouses, and Other Family Members").
- Provide clear information regarding tuition, fees, and both state and federal financial aid packages that may be available to student veterans. Give precise details about indirect costs such as books, supplies, transportation, and housing.
- Ensure that the Financial Aid website includes links to VA, military, and other federal forms (such as the Free Application for Federal

Student Aid [FAFSA]) that the student is likely to need to access his or her benefits. Provide links to web-based resources such as the Veterans Online Application (VONAPP) and GoArmyEd.

- Create a secure online account for students that contains a record of what payments have been received, which benefits have been processed, what benefits have been earned, and how much of the entitlement is left remaining (American Council on Education, 2010, p. 15).
- Develop proactive fiscal policies to aid student veterans whose VA benefits have been delayed in processing.

President Obama issued an executive order on April 27, 2012, that will transform some of these best practices into compulsory requirements (Obama, 2012). Specifically, the order states that institutions must

> provide prospective students who are eligible to receive Federal military and veterans educational benefits with a personalized and standardized form . . . to help those prospective students understand the total cost of the educational program, including tuition and fees; the amount of that cost that will be covered by Federal educational benefits; the type and amount of financial aid they may qualify for; their estimated student loan upon graduation; information about student outcomes, and other information to facilitate comparison of aid packages offered by different educational institutions. (Obama, 2012)

The law adopts principles from the Department of Education's "know before you owe" procedures but has not been fully implemented as of the writing of this book (Bergeron, 2012). Veterans' benefits can be complex, and the inherent lag time in working through the federal bureaucracy can frustrate both students and staff. Offices that implement the preceding best practices will reduce the number of frustrating episodes and will help alleviate student veterans' stress and anxiety about paying for their education.

Academic Advising

Academic advisers play a unique role, often bridging the gap between students' academic careers and personal lives. This is true for student veterans as well. Academic advisers may have sustained contact with student veterans, and it is important for them to understand the complexity of issues this student population must confront:

> To begin, academic advisors must understand the unique challenges this student population faces while transitioning to higher education, particu-

larly in terms of administrative (e.g., admissions process, financial benefits, transfer credit), transitional (e.g., identity development, community involvement, coping skills), and personal challenges (e.g., reluctance to seek assistance and understanding limitations). The second challenge is to assist military-affiliated students in recognizing and navigating through institutional roadblocks. (Shannon & Bucci, 2012)

Academic advisers have opportunities for one-on-one interactions with students that place them in a unique position to identify and help students overcome individual barriers to graduation. They are part instructor, part administrator, and an indispensable part of the learning process (Kelley, 2008, p. 27).

Academic advisers must have a detailed knowledge of a broad range of institutional policies and practices. They should be aware, for example, that students using the GI Bill or federal tuition assistance must take only classes that count toward their degrees and need to report any changes in their majors to Veterans Services. Failure to do either may affect their VA benefits. Academic advisers should also be aware that student veterans in need of tutoring services may have the VA pay up to $100 a month for tutors. This can be a helpful supplement to on-campus resources.

Best practices for academic advisers include the following:

- Establish processes to identify whether or not a student is a veteran or a dependent using VA educational benefits.
- Know basic military acronyms and what questions should and should not be asked of student veterans.
- Learn how student veterans differ from the general student population in terms of transitions and potential disabilities.
- Understand how to create an open and welcoming atmosphere for student veterans, and understand how physical, emotional, and behavioral environments can enhance or detract from their success.
- Know what on-campus resources specifically serve the student veteran population.
- Be aware of policies that directly affect student veterans, such as guidelines regarding military transfer credits, withdrawal owing to deployment, and military-related absences from classes, and the basics of accommodations for students with disabilities.
- Establish clear communication links with Disabilities Services, Student Health and Counseling Centers, and Student Affairs.
- Assign one or more advisers to specifically serve student veterans.

Academic advisers can have a significant impact on the educational experiences of student veterans simply by establishing an open and welcoming atmosphere in which the students feel that they can be heard:

> Through the advising relationship, student-veterans can receive guidance . . . and be heard. . . . Advisors should not overlook the power of attentive listening because simply paying attention to a veteran's story can go a long way to making her or him feel a sense of belonging. Recognition does not always come in the form of ovations in front of a crowded room. Many veterans will enjoy the appreciation received when an advisor takes the time to hear their personal stories. (Ryan et al., 2011)

The academic adviser is an essential element of creating a campus environment that both builds on veterans' successes and helps identify and overcome individual challenges to educational attainment.

Career Services

The Career Services Office plays an important role for students at all stages of their academic careers. This office provides networking opportunities with potential employers, facilitates internships and externships, provides résumé writing assistance, and trains students in interviewing skills. Student veterans may benefit from all of these services. Students who join the military directly out of high school may have virtually no civilian work experience and may have little understanding of how to conduct an effective job search. Student veterans benefit from the Transition Assistance Program (TAP), but many have expressed concerns about the timing and effectiveness of the program and therefore still rely on institutional Career Services Offices (American Council on Education, 2010, p. 17).

The Department of Labor's local veterans employment representatives (LVERs) and Disabled Veterans Outreach Program specialists (DVOPs) can be important partners for Career Services Offices, especially at small institutions that lack the resources for veteran-specific programming. LVERs are state employees who reach out to employers and lobby hiring executives to increase employment opportunities for veterans. They are often available to offer workshops for veterans seeking employment. DVOPs provide "intensive services to meet the employment needs of disabled veterans and other eligible veterans" (U.S. Department of Labor, n.d.). These representatives should be kept appraised of the number and quality of an institution's graduating student veterans, and Career Services Offices should request to be on their list of recruitment notifications. TAP centers, despite the noted concerns, offer job-search assistance to veterans and are another resource that Career Services Offices should exploit. Developing a reciprocal relationship with TAP facilitators can enhance your center and make its programming even more effective (American Council on Education, 2010, p. 18).

Career services can enhance their service to student veterans by considering the following:

- Emphasize the value of internships, especially prior to a students' graduation year.
- Collaborate with local and VA resources that can connect military students to potential employers.
- Connect student veterans with local business mentors.
- Train student veterans to understand the difference between military and civilian workplaces and a military and a civilian employer.
- Teach student veterans how to convert military training into equivalent civilian experience and how to express this cogently on a résumé.
- Collaborate with local employers to host mock interview sessions and résumé reviews.

Student veterans, like many students, see education as a key element of their strategy to gain and maintain employment that allows them to live according to the lifestyle they choose. Career Services Offices play an important role in helping this to happen.

Student Health and Counseling

The length and intensity of deployments related to the current war on terrorism have placed enormous stress on military personnel. Many of the men and women in the armed forces cope successfully with the mental strain and emotional anxiety, but for some this stress manifests itself in increased divorce rates, spouse and child abuse, mental distress, substance abuse, and suicide (Ramchand, Acosta, Burns, Jaycox, & Pernin, 2011, p. xiii). The VA, through its regional hospitals and clinics, is typically the primary mental health care provider for veterans. Campus clinics should develop clear lines of communication and partnerships with the nearest center. Some veterans, however, have never applied for VA health care benefits and for a variety of reasons choose not to use the services provided by the VA. Campus clinics therefore need to be prepared to assist student veterans and family members of veterans who are in need of their services.

The first challenge for most campus clinics is to convince students who need the services of a professional counselor to seek one out. This can be especially problematic for student veterans who have been trained to "accomplish the mission" without excuses and regardless of personal cost. Student veterans may see a mental health diagnosis as a sign of weakness, and those students still in the active military or National Guard may consider it a career-ending mark on their record. Males especially may believe that they are the only ones among their peers who are struggling and often attempt to conceal psychological symptoms from each other (Lorber & Garcia, 2010, p. 298). Veterans may be concerned about the cost of mental health care and unaware that Operation Enduring Freedom (OEF) and Operation Iraqi Freedom (OIF) combat veterans are eligible for cost-free medical care for any condition related to their service in the Iraq and Afghanistan theaters for five years after the date of their discharge or release.

Higher education often fails to fully appreciate the wear and tear associated with deployment and combat. Rudd, Goulding, and Bryan (2011, p. 357) found the following in a nationally representative sample of 628 student veterans:

- 23.7% experienced severe depression
- 34.6% experienced severe anxiety
- 45.6% experienced significant symptoms of PTSD
- 46.0% reported thinking about suicide
- 20.0% reported planning their suicide
- 10.4% reported thinking of suicide often or very often
- 7.7% had attempted suicide
- 3.8% reported that they were likely or very likely to commit suicide in the future

Eighteen veterans commit suicide each day (Shinseki, 2010). Despite the obvious need for proactive outreach regarding mental health, counseling professionals sometimes experience resistance to their efforts. There is an inherent tension between the use of VA and campus mental health resources and aspects of military enculturation. Student veterans sometimes feel as though it is an unacceptable admission of failure to access these resources and as if they are letting their unit down by not "staying strong" (Hoge et al., 2004, pp. 20–21). There is no easy way to address this tension, other than to collaborate with veterans and veteran organizations when possible, to seek to understand their point of view, and to persist in providing the services these students need. It is important to note that when processes are developed to help student veterans (e.g., a suicide prevention campaign), those very same processes will often help a wide segment of the nonmilitary population as well.

Best practices for Student Health and Counseling Centers include the following:

- Train clinicians to use treatments that are demonstrated to be effective with combat-related PTSD and train staff to use suicide risk assessment procedures that will identify veterans with prominent PTSD symptoms (Rudd, Goulding, & Bryan, 2011, p. 359).
- Raise awareness among student veterans of the need for and appropriateness of seeking out mental health services.
- Train students to develop their own help-seeking behaviors (Ramchand et al., 2011, pp. xxiv–xxv).
- Place crisis hotline numbers for student veterans in prominent locations throughout the campus, including online locations.
- Include a question on intake forms that asks, "Are you now or have you ever been a member of the U.S. armed forces?"
- Develop collaborative relationships with other extracampus agencies that serve veterans and their families, including VA medical centers and the local vets center.
- Facilitate regular on-campus visits by a VA center counselor and advertise these visits to the veteran community.
- Find guest speakers to talk about issues such as PTSD, depression, traumatic brain injury (TBI), and suicide prevention. Send mental health care professionals to speak at veteran orientations and present to the student veteran organization.
- Understand that off-campus issues may have a significant impact on student veterans and that extended support networks (family or military-related) should be considered as a resource.
- Designate at least one professional in the center as a veteran specialist, and train that person to respond to their unique needs.
- Know basic military acronyms and what questions should and should not be asked of student veterans.
- Communicate regularly with VA representatives to be sure that campus health care officials are current on potential emergency and nonemergency referrals.

These practices help campus health services to reach out as fully as possible to student veterans. They can enhance the academic success of military students and, in the end, may literally save lives.

Reader Reflection: Responding to the Veteran Suicide Rate

Given the rate of veteran suicides, what can your institution do to help—both on campus and in the community?

Disabilities Services

Significant numbers of student veterans are returning to higher education with disabilities of various kinds—from hearing loss to PTSD. In addition, the Americans with Disabilities Act Amendments Act (ADAAA) has broadened the definition of *disability* so that there are fewer burdens for individuals trying to demonstrate the need for disabilities services in higher education. Disabilities services professionals, therefore, play a critical role in enabling student veterans to succeed, but they also face challenges similar to those faced by counseling professionals—student veterans often hesitate to acknowledge disabilities, do not identify with the term *disabled*, and may see it as an indication of mission failure to have to ask for assistance from the Disabilities Services Office. Veterans who incur injuries in a noncombat environment may be reluctant to talk about their needs because they perceive their disability as illegitimately acquired.

Veterans who have recently returned from active duty may be waiting for a disability rating from the VA and may be confused as to whether or not they qualify for services on campus. Student veterans may not even be aware that they have a disability:

> Many of these "wounded warriors" have acquired disabilities during their service, making them eligible for protection under the [ADAAA]. Unlike the vast majority of students with disabilities who attend college, warriors with disabilities often have no history of receiving disability-based accommodations in high school. Accordingly, they are less familiar with their disability-related rights and responsibilities. Most colleges and universities have not had a lot of experience in accommodating students with the types of disabilities common among wounded warriors, including post traumatic stress disorder, traumatic brain injury, late acquired blindness or deafness, significantly disfiguring burns, and multiple amputations, among others. (Monroe, 2008)

Students who have PTSD, depression, or TBI (whether veterans or not) may also be experiencing sleep deprivation, difficulty with time management, and emotional stress—all of which can boil over in a confusing or stressful office visit or classroom experience. Best practices for Disabilities Services include the following:

- Raise awareness among student veterans of the need and appropriateness of seeking out help from Disabilities Services.
- Send disabilities services professionals to speak at veteran orientations and present to the student veteran organization.
- Educate faculty on the need and appropriateness of classroom accommodations. Train faculty to recognize symptoms of learning disabilities. Train faculty to understand and value the principles of Universal Design (UD) (see chapters 8, 9, and 10).
- Develop policies that encourage statements about the ADAAA and Disabilities Services on every academic syllabus.
- Hire veterans as student employees or graduate assistants in Disabilities Services.

Disabilities services personnel are important in facilitating the transition and persistence of our military students. The student veteran population may be hesitant to use these services, however, or unaware of newly developed disabilities. Disabilities services personnel who can overcome those barriers and convince students to use their resources will significantly enhance the academic success of student veterans.

Example of Best Practices: University of Washington DO-IT Program's Online Veterans Center
The University of Washington's DO-IT Center is an award-winning program "promoting the success of individuals with disabilities in postsecondary education and careers." The program's online Veterans Center provides multiple resources to help faculty, staff, and administrators create classrooms that maximize learning for student veterans with disabilities. Links connect users to national and regional resources for veterans with disabilities, special projects and events, and a large amount of information on accommodations and UD. See www.washington.edu/doit/Veterans/

Conclusion

The offices and services described in chapters 4 and 5 are an integral part of the student veteran's learning experience outside the classroom. These resources should be clearly identifiable and accessible to all military students. Staff should understand how to build on the strengths of student veterans and help mitigate the challenges they face. For more information on creating staff development programs see chapter 11. The best practice of all is to operate these offices with caring, highly trained individuals who are committed to the success of student veterans.

Chapter Summary

The administrative offices described in this chapter are key components in serving student veterans. Colleges and universities have become increasingly aware of the need to create specialized services for student veterans, and they have steadily increased both the quantity and quality of these services. Institutions that are able to serve military students effectively and efficiently—from financial aid to disabilities services—will enhance the academic success of their student veterans.

Key Points

- Student veterans who transition into higher education must navigate through a complex array of administrative processes and procedures.
- Postsecondary institutions should assess their services—with the help of their own student veteran population—and provide changes as needed in policies and procedures.
- Clear communication between administrative offices is vital. Financial Aid, the Registrar, Academic Advising, Career Services, and all the rest must have a coordinated way of communicating with each other, particularly in regard to how students' actions affect their GI benefits.
- Student veterans should have access to a centralized resource (whether that be a person, office, or website) that provides concise information about who to contact in regard to common issues that student veterans face.
- Each office has its own set of best practices that can enhance service to veterans and facilitate their academic success.

References

American Council on Education. (2008a). *Serving those who serve: Higher education and America's veterans* [Issue brief]. Washington DC: Author. Retrieved from http://www.acenet.edu/Content/NavigationMenu/ProgramsServices/Military Programs/serving/Veterans_Issue_Brief_1108.pdf

American Council on Education. (2008b). *Serving those who serve: Making your institution veteran-friendly.* Washington DC: Author. Retrieved from http://www.acenet.edu/news-room/Pages/Georgetown-Summit.aspx

American Council on Education. (2010). *Veteran Success Jam: Ensuring success for returning veterans*. Washington DC: Author. Retrieved from http://www.acenet.edu/news-room/Pages/Veterans-Jam-2010.aspx

Bergeron, D. A. (2012, July 25). Financial Aid Shopping Sheet for 2013-14. Dear Colleague Letter. Washington DC: United States Department of Education. Retrieved from http://www.ifap.ed.gov/dpcletters/attachments/GEN1212.pdf

College Board Advocacy & Policy Center. (2012). *Trends in higher education series: Trends in student aid 2012*. New York: Author. Retrieved from http://trends.collegeboard.org/student-aid

Cook, B. J., & Kim, Y. (2009). *From soldier to student: Easing the transition of service members on campus*. Washington DC: American Council on Education.

Doenges, T. (2011). *Calling and meaningful work among student military veterans: Impact on well-being and experiences on campus* (Doctoral dissertation). Available from ProQuest Dissertations and Theses database. (UMI No. 3468765)

Greenhouse, L. (1986, November 3). Angry dispute left for new senate. *New York Times*. Available from ProQuest New York Times database. (Proquest document ID #110969490)

Hoge, C. W., Castro, C. A., Messer, S. C., McGurk, D., Cotting, D. I., & Koffman, R. (2004). Combat duty in Iraq and Afghanistan, mental health problems, and barriers to care. *New England Journal of Medicine, 351*(1), 13–22. doi:10.1056/NEJMoa040603

Iraq and Afghanistan Veterans of America. (2012). *IAVA 2012 member survey*. New York: Author. Retrieved from media.iava.org/iava_2012_member_survey.pdf

Kelley, B. (2008). Significant learning, significant advising. *NACADA Journal, 28*(1), 19–28.

Lorber, W., & Garcia, H. A. (2010). Not supposed to feel this: Traditional masculinity in psychotherapy with male veterans returning from Afghanistan and Iraq. *Psychotherapy: Theory, Research & Practice, 47*(3), 296–305.

McBain, L., Kim, Y., Cook, B., & Snead, K. (2012). *From soldier to student II: Assessing campus programs for veterans and service members*. Washington DC: American Council on Education. Retrieved from http://www.acenet.edu/news-room/Pages/From-Soldier-to-Student-II.aspx

Monroe, S. (2008). *Dear colleague letter, July 25, 2008*. Washington DC: U.S. Department of Education Office for Civil Rights. Retrieved from http://www2.ed.gov/about/offices/list/ocr/letters/colleague-20080725.html

Obama, B. (2012). Establishing principles of excellence for educational institutions serving service members, veterans, spouses, and other family members. Presidential Executive Order 13607. Washington DC: White House Office of the Press Secretary. Retrieved from http://www.whitehouse.gov/the-press-office/2012/04/27/executive-order-establishing-principles-excellence-educational-instituti

O'Herrin, E. (2011, Winter). Enhancing veteran success in higher education. *Peer Review, 13*(1), 15–18. Retrieved from http://www.aacu.org/peerreview/pr-wi11/prwi11_oherrin.cfm

Ramchand, R., Acosta, J., Burns, R., Jaycox, L., & Pernin, C. (2011). *The war within: Preventing suicide in the U.S. military*. Santa Monica, CA: RAND Corporation.

Rudd, D., Goulding, J., & Bryan, C. (2011). Student veterans: A national survey exploring psychological symptoms and suicide risk. *Professional Psychology: Research and Practice, 42*(5), 354–360.

Ryan, S. W., Carlstrom, A. H., Hughey, K. F., & Harris, B. S. (2011). From boots to books: Applying Schlossberg's model to transitioning American veterans. *NACADA Journal, 31*(1), 55–63.

Shannon, A., & Bucci, D. (2012). *Reaching for the stars: Helping student veterans achieve new heights in higher education.* Manhattan, KS: NACADA Clearinghouse. Retrieved from http://www.nacada.ksu.edu/clearinghouse/advisingissues/veterans.htm

Shinseki, E. K. (2010, January 11). Remarks by Secretary Eric K. Shinseki [transcript]. Department of Defense–Veterans Affairs Suicide Prevention Conference, Washington DC. Retrieved from http://www.va.gov/opa/speeches/2010/10_0111hold.asp

Student Veterans of America. (2010). *Veterans center handbook.* Retrieved from http://deanofstudents.unc.edu/student-support/veterans-resources/articles-and-best-practices

University of Iowa. (2009). *Veterans task force report.* Retrieved from http://www.registrar.uiowa.edu/Student/Veterans/tabid/71/ItemId/589/Default.aspx

U.S. Department of Labor. (n.d.). VETS employment services fact sheet 1. Retrieved from http://www.dol.gov/vets/programs/empserv/employment_services_fs.htm#.UMJAo4UyGs0

U.S. Department of Veterans Affairs. (2010). *The Post-9/11 Veterans Educational Assistance Act of 2008 (Chapter 33)* [PowerPoint]. Washington DC: Author. Retrieved from http://www2.acenet.edu/jam/schedule/

U.S. Department of Veterans Affairs. (2012). *U.S. Department of Veterans Affairs school certifying official handbook* (2nd ed.). Washington DC: Author. Retrieved from http://gibill.va.gov/documents/job_aids/SCO_Handbook_v2.pdf

6

ACADEMIC PROGRAMS FOR STUDENT VETERANS

Being a veteran at college feels lonely. So many people don't have the background you do. For me, it just felt like walking in a lonely hallway.

—Carlos, former Marine (Wheeler, 2011, p. 97–98)

The previous two chapters have examined best practices and innovative approaches to student and administrative services. This chapter examines a variety of academic programs that institutions have developed to help student veterans navigate the transition between their military and academic careers. These programs range from one-credit "transition" courses to learning communities to degrees in veteran studies. Some of these programs have demonstrably increased the retention and success of student veterans, but there is still much research to do in this area. This chapter also serves as a bridge between the campus- and department-level strategies described so far and a greater focus on the individual classroom and the role that instructors can play in enhancing student veterans' success.

Weber (2012) found that cultural congruity and social support strongly correlated with student veteran retention (p. i). Academic programs have intuitively moved in that direction and generally focus on two goals in that area. The first is to assist student veterans through the early transition process as they move from the military into higher education (establishing cultural congruity). The second goal is to put the student veterans in courses that allow them to make contact with other veterans (establishing social support). The hope is that improving cultural congruity and social support will dramatically improve retention and graduation rates and will improve overall academic success within the student veteran population.

Summer Bridge Programs

The typical summer bridge program is "a short, intense introduction to college designed to assist underprepared first-year students" (McCurrie, 2009, p. 28). Bridge programs are characterized by small class size, personalized mentoring, and increased interaction with faculty and staff advisers. They were initially developed for students who tested into precollege levels of math or English, and the model has been modified for other at-risk constituencies, such as first-generation students. The format can be readily adapted for student veterans, with two caveats. First, student veterans should not be combined with incoming freshmen—the culture gap between these two groups is significant. Second, care should be taken so that student veterans do not perceive the program as "remedial" in any way. It should be offered as a resource that helps them understand the differences between the military and higher education and assists them in obtaining their educational benefits.

> *Example: California State University–Sacramento*
> *Sacramento State hosts a late summer program for veterans called the Summer Success Academy. The program provides students with an overview of veterans' benefits; describes how to access federal, state, and local services; gives directions on how to navigate campus resources; and connects the students with other Sacramento State veterans. The program invites veterans to become campus leaders, encourages them to participate (as investigator or subject) in research projects, and celebrates the accomplishments that student veterans have already achieved. Finally, students who participate in this program receive a $100 credit on their student ID. See www.csus.edu/vets/Academic%20Resources%20-%20Courses%20-%20Links/Summer%20Success%20Academy.html*

Veterans' Transition Courses

The veterans' transition course takes many forms but is generally an elective that student veterans may take during the first semester that they return to higher education. These courses may be a subset of an institution's first-year-experience curriculum or may be a stand-alone course for veterans only. Whereas a bridge program may last for only a few days, these courses tend to last an entire semester (one variation is to make the classes half-term—generally eight weeks—long). Bridge programs have the advantage of preparing students prior to their general entry into the academic culture, but first-semester transition courses have the advantage of enhancing regular contact with instructors and staff members who are knowledgeable about both the strengths and the challenges veterans face as they return from deployment.

Transition courses provide a formalized environment in which to discuss resources that are available to veterans, to connect military students to each other, and to communicate important policies and procedures that pertain to military students. One such example is General Studies 250 from San Diego State University:

> Mission: The purpose of this class [is] to introduce military veterans and active duty personnel who are new students to a network of current students and staff who can assist them in learning about the academic culture, campus resources, and student services/activities available at [San Diego State University]. Students who actively participate in this class can expect to have an easier transition to the academic environment and campus community. (Roberts, 2012, p. 1)

Transition courses allow student veterans to explore difficult topics from an academic perspective. The class might review literature that explores specifically how veterans experience and overcome disabilities, for example, or might reflectively examine how to adjust to life in a civilian world. Some veterans feel as though they are the only ones suffering with academic insecurities, invisible disabilities, or psychological symptoms (Lorber & Garcia, 2010, p. 298). Courses such as this can help them understand that they are not alone. Offices that are underutilized or misunderstood by student veterans—such as the Student Health and Counseling Center or Disabilities Services—can be emphasized as part of a mission-centered support team rather than as a crutch for individuals who cannot make it in the real world.

Courses that focus on the transition process will often directly or indirectly explore the cultural incongruities that exist between the military and higher education. Chapter 2 identified a number of these incongruities (see Table 2.3). Even the pace and timing of the college course schedule can initially seem strange:

> When I had to go to school for the military it was one topic, eight hours a day for three or four months straight. So you really get it crammed into your head and then [at college] when you have to do different classes for only an hour it's easy for me to lose information throughout the week. I almost wish it was one class, eight hours a day for like three weeks and then once you were all done, then you went to the next one. (Wheeler, 2011, p. 95)

Strategies for adjusting to this new, decidedly unmilitary environment are presented (often through the testimony of former class members).

Transition courses can also emphasize the reflective culture of academia. Academic modes of communication differ dramatically from those of the military.

The goal and purpose of reflective communication can be explained, and groundwork can be laid for student veterans to become familiar and comfortable with resources such as the library and the writing center. A transition course can also examine the personal transformation that occurs when student veterans go from being a valued member of a military team with a specific purpose and goal to the less structured (and, according to some student veterans, less purposeful) life of the college student. Student veterans must negotiate numerous incongruities between military and academic life. Transition courses can provide student veterans with the time and resources they need to bridge the two cultures.

Transition courses allow student veterans to connect to other military students and veteran organizations. Wheeler (2011) found that the student veterans in her study relied heavily on their fellow service members for support (p. 114). College can be a lonely experience for veterans who have not yet connected with other military students, as the opening quote of this chapter reveals. Students enrolled in transition courses can be easily introduced to other veterans on campus, including members of the faculty and staff. Members of student veteran organizations (SVOs) are often willing to come to class to encourage others to join their groups, and members of community veteran groups can be invited in to connect with the new students as well. Students who take transition courses should come out of the class with an extensive web of personal connections that they can draw on for the rest of their academic career.

Example: University of South Dakota
   The University of South Dakota has developed a special veterans' transition course that accomplishes many of the goals identified previously. The course was adapted from curriculum created by Philip Callahan and Michael Marks for the Supportive Education for the Returning Veteran (SERV) Program at the University of Arizona. The one-credit course is titled Veteran Service to Service: Building Transitional Resiliency. The class is taught by an instructor who is an expert in veterans' services. One graduate teaching assistant, who must be a student veteran, is assigned to assist the course. The course capitalizes on veterans' propensity for civic engagement and public service and uses service-learning as a key element for the course. The curriculum contains an intentional focus on resiliency and stress management and also taps into the unique capabilities of those who have served in the U.S. military. As stated in the syllabus, "We call this veteranism: the wisdom, experience, composure, and effective contributions that can only be provided by veterans." (Urban Dictionary, 2012)

Veterans' General Education Courses

Veteran-only sections of general education courses have had documented success in improving student veteran persistence and academic success. Student veterans respond positively to the opportunity to take course sections that are made up of men and women who have a shared military background, who are above the traditional age of most students taking general education courses, and who share a common understanding of what the classroom environment should be like. A variation of this is to have sections in which veterans predominate but which are not exclusively made up of military students. There are some benefits to this variation. Military dependents, for example, may appreciate such an environment, and sections with mixed veteran/nonveteran populations are easier to fully enroll.

Veteran-only sections allow students to speak freely about their experiences, especially if they have served in combat. They are able to help each other find answers to common questions outside the classroom and are able to develop study groups made up of other veterans. Although the veteran-only general education classes have shown success, this strategy is limited. This program works well only with those few classes that most student veterans must take—Introductory Speech, English 101, lower-level mathematics courses, and perhaps some of the general sciences. It also works best with courses that have stand-alone sections, rather than recitations built off a larger lecture course. Finally, there are mixed opinions from campus administrators and student veterans alike on the symbolic separation of veterans from the rest of the student population.

Example: SERV Program (Youngstown State University, University of Hawai'i at Mānoa, Thiel College, and Others)

The SERV Program, developed by John Schupp at Cleveland State University, creates veteran-only general education courses. Depending on the number and type of classes offered, a student veteran's first-semester schedule might consist solely of veteran-only courses, creating a unique first semester experience. Initial data has shown strong first- to second-year retention rates, ranging from 70–80%, for students who have gone through this program. When the SERV Program is combined with a learning community (see the following section), it seems to be even more effective (Schupp, 2009).

Veterans' Learning Communities

The concept of learning communities was developed in the 1980s, and learning communities are now recognized as a high-impact educational practice (Rocconi, 2010, p. 178). Learning communities share two common goals: The first is to create opportunities for collaborative learning through a shared core curriculum. The second is to integrate learning across the curriculum by organizing the core courses around a central theme. Learning communities have been linked to numerous positive educational outcomes, including some that are directly relevant to the experiences of student veterans, for example, transition to college, satisfaction with college, greater student-faculty interactions, perceptions of supportive campus environments, and persistence and graduation (Rocconi, 2010, p. 179).

Courses in veterans' learning communities are often focused around themes that are important to veterans, such as leadership, loss, or perseverance. The learning communities also allow student veterans to meet each other and to participate in at least one class in which student veterans predominate. They may or may not directly address transitional issues; instead they focus on curricular issues of interest to many veterans. They may or may not have a residential requirement. Veterans' learning communities can play a powerful role in helping student veterans connect with fellow students in courses that meet graduation requirements.

> *Example: The Ohio State University's Veterans' Learning Community*
>
> *Ohio State's learning community combines academic advice and assistance with limited-enrollment general education courses, special programming, and opportunities to link to the broader veterans' community. The general education courses include an introduction to the humanities, a comparative studies literature class, and an advanced writing course. A freshman seminar is also available. All courses are centered on military themes. The comparative studies course, for example, is titled Experiences of War and examines representations of the war experience in art, literature, and film from diverse cultures. The freshman seminar is titled Folklore of War and Wartime and provides an introduction to folklore studies with the military, war, and wartime as its theme (Ohio State University, 2010).*

Veterans' Curriculum

Some institutions have developed an in-depth curriculum that is designed to help student veterans transition into higher education and increase their resiliency and ability to deal with stress in healthy ways. These programs generally consist of three to five courses that are specific to veterans and go beyond (but generally count as) general education courses. They are in many respects a combination of the transition course and veterans' learning community strategies. This curriculum provides many of the benefits of the programs listed previously but is an even more intensive time commitment for student veterans.

> *Example: The University of Arizona*
>
> *The University of Arizona combines the SERV model of cohort-based veterans education with a curriculum that emphasizes resiliency. This emphasis seems to be having an impact: research has shown that students who have participated in the program have demonstrated significant improvements in*

resiliency scores from the beginning to the end of the semester (University of Arizona, 2012). The program consists of three 3-credit courses: Resiliency and Human Potential, Leadership Principles and Practices, and Transitional Resiliency. These courses count as general education courses and are offered to veterans as a block of courses their first semester at the university. The courses are taught by faculty members who are familiar with the challenges that veterans face as they transition into higher education and use alumni from previous semesters as teaching assistants. See http://registrar.arizona.edu/vets/serv-classes

Veterans Studies Program

A few institutions have recently developed cross-disciplinary majors, minors, or certificates related to veterans. These veterans studies programs are similar in scope to women's studies, Hispanic studies, or Black studies programs. Although they emphasize a curriculum that is focused on an understanding of veterans and the military in general, they are not necessarily directed at student veterans themselves.

> *Example: Eastern Kentucky University Veterans Studies Program*
> *Eastern Kentucky has developed "a unique, multi-disciplinary program that provides veterans and non-veteran students a foundation of understanding regarding military structure, culture, combat, and the psychological and physiological changes resulting from military service" (Eastern Kentucky University, 2012). Students can get a certificate or a minor in the program. The curriculum consists of a core course titled Introduction to Veterans Studies, three or four elective courses taken from a series of options that range from Shakespeare at War to Stress and Military Family Resilience, and a capstone course. See http://va.eku.edu/vsp*

Challenges to Veteran-Specific Academic Programming

Institutions may face a number of challenges as they plan veteran-specific academic programs. Perhaps the most significant challenge is to get the veterans to enroll in the programs in the first place. Student veterans are often reluctant to take elective courses because they consider them a waste of time and money. If institutions spend the resources to develop and offer these programs, they also need to allot resources to advertise and market them. The benefits of the program should be clearly described online and further explicated during orientation and class registration sessions. Student veterans who have already matriculated through the course or courses can be invaluable in testifying to the value of such programs, and it would serve institutions well to include them in registration sessions if possible.

Designing courses that count as part of the general educational curriculum will help veterans see their value.

If student veterans are reluctant to take courses that don't count toward graduation, they are doubly reluctant to take courses that suggest that they have some sort of academic deficit or that treat them as "problems" that need to be "fixed." Institutions should be careful in how they structure their veteran-specific programs. Curricula should focus on the strengths, as well as the challenges, of being a student veteran. A course titled Building on Veterans' Strengths is going to be more popular than one called Resources for Solving Veterans' Issues. Finally, many student veterans come into higher education with credit for the most common first-year courses. Programs that focus solely on those classes may miss a significant number of military transfer students.

Women veterans tend to experience the transition process differently than their male counterparts, and this can have an impact on the effectiveness of and participation levels in some programs. Nearly 20% of the veterans return-ing to higher education are women, but it is not common for them to take part in campus programs for veterans in significant numbers. Women veter-ans under the age of 35 are more likely than their nonveteran peers to have children and to be single parents, which can limit their involvement. Women who have experienced military sexual trauma (MST) may not want to partici-pate in male-dominated veteran programs (Sander, 2012). A few institutions have begun to offer programs specifically for women veterans to better serve their needs. At the very least, institutions should attempt to connect incom-ing women veterans to women veterans already on campus so that they may provide models of academic success (Baechtold & DeSawal, 2009, p. 40).

In this era of restricted fiscal budgets, institutions of higher education must often weigh the costs of expanded academic services for particular stu-dent populations against the benefits of using those resources to serve the overall student population. Some academic programs for student veterans, even when shown to be highly successful, have been eliminated:

> [At] Cleveland State University, for instance, where the model for many institutions' veterans-only classes developed, the courses have been done away with (that structure, called Supportive Education for the Returning Veteran, is still in place at a handful of others, including the University of Arizona and Youngstown State University). The classes were also discontin-ued at Ohio State University. Though officials decline to say why, staff at other campuses point to issues with logistics and demand. (Grasgreen, 2012)

Programs that are not well marketed or that are perceived as having lim-ited value may have trouble filling courses. This is especially true for elective-type transition classes that student veterans may believe will cost them both time and money with no appreciable benefit. If institutions such as Cleveland State University (with a student population of more than 16,000) and Ohio State University (with a student population of more than 64,000) struggle to fill these specialized classes, it is easy to understand how smaller institutions might find such courses financially unsustainable. Academic programs, regardless of their size and type, should be closely assessed for effectiveness. At the very least, retention rates by semester for student veterans who participate in these programs and those who don't should be compared. It may be the case that even a small percentage increase in retention will allow the program to pay for itself. Administrators, however, also have to balance the cost of offering these programs against the cost of providing more direct support to student veterans, such as funding a veterans' resource center. Finally, few programs exist for the dependents of those who have served in the war on terrorism. The latest version of the GI Bill allows educational benefits to be transferred to spouses and dependents, and many military families are using the benefits in this way. Institutions may want to consider allowing these dependents to participate fully in those academic programs that are focused on student veterans.

Chapter Summary

Recent research has shown that cultural congruity and social support are highly important factors in the retention of student veterans. Academic programs can provide support in these areas by helping student veterans negotiate the challenges of transition and connecting them to the broader veterans' community. Academic programs take many forms, from summer bridge programs to full-blown curricula that incorporate veterans' learning communities. Research has shown that some of these programs are highly effective, but there are still significant gaps in our knowledge of what really works for military students.

Key Points

- Academic programs typically focus on two goals: assisting student veterans through the transition process and connecting them with other veterans.
- Transition courses can help veterans understand the value of resources that they may be hesitant to use.
- Some veterans will be hesitant to take courses that are elective, so institutions should strongly consider developing transition courses that fulfill general education requirements.

- Women who have served for three or more years in the military's male-dominated environment may wish to distance themselves from other student veterans and may be hesitant to participate in academic programs for military students.
- Research is still behind practice in terms of knowing what works best. Programs that have been developed to assist student veterans should be assessed and the data published so that the entire higher educational community can better understand how to serve these students.

References

Baechtold, M., & DeSawal, D. M. (2009). Meeting the needs of women veterans. In R. Ackerman & D. DiRamio (Eds.), *Creating a veteran-friendly campus: Strategies for transition and success* (pp. 35–43). San Francisco: Jossey-Bass. doi:10.1002/ss.314

Eastern Kentucky University. (2012). *Veterans Studies Program* [brochure]. Richmond: Author. Retrieved from http://va.eku.edu/vspbrochure

Grasgreen, A. (2012, January 4). Veterans only classes both expanding and closing. *Inside Higher Education*. Retrieved from http://www.insidehighered.com/news/2012/01/04/veterans-only classes-both-expanding-and-closing#.TwW _JxmDCI4.email#ixzz1ic2oHyp4

Lorber, W., & Garcia, H. A. (2010). Not supposed to feel this: Traditional masculinity in psychotherapy with male veterans returning from Afghanistan and Iraq. *Psychotherapy: Theory, Research & Practice, 47*(3), 296–305.

McCurrie, M. K. (2009). Measuring success in summer bridge programs: Retention efforts and basic writing. *Journal of Basic Writing 28*(2), 28–49.

Ohio State University. (2010). *Veterans learning community: Repurposing shared knowledge and common experiences.* Columbus: Author. Retrieved from cfs.osu.edu/files/cfs/VLC%20Brochure%205_27_10.pdf

Roberts, F. (2012). General Studies 250 for Military and Veterans [syllabus]. San Diego State University. Personnel correspondence, August 27, 2012.

Rocconi, L. M. (2010). The impact of learning communities on first year students' growth and development in college. *Research in Higher Education, 52*(2), 178–193.

Sander, L. (2012, July 30). Female veterans on campuses can be hard to spot, and to help. *The Chronicle*. Retrieved from http://chronicle.com/article/Female -Veterans-Can-Be-Hard-to/133205/

Schupp, J. (2009). SERV: Helping America's best, brightest, and bravest get their degree [PowerPoint]. Retrieved from www.veterans.usf.edu/pdfs/conf09/Schupp.pdf

University of Arizona. (2012). *Program overview.* Supportive Education for Returning Veterans (SERV) program. Retrieved from http://cals.arizona.edu/aed/ProgramSummary.pdf

Veteranism. (n.d.). In *Urban Dictionary*. Retrieved from http://www.urbandictionary .com/define.php?term=veteranism

Weber, D. (2012). *Academic success and well-being following OEF/OIF deployment* (Doctoral dissertation). Available from ProQuest Dissertations & Theses data-base. (UMI No. 3495315)

Wheeler, H. A. (2011). *From soldier to student: A case study of veterans' transitions to first-time community college students* (Doctoral dissertation). Available from Pro-Quest Dissertations & Theses database. (UMI No. 3465899)

7

STUDENT VETERANS IN OUR COMMUNITY COLLEGES

Holly Wheeler, Monroe Community College of Rochester, New York

The Navy broke me down and built me back up again. Then I get here and I'm not good enough to take College Algebra? I get that I have to do the work and that I've forgotten things, but when you've seen people killed and survived, having to take these classes feels like a slap in the face.

—William, Navy veteran[1]

From their humble beginnings as junior colleges, envisioned in the late nineteenth century by the University of Chicago's founding president William Rainey Harper, two-year institutions have moved to the forefront of higher education. Two-year institutions have grown for many reasons, including Great Depression–era government aid and the subsequent demand for terminal degrees and vocational training (Witt, Wattenbarger, Gollattscheck, & Suppiger, 1994), an increased need for skilled workers, and a desire to provide access to higher education to a larger percentage of the population (Cohen & Brawer, 2003). Increases in high school populations, demand for part-time status, financial aid availability, and calls for educational access for students who struggled academically or who otherwise had been traditionally excluded from higher education have also driven institutional growth (Vaughan, 2006). Community colleges have increasingly been seen as a key component for solving a host of societal problems, including racial segregation, unemployment, and inequitable income (Cohen & Brawer, 2003). Community colleges have continued to evolve, and according to the American Association of Community Colleges (AACC; 2012), approximately 13 million students are enrolled at 1,132 two-year colleges in America today. Eight million of these students are enrolled in credit-bearing courses.

Military service members have been a crucial component in both the historical and current growth of community colleges. Two-year colleges developed courses to support the war effort during World War II, and the 1944 Servicemen's Readjustment Act flooded higher education with new college students, including those who chose two-year institutions (Vaughan, 2006). Community colleges began to serve military students in greater numbers following World War II. The original GI Bill provided World War II veterans with living expenses and tuition paid directly to the institution of higher education (Breedin, 1972; U.S. Congress, 1972); at the time, the benefits were sufficient for a veteran to attend an Ivy League school (Bound & Turner, 2002; Humes, 2006). Those veterans who chose two-year institutions did so for two reasons: vocational training and the ability to earn a degree in a short period of time (Brookover, 1945; Kinzer, 1946; Lee, 1946; Mettler, 2005).

Service members returning home from Vietnam were faced with a very different GI Bill. College costs had risen 300% since World War II, but federal support for veterans had only increased 30% (Breedin, 1972). Vietnam veterans did not attend college at the same rate as previous veterans as a result, but 80% of those who did chose community colleges for their flexibility and affordability (Breedin, 1972). Two-year colleges responded to the needs of these veterans: using a 1969 Carnegie Corporation grant, the American Association of Junior Colleges developed a nationwide program to encourage military service members to attend two-year colleges by tailoring courses of study to veterans and focusing on those veterans who were educationally disadvantaged (Stephens & Stenger, 1973).

With open admission policies and low-cost tuition, community college enrollment is likely to continue to increase. Today's comprehensive community college serves four main functions, which are different from those of four-year institutions: vocational training for the local workforce, remediation for students not yet ready for college-level work, continuing education for the community, and a liberal arts education designed to prepare students for transfer to four-year institutions. Located in urban, suburban, rural, and even in virtual space across America, community colleges are vital in the higher education landscape. Radford and Wun (2009, p. 6) found that 43.3% of all student veterans are enrolled in public two-year colleges.

Specific job training and certifications have made community colleges crucial to local labor forces and attractive to student veterans since the 1920s (Horn, McCoy, Campbell, & Brock, 2009; Porchea, Allen, Robbins, & Phelps, 2010). Employers look to community colleges to retrain displaced workers, teach current employees new skills, and keep up with the need for workers in high-demand fields. A survey of community colleges across the country reveals the diversity of their offerings. Students can earn degrees in nursing, radiological technologies, fire protection technology, dental assisting, heating and cooling repair, early childhood education, human services, optical systems technology, and accounting, among others. Cohen and Brawer (2003) indicate that these are "programs designed to lead to initial job entry with no further schooling or to modify the skills of people who have already been employed" (p. 220).

This function sets community colleges apart from their four-year counterparts. Community colleges, for example, train and certify more first responders than four-year institutions: roughly 80% of firefighters, nurses, emergency medical technicians, and police officers receive their training and credentials at community colleges (American Association of Community Colleges, 2006). Two-year institutions are responsive to their communities in a way four-year institutions are typically not. If a local manufacturing company needs skilled workers for a plant expansion, for example, they will work with their local community college to meet the needs of the workforce. This is not to say that four-year institutions do not work with their constituencies, but community colleges by design respond directly to the needs of their respective communities.

Remediation is a major component of today's community college offerings. Estimates of community college students who need to take precollege-level classes are as high as 50% (Bettinger & Long, 2005; Horn et al., 2009; Oudenoven, 2002). Also called developmental education, remedial courses prepare students for entry into college-level classes. Community college students may not yet be ready for college-level courses for a variety of reasons. Some students are returning to school after more than ten or twenty years and need refreshers to bring their skills back to where they once were (Vaughn, 2006), whereas other students may lack basic skills because of language barriers (Deegan, Tillery, & Associates, 1985; Vaughn, 2006). Still others may not have a strong enough academic background to be ready for college courses upon arrival (Cohen & Brawer, 2003; Deegan, Tillery, & Associates, 1985).

Serving a disproportionate number of underprepared students is a challenge for community colleges. The cost of offering such courses has led some local sponsors to voice concerns about the numbers of these courses, especially those that serve recent high school graduates (Levin & Calcagno, 2008; Oudenhoven, 2002). To further complicate matters, studies indicate that students who enroll in remedial courses are at a greater risk for noncompletion than those students who do not take remedial classes (Adelman, 1996; Bettinger & Long, 2005; Porchea et al., 2010; Rosenbaum & Person, 2003).

The last two main ways in which community colleges differ from four-year institutions are their foci on continuing education for the community and general education. The community education function covers multiple areas, including adult, continuing, and community-based education; lifelong learning; and contract training. Courses in this category may be for credit or not, vary in duration, be provided on or off campus, be sponsored by the college with another group, or develop in a variety of other permutations

(Cohen & Brawer, 2003). Students served by these courses and programs have different goals than other students at the same institution because they are typically interested in specific courses, rather than degree programs. These students are often older than other students, and there can be a huge variation in their academic preparation and background. Some may have already completed degrees, whereas others may not have even graduated from high school. Community education is often fully funded, either through tuition or grants. Institutions may, for example, enroll retirees in courses for credit to satisfy curiosity or to help them manage their retirement funds, or a group of employees may be required to attend a series of classes to develop a highly focused set of skills required for their jobs.

The last curricular function of the community college is in liberal arts general studies. Courses in the humanities, sciences, social sciences, and mathematics offered at the 100 and 200 level are considered a basic foundation for students who plan to transfer from two-year to four-year institutions. Many community colleges have developed articulation agreements with four-year institutions that guarantee transfer of a certain set of courses into a four-year degree program. This partnership is, according to Cohen and Brawer (2003), sometimes the reason for curricular change at the two-year level. The transfer function of community colleges has become more important in recent years as four-year institutions have become too expensive for many segments of the population.

In addition to their differing missions and relationship to the community, community colleges and four-year institutions offer wholly different experiences. University students have the opportunity to live on campus, which provides easy access to on-campus services, events, and activities. Students who live on campus are invested in the social aspect of their education in a way not often possible at community colleges, and they forge strong bonds and participate in campus life more regularly than students who do not live on campus. Few two-year institutions have residence halls, and students often do not stay on campus after classes and thus do not participate in on-campus social activities.

Although they differ from four-year institutions in many ways, community colleges have taken similar steps to increase the number of programs, services, and opportunities that they provide for their student veterans. McBain, Kim, Cook, and Snead (2012) found the following in the community colleges they surveyed:

- 54.6% have undertaken initiatives to provide professional development for staff.
- 49.3% have increased the number of services and programs they offer for student veterans.

- 43.6% have undertaken initiatives to provide professional development for faculty.
- 42.6% trained counseling staff to assist students with posttraumatic stress disorder (PTSD), brain injuries, and other health issues.
- 40.5% have added staff to specifically serve student veteran needs. (p. 14)

While programs, services, and opportunities differ between two-year and four-year institutions, the most significant difference between them is the type of students they serve.

Community College Students

Given their mission to emphasize accessibility and affordability, it is not surprising that community colleges currently enroll 44% of the nation's undergraduates and educate 43% of first-time freshmen and 42% of all first-generation college students (American Association of Community Colleges, 2012). Students who attend community colleges are more likely to be over 24 years of age, female, Black or Hispanic, and from lower income families than are students attending four-year institutions (Horn, Nevill, & Griffith, 2006). Sixty-one percent of community college students are financially independent, compared with 35% of students at four-year institutions (Horn et al., 2006). Furthermore, one-third are married with children, and one-fourth are single parents (Horn et al., 2006). These statistics set community college students apart from those at four-year institutions and are clearly mirrored in the population of veterans who attend college. These traits are also strikingly similar to those of military students presented in chapter 1.

Students who attend community college are more likely to enroll part-time, a characteristic shared by student veterans; more than two-thirds of community college students attended part-time in 2003–2004 (Horn et al., 2006). Seventy-nine percent of community college students work, and 41% of them work full-time while attending classes (Horn et al., 2006). This, too, is common for military students who attend community colleges. They are more likely to be married and often have to work as they attend school. Finally, according to the AACC (2012), approximately 45% of students with disabilities, a population less likely to remain in college through degree completion, attend community colleges (Horn et al., 2006).

A report titled *Profile of Undergraduates in U.S. Postsecondary Education Institutions, 1992–1993* (Horn & Premo, 1995), although two decades old, provides an explanation of risk factors that are still relevant to today's military and nonmilitary community college students. The term *risk* indicates factors that could negatively affect a student's completion of a postsecondary educational program. The seven risk factors identified in the report are (1) part-time enrollment, (2) delayed enrollment, (3) full-time work, (4) having dependents, (5) financial independence, (6) single parenting, and (7) not graduating from high school (Horn & Premo, 1995). These factors are consistent with later findings of other researchers (Hawley & Harris, 2005; Schmid & Abell, 2003). The report addresses risk at all postsecondary institutions, but these risks are especially significant for community college students. In fact, three-fourths of community college undergraduates have at least one of the risk factors, whereas 70% of students entering four-year institutions did not have any (Schmid & Abell, 2003). The current statistics provided by AACC (2012) support the relationship between community colleges and risk factors.

Military students share these risk factors with their nonmilitary peers. Military undergraduates have clearly delayed their entry into postsecondary education, and 97% of them are financially independent. Military students are often parents; in 2008, for example, 33% of military undergraduates were married with children and 14% were single parents (Radford, 2009). The demographics of military students at community colleges clearly mirror the typical community college student; these two groups share characteristics that stand in stark contrast to student demographics at four-year institutions.

What sets student veterans apart from their nonmilitary peers with regard to risk factors is, of course, their military service. Military deployment and combat experience have few corollaries in the civilian world. The transition military students experience is destabilizing and overwhelming and presents a significant risk in their educational endeavors. Some institutions of higher education are unprepared to serve veterans, and this further complicates military students' educational endeavors (McBain et al., 2012; Ryan, Carlstom, Hughey, & Harris, 2011).

Serving Military Students in Community Colleges

Cost and convenience are two of the most important features that lead students to enroll in community colleges, and these features are equally appealing to veterans (Field, 2008; Sewall, 2010). According to the literature, military students also choose community college for several other reasons, including geography (Radford, 2009; Steele, Salcedo, & Coley, 2010) and available programs (Radford, 2009). Although community colleges are accustomed to serving varied populations, veterans are markedly different from typical students because of their experiences in the armed forces. Factors discussed in previous chapters, such as the shift from military to academic culture, injuries and disabilities, and difficulty in identifying and accessing benefits, all set student veterans apart from their peers.

Serving the military student population presents community colleges with both challenges and opportunities. The transition from active-duty soldier to full- or part-time student is difficult regardless of the service branch, the time served, or personal experience. After having returned from six years of service, Jim said that his transition was "dark" and "confusing" and that attending community college was "overwhelming" and "intimidating." Carlos said his attendance at community college was immediately "weird." He continued,

> I had PTSD; I still do to a point. Certain things just bother me. Whereas in the military . . . amongst my guys in the Marines, you know, we all wear the same uniform so I feel comfortable. Now everybody comes here and they are all shapes and sizes and I have to size everybody up quite fast. It's a constant thing with me.

Other student veterans feel that the community college environment is a perfect fit. They are used to working with people from diverse backgrounds and need flexibility in their scheduling, both of which are common in the community college environment.

Challenges for Community Colleges Educating Student Veterans

Student veterans in community colleges share some similarities with their four-year counterparts: they want to know how to navigate the confusing system of higher education, how to access their benefits, where to find a veteran-specific contact on campus, and what resources and services are available to them. Community colleges should offer student veterans basic services—a school certifying official (SCO); a main point of administrative contact for student veterans; staff members that are knowledgeable about PTSD, depression, traumatic brain injury (TBI), and other issues military students face; a veterans' resource center; and dedicated programs and services (McBain et al., 2012; Persky & Oliver, 2011; Radford, 2009).

In one of the first studies on post-9/11 military students, DiRamio, Ackerman, and Mitchell (2008) reported that many veterans attending postsecondary institutions did not have strong academic skills, regardless of whether they were reenrolling or were new students. Some studies have found that student veterans have lower graduation rates (Ryan et al., 2011), and retention and degree completion are some of the top challenges facing military students (McBain et al., 2012). Sixty-nine percent of student veterans in one study indicated that they needed to relearn material they had forgotten, but once they made the transition to higher education, they were more successful than their peers (Cate, Gerber, & Holmes, 2010). Blake "had such a big gap between high school and college" that he "had to take [math] twice" in order to pass the first entry-level course. This gap in education is further complicated by military students' previous experiences in education. A recent study found that veterans who had self-advocacy skills before enlisting in the military had an easier time with the transition than those who did not (Wheeler, 2012). Those military students who did not have these skills before their service did not develop them during their enlistment, so they floundered when faced with the options and relative freedom of community college life.

Enrolling in remedial courses is often a blow to a student's self-esteem, and military students may be more sensitive than other students in this area. In the military, service members are broken down quickly at basic training, only to be built up again just a few weeks later. Service members take pride in their accomplishments and are rewarded for their successes. Enlisted service members take the Armed Services Vocational Aptitude Battery (ASVAB), a multiple-choice test measuring aptitude in the verbal, math, science, technical, and spatial domains (U.S. Department of Defense, n.d.). The purpose of the test is to predict a service member's future occupational success, and after the test, a list of possible career paths in the military is developed for each applicant. With hundreds of military occupational specialties (MOSs) in the Army and Marines, a recruit's results can provide a positive focus on a variety of occupations for which he or she qualifies. Military service members who take college placement tests such as Accuplacer or the College Placement Test, however, may feel like they have failed because they do not place into college-level classes. Carlos was "so pissed off" about needing to take remedial math and English that he "considered dropping out." The opening quote of this chapter speaks to this:

> The Navy broke me down and built me back up again. Then I get here and I'm not good enough to take College Algebra? I get that I have to do the work and that I've forgotten things, but when you've seen people killed and survived, having to take these classes feels like a slap in the face.

Student veterans have served their country, sometimes in combat, and take pride in their accomplishments and service. Being deemed unready for college-level courses is a blow to self-esteem that some student veterans cannot easily overlook.

Another difference between two-year and four-year institutions with regard to services for military students is the students themselves. A comprehensive report of military students in higher education is not available despite the increasing attention to this population. Creating a portrait of those attending community college is even more complicated because research on those military students attending two-year institutions has not kept pace with studies that focus on four-year institutions. Of the studies that ushered in research on military students in community colleges (Rumann, 2010; Wheeler, 2011; Zinger & Cohen, 2010), only one (Wheeler, 2011) addressed military students' status as first-time students; other studies have not addressed whether or not those attending two-year institutions have previous college experiences. Anecdotal evidence and some statistical data, however, provide support for the contention that military students who attend community colleges are different from those who attend four-year institutions. Since military students are more likely to pursue an associate's degree or a certificate than a bachelor's or graduate degree (Radford, 2009) and tend to have lower high school grade point averages (GPAs) and need remedial preparation (HERI, 2009), it follows that military students attend community colleges at higher percentages than they attend four-year institutions.

Military students who attend community colleges are often enlisted (nonofficer) service members who have not attended college prior to enlistment, who may have had unsuccessful high school experiences, or who may have taken vocational-track, rather than college preparatory, classes in high school. Eighty-three percent of military service members are enlisted men and women who serve in direct combat, operate and maintain equipment, and serve as specialists in diverse fields (U.S. Department of Labor, 2012). Officers almost always already have at least a bachelor's degree and generally do not enroll in two-year institutions. Officers must demonstrate the ability to be successful and focused—skills that are enhanced with additional training in the military. Former officers have supervised and managed enlisted personnel, developed leadership skills, and held jobs in the medical, legal, and engineering fields, among others. Officers benefit from their previous educational experiences, both in higher education and the military.

Military training and education for enlisted service members does not directly mirror what they will encounter in higher education. An enlisted member of the Army, for example, graduates from basic training and enters advanced individual training (AIT), which provides specialized training and coursework for their specific MOS. Military service members in AIT attend classes; take and, if necessary, retake multiple-choice tests requiring a 70% pass rate; and prepare to perform tasks in the field. The classroom work is designed to apply directly to job performance in the field. Students are accustomed to taking constant direction, following orders, taking multiple-choice tests, and engaging in team-based hands-on learning in the rigid structure of the military—an experience that does not typically have a direct corollary in the seemingly chaotic system of higher education. Postsecondary educators can structure their courses to build on these experiences, however, and enhance the chances of academic success for our student veterans (see chapters 8, 9, and 10).

Most military students on community college campuses are younger than 25, and although they may have peers on campus who are the same age, those peers do not have the same life experiences. These student veterans simply feel out of place. Additionally, the high school peers of military students are much further along or finished with their college degrees by the time the student veterans enter higher education, which leaves them feeling like they have to catch up or make up for lost time. Their desire to finish a degree with practical application in a timely manner reflects the desires of military students from previous generations.

A final challenge facing community colleges is that suicide among military service members is at an all-time high. According to recent figures, more military service people have died by their own hand than from the fighting in Afghanistan (Thompson & Gibbs, 2012). The statistics are sobering: 95% of military suicides are enlisted men, 47% of whom are under 25 years old (Thompson & Gibbs, 2012). Younger enlisted men make up the majority of the population of student veterans at community colleges. The Pentagon is allocating increased funding to mental health services for veterans, but clearly this is a tremendous challenge for community colleges with student veteran populations—a problem for which no one seems to be able to find a satisfactory solution.

Opportunities for Community Colleges Serving Military Students

Community colleges are poised to be the higher education institutions of choice for returning student veterans, and they therefore have tremendous opportunities to serve this growing population. Two-year institutions have already demonstrated their responsiveness to military students, as shown in the two American Council on Education (ACE) *From Soldier to Student* reports (Cook & Kim, 2009; McBain et al., 2012). According to the 2012 study, 85% of responding community colleges have increased their efforts to serve military students, and they are more likely than four-year institutions to provide military-specific programs. Community colleges also offer more flexible scheduling and more varied delivery modes than four-year institutions (McBain et al., 2012).

One area in which higher education rarely serves military students well is in transfer credit for military experience. ACE indicated that 83% of responding institutions awarded college credit for military training and 63% for military occupational experience (McBain et al., 2012), but institutions did not indicate what kind of credit was common or how often credit was actually awarded. It is often unclear how much credit will be transferred to any particular institution, and it can be confusing for a student to determine how transferable credits may be applied to specific programs (Steele et al., 2010). A military student receiving 15 hours of general elective credit for military training, for example, may be 15 hours closer to a degree, but those hours may not help him or her with the classes needed for a degree program. The Sailor/Marine American Council on Education Registry Transcript (SMART) and the Army/American Council on Education Registry Transcript System (AARTS) provide a description of military training, the outcomes of that experience, and a recommendation for college credit (American Council on Education, 2009). In an example of how these services work, ACE provides an authentic transcript that recommends three semester hours at the undergraduate level in environmental science for a one-week, 45-hour hazardous waste operations course. The transferring institution can accept, modify, or reject these recommendations based on how closely the outcomes of the course in the military match the institution's environmental science course. Military training does not always align with college courses in a way that allows institutions to grant credit. Paul, for example, spent 22 weeks training full-time in psychological operations in the U.S. Army. He then spent one year working in that field in Bosnia. When he subsequently enrolled in a community college, he was offered only three credits of Introduction to Psychology because his training and experience did not match exactly with the college's psychology curriculum.

Greg's experience was even more dramatic. Greg spent ten years in the Army and came to college with more schooling, training, and experience than many of his peers. He received training at the Army's Chemical, Biological, Radiological, and Nuclear School and took additional courses in air assault, hazardous materials, and various other specialties. Greg amassed an astounding 700 military education credits. Despite this training, his AARTS transcript recommended that he receive only 16 total credits in the following areas: leadership, science, technical education, public speaking, and communication. Even worse, when he enrolled at a local community college, his experience and schooling in the Army did not line up with the college curriculum, and he earned just three credits—in physical education. Greg was a sergeant first class in the Special Forces who received, among other awards, a Naval Commendation Medal in Combat with Valor for his service during Operation Black Thunder. He had hundreds of hours of education and ten years of active service, and yet he received just three credits of physical education; meanwhile, a high school student taking advanced placement

(AP) courses as a junior or senior can enter community college with 30 credit hours of specific transfer equivalents. High school students taking AP classes obviously do the work to earn their credits, but there seems to be incongruity in how higher education treats prior educational experiences for the members of the military.

Community colleges' inherent flexibility should allow them to find innovative approaches to awarding appropriate credit for military students' training. There are hundreds of MOSs with related outcomes for college courses, but few institutions have seized this opportunity to ease the transfer of military experience. Two-year institutions should provide ways to quickly and easily transfer military credits into specific institutional credits. This would go a long way to demonstrate support for student veterans and would help them reach their academic goals.

Community colleges have an opportunity to model environments with which student veterans are familiar and comfortable. Enlisted service members are accustomed to structure. They are given a mission, are shown how to complete it, and know what the expectations are for completion. When they arrive at college, they expect the same structure. They are looking for an established procedure that tells them how to enroll, when to enroll, and where to turn in their paperwork. Providing a clear location and a point of contact for military students is the first step toward modeling the environment military students have become used to. Community colleges can also structure their courses to more closely mirror student veterans' previous educational experiences. Military training is undertaken in groups, and group members work together to achieve a common goal. Courses that are designed specifically for student veterans and block scheduling for specific programs would streamline degree completion for these students and would enhance their academic success (Persky & Oliver, 2011).

Finally, two-year institutions have an opportunity to maximize the flexibility of withdrawal and reenrollment policies for students who are deployed in the middle of an academic term. Military service members who have time left on their contracts may be activated, National Guard members can be required to report to duty, and reservists can be mobilized—all while they are enrolled in college. Institutions of higher education know that this is a distinct possibility, yet only 28% of them report that they have a process to ease the withdrawal and reenrollment process for military students (McBain et al., 2012). These students are instead asked to withdraw and then reapply, which can cause significant delays in their pursuit of higher education. Community colleges should develop flexible procedures to facilitate the reentry of student veterans into higher education.

Best Practices in Community Colleges

This chapter closes by highlighting a few institutions that are establishing innovative and effective ways to serve student veterans. These institutions stand as exemplars that the rest of higher education should closely examine and model.

Bismarck State College, Bismarck, North Dakota

Recognizing that military students need flexibility, Bismarck State College (BSC) offers a variety of two-year degrees and certificates that can be completed entirely online, including eight different degree programs in energy technology and ten degrees in criminal justice and human services. BSC also offers two services to specific branches of the armed forces. Through a partnership with the Army, BSC grants credit toward an AAS in an energy program for specific training at the Army Prime Power School. Additionally, BSC is part of the General Education Mobile Program, which creates a block of general education courses at BSC for those in the Air Force who transfer through a partnership with the Community College of the Air Force. This service allows airmen the ability to complete five general education courses in a block sequence at BSC and then apply them toward a degree from the Community College of the Air Force. See www.bscmilitaryonline.com

Clackamas Community College, Oregon City, Oregon

Awarded an ACE Success for Veterans Grant, Clackamas Community College (CCC) identified programs with the potential to be condensed and combined with the military training for their military students. After correlating MOSs with their existing degree programs, they developed a total of twenty-one courses to bridge military training to a degree program (American Council on Education, n.d.). CCC was able to accelerate student veterans' work in programs such as law enforcement, human services, and business administration by recognizing and rewarding prior military training. CCC has further demonstrated its commitment to serving military students with its partnership with Army Strong, an organization that serves all branches of the military and provides information and resources regarding benefits, deployment, and readjustment. The first Army Strong Community Center west of the Mississippi River and located at a community college is on the CCC Oregon City Campus. See http://depts.clackamas.edu/veterans

Monroe Community College, Rochester, New York

Monroe Community College (MCC) has developed a multipronged approach to veteran services in response to its increasing student veteran population. Veterans Services provides a one-stop shop where military students can receive help with admissions, financial aid, benefits counseling, military-specific academic advising, and other resources. MCC also has a Military Mentoring Program that pairs service members or their family members with a faculty or staff member with considerable experience working with student veterans. A student veteran organization and partnerships with local organizations, including Army Strong, the Rochester Vet Center, and the Veterans Outreach Center, which has an educational specialist on MCC's campuses three days a week, further demonstrates MCC's commitment to military students. Finally, MCC also has a program called Supporting Transitioning and Returning Service Members (STARS), which is a training program developed to educate administrators, faculty, and staff on topics such as military culture, transition to higher education, benefits, health concerns, and veterans in the classroom. Attending four 90-minute sessions earns the attendee a "STARS Veteran-Friendly Designation," which provides a strong and visible network of support for military students. See www.monroecc.edu/depts/counsel/vetacademy

Tidewater Community College, Norfolk, Virginia

Tidewater Community College (TCC) serves hundreds of military students and offers classes on each of the ten military bases in its vicinity. It also offers specialized closed courses for military students. Further, as a member of the Army Concurrent Admissions Program, new recruits in the Army can be matched with TCC at the time of their enlistment and receive a plan for their education once they have completed their service. See www.tcc.edu/students/veterans/

Conclusion

Community colleges are in a unique position with regard to military students. They are poised to see enrollments rise as military students increasingly choose higher education as a postdeployment option. Community colleges have the flexibility to respond in a way that four-year institutions do not. To meet the needs of military students and help them on their road to completion, two-year institutions need to do what they were designed to do: offer flexible options, create innovative programs and services, and prepare students for their next step: a career or transfer to a four-year institution.

Chapter Summary

Community colleges have grown and changed in response to their respective communities throughout their histories. Although military students who attend community colleges present challenges, they also provide great opportunities for the institutions they attend—opportunities community colleges must seize in order to best serve this increasing and unique population.

Key Points

- Military service members have always contributed to the growth of two-year institutions; today's increase in military students at community colleges continues that trend.
- Community colleges serve four main functions: vocational training, remediation, community education, and general education in the liberal arts designed for transfer to four-year institutions.
- Students who attend community colleges differ significantly from students who attend four-year institutions and are at risk for noncompletion.
- Risk factors common to military students include delayed entry, financial independence, dependents, and disabilities.
- Community colleges face multiple challenges in educating military students, including remediation, suicide risk, and lack of degree completion.
- Community colleges have the flexibility to provide multiple curricular options to the military student population. These options include the acceptance of military training for degree program requirements, bridge classes that connect military training to specific courses, block scheduling, online programs, veteran-specific courses, and courses offered on military installations.
- Additional best practices include on-campus partnerships with community veteran organizations, mentoring programs, and training for faculty and staff.

Note

1. Uncited quotations from student veterans originate from the author's personal research.

References

Adelman, C. (1996, October 4). The truth about remedial work. *Chronicle of Higher Education, 43*(6), A.56. Retrieved from http://chronicle.com/article/The-Truth-About-Remedial-Work/74884/

American Association of Community Colleges. (2006). *First responders: Community colleges on the front line of security*. Washington DC: Author. Retrieved from http://www.aacc.nche.edu/Publications/Reports/Documents/firstresponders.pdf

American Association of Community Colleges. (2012). *2012 fact sheet.* Retrieved from http://www.aacc.nche.edu

American Council on Education. (2009). *A transfer guide: Understanding your military transcript and ACE credit recommendations.* Washington DC: Author. Retrieved from http://www.acenet.edu/news-room/Pages/Military-Transfer-Guide.aspx

American Council on Education. (n.d.). *Promising practices in veterans' education: Outcomes and recommendations from the Success for Veterans Awards Grant.* Washington DC: Author. Retrieved from http://www.acenet.edu/news-room/Pages/ACE-Walmart-Success-for-Veterans-Grants.aspx

Bettinger, E. P., & Long, B. T. (2005). Remediation at the community college: Student participation and outcomes. *New directions for community colleges, 129,* 17–26.

Bound, J., & Turner, S. (2002). Going to war and going to college: Did World War II and the GI Bill increase educational attainment for returning veterans? *Journal of Labor Economics, 20*(4), 784–815.

Breedin, B. (1972, March 1). Veterans in college. *Research Currents.*

Brookover, W. B. (1945). The adjustment of veterans to civilian life. *American Sociological Review, 10*(5), 579–586.

Cate, C. A., Gerber, M., & Holmes, D. L. (2010). *A new generation of student veterans: A pilot study.* Santa Barbara: University of California, Santa Barbara Institute for Social, Behavioral, and Economic Research. Retrieved from www.uweb.ucsb.edu/~chriscate/PilotReport09.pdf

Cohen, A. M., & Brawer, F. B. (2003). *The American community college* (4th ed.). San Francisco: Jossey-Bass.

Cook, B. J., & Kim, Y. (2009). *From soldier to student: Easing the transition of service members on campus.* Washington DC: American Council on Education.

Deegan, L., Tillery, D., & Associates. (1985). *Renewing the American community college: Priorities and strategies for effective leadership.* San Francisco: Jossey-Bass.

DiRamio, D., Ackerman, R., & Mitchell, R. L. (2008). From combat to campus: Voices of student-veterans. *NASPA Journal, 45*(1), 73–102. doi:10.2202/1949-6605.1908

Field, K. (2008, July 25). Cost, convenience drive veterans' college choices. *Chronicle of Higher Education, 54*(46), A.1. Retrieved from http://chronicle.com/article/Cost-Convenience-Drive/20381

Hawley, T. H., & Harris, T. A. (2005). Student characteristics related to persistence for first-year community college students. *Journal of College Student Retention, 7*(12), 117.

Higher Education Research Institute (2009). *The American Freshman National Norms Fall 2008.* Los Angeles, CA. Retrieved from http://www.heri.ucla.edu/PDFs/pubs/TFS/Norms/Monographs/TheAmericanFreshman2009.pdf

Horn, C., McCoy, Z., Campbell, L., & Brock, C. (2009). Remedial testing and placement in community colleges. *Community College Journal of Research & Practice, 33*(6), 510–526. doi:10.1080/10668920802662412

Horn, L., Nevill, S., & Griffith, J. (2006). *Profile of undergraduates in U.S. postsecondary education institutions, 2003–04: With a special analysis of community college students.* National Center for Education Statistics (NCES 2006–184). Washington DC: U.S. Government Printing Office.

Horn, L., & Premo, M. (1995). *Profile of undergraduates in U.S. postsecondary education institutions, 1992–1993: With a special essay on undergraduates at risk.* National Center for Education Statistics (NCES 96-237). Washington DC: U.S. Government Printing Office.

Humes, E. (2006). *Over here: How the GI Bill transformed the American dream.* Orlando, FL: Harcourt.

Kinzer, J. R. (1946). The veteran and academic adjustment. *Educational Research Bulletin, 25*(1), 8–12.

Lee, K. (1946, July). War veterans in civil life. *Editorial Research Reports, 1946, 11.* Retrieved from http://library.cqpress.com/cqresearher

Levin, H. M., & Calcagno, J. C. (2008). Remediation in the community college. *Community college review, 35*(10), 181–207. doi:10.1177/0091552107310118

McBain, L., Kim, Y., Cook, B., & Snead, K. (2012). *From soldier to student II: Assessing campus programs for veterans and service members.* Washington DC: American Council on Education. Retrieved from http://www.acenet.edu/news-room/Pages/From-Soldier-to-Student-II.aspx

Mettler, S. (2005). *Soldiers to citizens: The GI Bill and the making of the greatest generation.* New York: Oxford University Press.

Oudenhoven, B. (2002). Remediation at the community college: Pressing issues, uncertain solutions. *New Directions for Community Colleges, 117,* 35–45.

Persky, K. R., & Oliver, D. E. (2011). Veterans coming home to the community college: Linking research to practice. *Community College Journal of Research and Practice, 24,* 111–120. doi:10.1080/10668926.2011.525184.

Porchea, S. F., Allen, J., Robbins, S., & Phelps, R. P. (2010). Predictors of long-term enrollment and degree outcomes for community college students: Integrating academic, psychosocial, socio-demographic, and situational factors. *Journal of Higher Education, 81*(6), 750–778.

Radford, A. W. (2009). *Military service members and veterans in higher education: What the new GI Bill may mean for post-secondary institutions.* Washington DC: American Council on Education. Retrieved from http://www.acenet.edu/news-room/Pages/Military-Service-Members-and-Veterans-in-Higher-Education-What-the-New-GI-Bill-May-Mean-for-Postsecondary-Institutions-.aspx

Radford, A. W., & Wun, J. (2009). *Issue tables: A profile of military service members and veterans enrolled in postsecondary education in 2007–08* (Issue Tables NCES 2009182). Washington DC: National Center for Educational Statistics. Retrieved from http://nces.ed.gov/pubs2011/2011163.pdf

Rosenbaum, J. E., & Person, A. E. (2003). Beyond college for all: Policies and practices to improve transitions into college and jobs. *Professional School Counseling, 6*(4), 252–260.

Rumann, C. B. (2010). *Student veterans return to community college: Understanding their transitions* (Doctoral dissertation). Available from ProQuest Dissertations and Theses. (UMI No. 3403830)

Ryan, S. W., Carlstrom, A. H., Hughey, K. F., & Harris, B. S. (2011). From boots to books: Applying Schlossberg's model to transitioning American veterans. *NACADA Journal, 31*(1), 55–63.

Schmid, C., & Abell, P. (2003). Demographic risk factors, study patterns, and campus involvement as related to student success among Guilford Technical Community College students. *Community College Review, 31*(1), 1–16.

Sewall, M. (2010, August 5). Bill to expand veterans' education benefits begins moving through Congress. *Chronicle of Higher Education, 56*(38). Retrieved from http://chronicle.com/article/Bill-to-Expand-Veterans-Ed/123789/

Steele, J. L., Salcedo, N., & Coley, J. (2010). *Service members in school: Military veterans' experiences using the post 9/11 GI Bill and pursuing postsecondary education.* Santa Monica, CA: Rand Corporation.

Stephens, E. R., & Stenger, C. A. (1973). The opportunity and challenge of the Vietnam era veteran to American educators. *Journal of Higher Education, 43*(4), 303–307.

Thompson, M., & Gibbs, N. (2012, July). The war on suicide? *Time, 180*(4), 22–31.

U.S. Congress. (1972). *Educational benefits available for returning Vietnam era veterans: Hearings before the subcommittee on readjustment, education, and employment of the Committee on Veterans' Affairs, United States Senate.* Washington DC: U.S. Government Printing Office.

U.S. Department of Defense. (n.d.). *ASVAB fact sheet.* Retrieved from http://official-asvab.com

U.S. Department of Labor. (2012). Military careers. *Occupational outlook handbook.* Washington DC: Author. Retrieved from http://www.bls.gov

Vaughn, G. B. (2006). *The community college story* (3rd ed.). Washington DC: American Association of Community Colleges.

Wheeler, H. A. (2011). *From soldier to student: A case study of veterans' transitions to first-time community college students* (Doctoral dissertation). Available from ProQuest Dissertations and Theses database. (UMI No. 3465899)

Wheeler, H. A. (2012). Veterans' transitions to community college: A case study. *Community College Journal of Research and Practice, 36*(10), 775–92. doi:10.1080/10668926.2012.679457

Witt, A. A., Wattenbarger, J. L., Gollattscheck, J. F., & Suppiger, J. E. (1994). *American's community colleges: The first century.* Washington DC: American Association of Community Colleges.

Zinger, L., & Cohen, A. (2010). Veterans returning from war into the classroom: How can colleges be better prepared to meet their needs. *Contemporary Issues in Education Research, 3*(1), 39–51.

PART THREE

INNOVATIVE APPROACHES TO SERVING VETERANS IN THE CLASSROOM

8

COURSE STRUCTURE AND DESIGN

My goals are different [from other students] and I don't care about this Friday. I care about ten years down the line Friday.

—Martin, Air Force veteran (Wheeler, 2011, p. 107)

Astudent's journey through higher education comprises a myriad of activities and events. Regardless of the type of education a student veteran chooses—two year or four year, private or public, online or face-to-face—one of his or her most essential experiences is that of taking classes. Graduate teaching assistants (GTAs), instructional staff, adjuncts, and professors at all ranks should understand what they can do to improve the success of student veterans. The next three chapters explore specific ideas for teachers and other course designers, building off of Fink's (2003) model of course design. This chapter provides a strategic overview by exploring the military's own educational paradigm and examining broad issues related to course structure and design, including situational factors, the formation of learning goals, and feedback and assessment procedures. Chapter 9 examines how teaching and learning activities can enhance (or frustrate) student veterans' educational experiences, and chapter 10 explores how physical, emotional, and behavioral environments can affect the academic success of our students, including those taking classes online.

The Military's Educational Experience

The military provides a specific and effective educational experience that transforms its "students" into a team capable of achieving incredibly complex and hazardous missions. The Coast Guard's *Performance, Training and*

Education Manual states, "The mission of the Training and Education System is to systematically improve performance to achieve excellence in mission execution" (U.S. Coast Guard, 2009, p. 1-1).

The Army's vision of education is similar:

> The Army prepares every Soldier to be a warrior. Army training seeks to replicate the stark realities of combat. The Army has changed its training systems to reflect the conditions of the current operational environment and better prepare Soldiers for them. The goal is to build Soldiers' confidence in themselves and their equipment, leaders, and fellow Soldiers. (U.S. Department of the Army, 2005, p. 4-11)

The military accepts applicants from all walks of life and then molds them into a cohesive team, shaped by core values (see Figures 8.1 and 8.2).

Educational training in the armed forces is, above all else, purposeful. The preface of the Army's *Training the Force* manual (U.S. Department of the Army, 2002, p. iv) states,

Figure 8.1 The Army Values (U.S. Department of the Army, 2005, p. 1-16).

- Loyalty: Bear true faith and allegiance to the U.S. Constitution, the Army, your unit, and other soldiers.
- Duty: Fulfill your obligations.
- Respect: Treat people as they should be treated.
- Selfless service: Put the welfare of the nation, the Army, and subordinates before your own.
- Honor: Live up to all the Army values.
- Integrity: Do what's right—legally and morally.
- Personal courage: Face fear, danger, or adversity (physical or moral).

Figure 8.2 The Sailor's Creed (U.S. Department of the Navy, 1999, p. iii).

I am a United States Sailor.
I will support and defend the Constitution of the United States of America and I will obey the orders of those appointed over me.
I represent the fighting spirit of the Navy and those who have gone before me to defend freedom and democracy around the world.
I proudly serve my country's Navy combat team with Honor, Courage, and Commitment.
I am committed to excellence and the fair treatment of all.

The U. S. Army exists for one reason—to serve the Nation. From the earliest days of its creation, the Army has embodied and defended the American way of life and its constitutional system of government. . . . The Army will do whatever the Nation asks it to do, from decisively winning wars to promoting and keeping the peace.

The military trains its personnel to evaluate and act, whereas postsecondary courses can be more reflective, perhaps even esoteric. Classes run the risk of seeming pointless and useless (i.e., no direct application) to a student veteran. Military training involves a seriousness and commitment that is typically not found in postsecondary educational settings, a commitment the Army refers to as the "Warrior Ethos":

The Warrior Ethos inspires the refusal to accept failure and conviction that military service is much more than a job. It generates an unfailing commitment to win. . . . The Warrior Ethos instills a "mission first—never quit" mental toughness in Soldiers. Training as tough as combat reinforces the Warrior Ethos. . . . Soldiers combine the Warrior Ethos with initiative, decisiveness, and mental agility to succeed in the complex, often irregular environments in which they operate. Soldiers and leaders who exemplify the Warrior Ethos accomplish the mission regardless of obstacles. (U.S. Department of the Army, 2005, pp. 4-11 to 4-12)

Military training generally uses a "crawl-walk-run" process:

Training starts at the basic level. Crawl events are relatively simple to conduct and require minimum support from the unit. After the crawl stage, training becomes incrementally more difficult, requiring more resources from the unit and home station, and increasing the level of realism. At the run stage, the level of difficulty for the training event intensifies. Run stage training requires optimum resources and ideally approaches the level of realism expected in combat. (U.S. Department of the Army, 2002, p. 5-3)

This process of moving from simple to more complex is common for many courses in higher education, although the level of immediate practicality may not be as pronounced.

As mentioned in chapter 2, military personnel typically proceed from basic training to some sort of advanced training (see Table 2.1). The areas represented by this training can be quite broad. In the Army, for example, training occurs in areas that range from human resources (Adjutant General Corps School) and finance and accounting (Finance Corps School) to detecting and defending against nuclear, biological, and chemical agents (Chemical School) and armored warfare (U.S. Army Armor Center)

(GoArmy, n.d.). This training provides content knowledge and hands-on skills that may be highly related to programs of study in higher education and to civilian jobs. The Finance Corps School, for example, trains its graduates to provide the Army with timely and accurate finance and accounting support and teaches them processes related to payroll, travel preparation and payment, commercial vendor vouchers, and the disbursement of public funds. There is recognition also that the training process—like all learning—is a lifelong endeavor, involving "day-to-day experience, education, self-development, developmental counseling, coaching, and mentoring" (U.S. Department of the Army, 2006, p. 4-12).

The military sees itself as an innovative leader in negotiating the constantly changing world and an entity that fosters strong leaders with the ability to think creatively:

> The Army's practice of learning and changing continually while performing its mission has historical roots. Since the 1980s, the Army has been a national leader in anticipating and leading change. Its deliberate study of technical and professional developments, focused collection and analysis of data from operations and training events, free-ranging experimentation, and transforming processes have made it a model of effective innovation. Army leaders are continuing to foster creative thinking. They are challenging inflexible ways of thinking, removing impediments to institutional innovation, and underwriting the risks associated with bold change. (U.S. Department of the Army, 2005, p. 4-10)

Innovation occurs within an environment of communication and engagement between soldiers and leaders:

> It tests new ideas, concepts, and ways of conducting operations. Engagement includes methodically collecting and analyzing data and conducting informed discussions. It experiments with new ideas and creates opportunities to learn from critics. Army leaders are seeking to innovate radically. They want to move beyond incremental improvements to transformational changes. They continue to identify and test the best practices in industrial and commercial enterprises, the other Services, and foreign military establishments. They review history for insights and cautions. Consistent with security, they share information and ideas across organizational, public, private, and academic boundaries. (U.S. Department of the Army, 2005, p. 4-10)

Faculty, staff, and administrators in higher education often fail to appreciate the educational mission of the military services. Although the services' goals are different from those of most colleges and universities, the military has invested a great deal of thought, time, and effort to ensure that its personnel are sufficiently educated for the missions that they must perform.

There are five ways to combine active-duty service and higher education, which Asch, Kilburn, and Klerman (1999, p. 19) have called "tracks." An individual is on the *officer track* if he or she first attends a four-year college and then enters the service as an officer. Reserve Officers' Training Corps (ROTC), Officer Candidate Training, Officer Candidate School, and the service academies provide this type of opportunity. An individual is on the *college-enlisted track* if he or she first attends college or receives some college credit and then enters the service as an enlistee. An individual is on the *enlisted-college track* if he or she enters the service as a high school graduate, completes a service obligation, leaves the service, and then attends college as a veteran or, in some cases, as a member of a reserve or guard component. Students in this track are eligible for financial benefits under the various GI bills. An individual is on the *enlisted-officer track* if he or she enters the service as an enlisted member and then, during his or her enlisted career, leaves the service temporarily to attend a four-year college. Upon receiving a degree, the member returns to serve as an officer. Finally, an individual is on the *concurrent track* if he or she obtains college credits while in the service, that is postsecondary education and service are simultaneous (Asch et al., pp. 20–27). This option has become far more common with the rapid growth of online educational opportunities.

Education within the U.S. armed forces is intentional to the extreme. Few experiences in higher education have undergone such rigorous evaluation and revision. The experience is intense because lives literally hang in the balance. Putting aside the obvious dangers of conflict, human error in any number of ways can cause injury and death when one is operating machinery with the complexity and heft of, for example, tanks and weapon systems. Student veterans are the recipients of this educational experience and return to higher education with practical skill sets that may be directly related to specific programs and majors. They have also experienced processes and internalized learning routines that may not serve them well as they transition into higher education. As mentioned in the previous chapter, military training differs in significant ways from academic coursework:

> In addition to the cultural adjustments that student-veterans must make— becoming acclimated to civilian and campus life and overcoming feelings of isolation or homesickness familiar only to those who have also experienced deployment or combat—student-veterans must also change the way they approach learning. When military service members aren't actively engaged

in combat operations, they are learning and training—both as individuals and as units—and they are doing so according to strict procedural guidelines and requirements in order to meet official, known, and measurable performance standards. (Dalton, 2010, p. 13)

Instructors need to remember this as they consider how to design courses to best serve student veterans who have already had formative—and formidable—educational experiences.

Course Structure and Design

Faculty members often receive little structured training in how to design and teach courses. At best, they have had the experience of being a GTA, but few graduate students—even if identified as the instructor of record—actually exercise complete control over designing and managing courses. Fink's (2003) theory of integrated course design provides a framework to help faculty develop courses that enhance opportunities for significant learning for all their students. Fink identifies four core components of teaching, which are outlined in Table 8.1.

Instructors who teach online classes must add a fifth core component, which occurs prior to the start of instruction: obtain working knowledge of the technology used to deliver the course and its content. Graduate education provides instructors with knowledge of the subject matter, but new faculty often receive limited training in the other components prior to being assigned their teaching duties. A well-designed course, however, can significantly improve teacher-student interactions and the management of the course.

Reader Reflection: Preparation for Teaching in Higher Education

Consider your own preparation for teaching in higher education.

1. How much training did you receive in designing courses?
2. What surprised you the most when you first taught a course on your own?

Fink's integrated model of course design is a three-stage process that first considers situational factors, the learning goals of the course, and how those learning goals will be accomplished and assessed. The second stage develops more fully the sequencing of specific learning activities and the application of instructional strategies, and the third stage addresses grading schemes and syllabi construction (Fink, 2003, p. 67). This chapter will examine three of the first-stage components more closely (situational factors, learning goals, and feedback and assessment procedures), while the next chapter will look

TABLE 8.1 The Four Components of Teaching (Fink, 2003, p. 22)	
Components That Occur Primarily Before Instruction Begins	*Components That Occur Primarily After Instruction Begins*
Obtain Knowledge of the Subject Matter	Teacher-Student Interactions
Design of the Course	Management of the Course

at how the fourth of these components—the development of teaching and learning activities—adds to an overall instructional strategy that can better serve our student veterans.

The Components of Extraordinary Course Design

Situational factors are specific characteristics of your course that will affect the class, and they must be accounted for in the course design. This could include the specific context of the teaching and learning situation, the expectations of external groups, the nature of the subject, the characteristics of the learners, the characteristics of the teacher, and special pedagogical challenges that might be inherent to the course (Fink, 2003, p. 69). All of these factors should be considered with the student veteran in mind:

Specific Context of the Teaching and Learning Situation

- How many student veterans might be in the class?
- Are these veterans likely to be taking this class the first semester after their return from deployment?
- Does the layout of the classroom cause any potential hurdles for student veterans (multiple exits, glass windows/walls, areas inaccessible to students with restricted mobility, etc.)?
- If the course is online, are there likely to be active-duty military personnel taking the course, and if so, what might be the ramifications?

Expectations of External Groups

- Are the retention rates of student veterans under scrutiny by state or university initiatives?
- Is this a course that student veterans should receive credit for based on the educational experiences they have had in the military?
- Would previous military experience count as fulfilling any prerequisite for the course, allowing student veterans to enroll in it directly?

Nature of the Subject

- Does the content require special consideration, given what we know about the general characteristics of student veterans?
- Does the content of the course require that students closely examine issues such as death or loss?
- Does the course cover geographical areas or cultures in which student veterans may have some expertise (remember that the United States has significant troop deployments in many areas of the world, and not just the Middle East)?
- Does the course content cover leadership theory or have a significant ethics component that student veterans may have had previous training in?

Characteristics of the Learners

- Student veterans may be experiencing significant transitional challenges as they move between active duty and higher education.
- Student veterans may come into a course with significant practical experience (an Army medic taking nursing courses, for example).
- Student veterans may have disabilities (including some that they themselves are unaware of) that create challenges for their learning success.

Characteristics of the Teacher

- What prior experience does the teacher have with the military, and is it positive or negative?
- What stereotypes about military students or the military itself must the teacher overcome?
- Does the teacher understand best practices in educating student veterans?

Special Pedagogical Challenges

- Student veterans tend to volunteer more of their time to service projects than any other group. Would a service-learning project be appropriate for the course?
- Team-based learning can be both a positive and a negative experience for student veterans. Have team-based learning exercises been examined to make sure assignments are clearly defined and have unambiguous goals?

- Does the course use the principles of Universal Design (UD)?
- Does the course use modes of communication that are radically different from military protocol?
- Are there contingency plans for students who are taking online courses overseas and who may have course activities disrupted by their military duties?

There are large numbers of veterans returning to higher education, and all faculty members should consider the presence of military students as one of the situational factors of course design.

Course Design: The Integrated Components

In Fink's model, once the situational factors for a course have been identified, faculty members develop learning goals, and feedback and assessment procedures, and teaching and learning activities. It is important that course designers understand the synergy that exists between these components (Fink, 2003, p. 66). Strong learning goals must be matched with feedback and assessment activities that adequately measure progress toward or attainment of those goals. Teaching and learning activities should engage the students in such a way that they are able to show progress on the measures of feedback and assessment. The process is recursive—as course designers consider assessment procedures and learning activities, new learning goals may suggest themselves. In the end, a well-designed course balances and integrates each of the components, based on an honest assessment of the situational factors of the course.

Learning goals are the product of a learner-centered pedagogy that identifies exactly what the instructor hopes the students will receive by taking his or her course. Learning goals include, but also transcend, the content of the course. Every class has the potential to offer students multiple ways to experience extraordinary learning opportunities. Although the phrase "significant learning" has become a catchword in much of today's pedagogical literature, its meaning is often ill-defined. Fink's (2003) multilayered examination of what constitutes significant learning provides a crucial foundation for this chapter and reveals some unique ways in which faculty might better connect with student veterans as they prepare learning activities for their classroom.

Fink recognizes the usefulness of Bloom's (1956, pp. 201–207) traditional (cognitive) content-centered learning taxonomy. Bloom's taxonomy provides a hierarchical ordering of six types of learning (see Figure 8.3), all based on a student's ability to manipulate and restate learned content.

Figure 8.3 Bloom's Hierarchical Sequence of Educational Objectives.

Evaluation	Highest level of learning
Synthesis	
Analysis	
Application	
Comprehension	
Knowledge	Lowest level of learning

Fink, however, proposes a new taxonomy that emphasizes multiple dimensions of learning. These dimensions go beyond the content-centered focus of Bloom's theory and address the need to give expression to types of learning such as the development of character, leadership, and the ability to teach oneself. Fink defines *significant learning* as that which causes change in the learner (Fink, 2003, p. 29, 56). Content (which Fink calls "foundational knowledge") becomes just one of six major categories of significant learning; the other categories are application, integration, human dimension, caring, and learning how to learn. These types of learning are described in the following list (Fink, 2003, pp. 30–32). Interestingly, the training literature of the armed forces includes strong analogs to Fink's categories, and these are also included in the list.

- *Foundational knowledge*: Understanding and remembering specific information and ideas. This type of learning provides a basic understanding of a particular subject.

  Domain knowledge requires possessing facts, beliefs, and logical assumptions in many areas. Tactical knowledge is an understanding of military tactics related to securing a designated objective through military means. Technical knowledge consists of the specialized information associated with a particular function or system. Joint knowledge is an understanding of joint organizations, their procedures, and their roles in national defense. Cultural and geopolitical knowledge is awareness of cultural, geographic, and political differences and sensitivities. (U.S. Department of the Army, 2006, p. 6-5)

- *Application*: Learning how to engage in some new type of intellectual, physical, or social action. This type of learning allows the other types of learning to be useful.

  Character and knowledge—while absolutely necessary—are not enough. Leadership demands action—the self-discipline to DO what feels or is known to be right. . . . Leadership is a lifelong learning process for Army leaders, but action is its essence. (U.S. Department of the Army, 2005, pp. 1-19)

- *Integration*: Connecting learned material with other ideas, people, or realms of life. This type of learning allows students to draw parallels and connections between ideas or actions that may have seemed disparate at first, strengthening the web of meaning through inter-relatedness.

  Sometimes a new problem presents itself or an old problem requires a new solution. Army leaders should seize such opportunities to think creatively and to innovate. The key concept for creative thinking is developing new ideas and ways to challenge subordinates with new approaches and ideas. (U.S. Department of the Army, 2006, p. 6-2)

- *Human dimension*: Learning something important about oneself or others. This type of learning allows students to discover personal and social implications for what they are studying. "An Army leader's self-control, balance, and stability greatly influence his ability to interact with others. People are human beings with hopes, fears, concerns, and dreams" (U.S. Department of the Army, 2006, p. 6-4).

- *Caring*: Developing new feelings, interests, and values. This type of learning allows students to interact with the subject on a personal level, creating new energy and enthusiasm for learning.

  Army leaders show a propensity to share experiences with the members of their organization. When planning and deciding, try to envision the impact on Soldiers and other subordinates. The ability to see something from another person's point of view, to identify with and enter into another person's feelings and emotions, enables the Army leader to better care for civilians, Soldiers, and their families. (U.S. Department of the Army, 2006, p. 4-9)

- *Learning how to learn*: Becoming a better student; learning how to be inquisitive and self-directed. This type of learning is important because it allows students to become lifelong learners and to engage in future studies with greater effectiveness and efficiency. "Leaders of character can develop only through continual study, reflection, experience, and feedback" (U.S. Department of the Army, 2006, p. 4-12).

These types of learning are interactive, rather than hierarchical, and this interactive model increases the potential for student learning. It represents, in some respects, the Army's own educational philosophy: "Competence develops from a balanced combination of institutional schooling, self-development, realistic training, and professional experience" (U.S. Department of the Army, 2006, p. 2-7). Fink's taxonomy provides a foundation from which classes can be designed to give student veterans significant learning experiences.

Well-designed courses have learning goals from each of the significant learning categories. In each case, course designers should ask themselves what they would like the students to remember, experience, or do a year or more after taking the course. Faculty members need to consider what outcomes are most important for their course—to identify the knowledge, skills, and aptitudes they wish their students to exhibit long after the course is finished. "Begin with the end in mind" is a familiar enough mantra (Covey, 2004, p. 95) and in the context of course design is often referred to as "backward design" (Wiggins, 1998). Overall learning goals will probably not change significantly in a course based on the presence or absence of student veterans. The primary objective is to make sure that student veterans have the same opportunities to achieve the learning goals as do nonveteran students.

Reader Reflection: Developing Course-Specific Learning Goals

Think about one course you will soon be teaching. Consider the overall goals you have for this course (Fink, 2005, p. 8):

1. What do you want your students to learn beyond the content?
2. What distinguishes a student who has taken your course from one who has not?
3. What would you want your students to remember from your course five years after they had taken it?

Feedback and assessment procedures are not simply a basis for student grades, but rather a means by which instructors can measure student achievement of the learning goals. Students have better opportunities to learn if the course includes feedback within each topic area that allows them to improve (formative assessment). Wiggins (1998) describes this process as "Educative" and Fink (2003) further defines this as a process that incorporates forward-looking assessment, self-assessment, and an adherence to valid criteria and standards. It contrasts with summative assessment, which measures student learning after a content area is over and which provides limited opportunities for student improvement. Educative assessment is administered frequently and provides students with immediate feedback.

It is delivered in such a way as to encourage student growth rather than to discourage it (Fink, 2003, p. 83).

Student veterans are quite familiar with assessment and evaluation, for the process is a vital component of military training and preparedness in both its formal and informal manifestations:

> All training must be evaluated to measure performance levels against the established Army standard. The evaluation can be as fundamental as an informal, internal evaluation performed by the leader conducting the training. Evaluation is conducted specifically to enable the unit or individual undergoing the training to know whether the training standard has been achieved. Commanders must establish a climate that encourages candid and accurate feedback for the purpose of developing leaders and trained units. (U.S. Department of the Army, 2002, p. 6-4)

Feedback in the military tends to be frequent and immediate: "A key element in developing leaders is immediate, positive feedback that coaches and leads subordinate leaders to achieve the Army standard. This is a tested and proven path to develop competent, confident adaptive leaders" (U.S. Department of the Army, 2002, p. 6-4). Assessment in the military can range in formality from a verbal debrief after a training exercise to a written evaluation from within the unit to an official evaluation from an external reviewer (Dalton, 2010, p. 14). Regardless of the source, assessment in the military is meant to be immediately applicable:

> Whatever the level of formality, however, the universal purpose of training assessment in the military is to analyze and catalog the "lessons learned" of previous training evolutions; when military personnel learn a particular procedure, they also learn *why* that procedure is best in a given situation, based on the previous experiences of others. (Dalton, 2010, pp. 14–15)

The assessment process is not about testing or grading, nor is it about punitive measures:

> Evaluation tells the unit or the soldier whether or not they achieved the Army standard and, therefore, assists them in determining the overall effectiveness of their training plans. Evaluation produces disciplined soldiers, leaders and units. Training without evaluation is a waste of time and resources. (U.S. Department of the Army, 2002, p. 6-4)

Student veterans have been taught to expect a certain type of feedback. They tend to want honest and direct evaluations from professors (and are likely to give the same) and understand the process as one that will help them achieve their goal of passing the course. However, they will also tend to want to know what the purpose of each activity itself is—in other words, what the "mission objective" is for any particular assignment (Dalton, 2010, p. 15). It is important for instructors to understand that student veterans who recently transitioned out of the military will need to adjust to the means and methods of academic assessment, but the instructors themselves can also reevaluate their own feedback processes by considering Fink's model of educative assessment and the military's evaluative activities. For a much deeper discussion on student-centered assessment in higher education, readers are strongly encouraged to refer to Wiggins (1998) and Fink (2003).

Universal Design

The process of helping students with different types of abilities succeed is often called Universal Design (UD). As indicated earlier in this book, perhaps as many as 40% of our student veterans may have disabilities of some sort. UD is a set of principles that can provide faculty with ways to better serve all students with disabilities, including our student veterans. The Assistive Technology Act of 1998 defines *UD* as

> a concept or philosophy for designing and delivering products and services that are usable by people with the widest possible range of functional capabilities, which include products and services that are directly usable (without requiring assistive technologies) and products and services that are made usable with assistive technologies. (Section 3.a.17)

This concept is especially important for student veterans. Most students with disabilities entering higher education have had those disabilities identified at an early age and are well informed about their own strengths and weaknesses. Student veterans, however, are often coping with newly acquired disabilities—some of which may not be identified until they are already heavily engaged with academic material. As Church (2009) writes,

> The UD paradigm addresses the needs of all veterans, including those who have not self identified, and designs course materials and classroom activities that are relevant to a diverse student body, rather than focusing exclusively on the needs of the students with disabilities. (p. 54)

UD broadly adopts the following guidelines (Connell et al., 1997):

- *Equitable use.* The design is useful and marketable to people with diverse abilities. It provides the same means of use for all users, identical whenever possible and equivalent when not; it avoids segregating or stigmatizing users; it makes provisions for privacy, security, and safety equally available to all users; and the design is appealing to all users.
- *Flexibility in use.* The design accommodates a wide range of individual preferences and abilities. It provides choice in the methods of use; accommodates right- or left-handed access and use; facilitates the user's accuracy and precision; and provides adaptability to the user's pace.
- *Simple and intuitive use.* The design is easy to understand, regardless of the user's experience, knowledge, language skills, or current concentration level. It eliminates unnecessary complexity, is consistent with user expectations and intuition, accommodates a wide range of literacy and language skills, arranges information consistent with its importance, and provides effective prompting and feedback during and after task completion.
- *Perceptible information.* The design communicates necessary information effectively to the user, regardless of ambient conditions or the user's sensory abilities. It uses different modes (pictorial, verbal, tactile) for redundant presentation of essential information, maximizes the legibility of essential information, differentiates elements in ways that can be described (i.e., it is easy to give instructions or directions), and provides compatibility with a variety of techniques or devices used by people with sensory limitations.
- *Tolerance for error.* The design minimizes hazards and the adverse consequences of accidental or unintended actions. It arranges elements to minimize hazards and errors, provides warnings of hazards and errors, provides fail-safe features, and discourages unconscious action in tasks that require vigilance.
- *Low physical effort.* The design can be used efficiently and comfortably and with a minimum of fatigue. It allows students to maintain a neutral body position and use reasonable operating forces and it minimizes repetitive actions and sustained physical effort.
- *Size and space for approach and use.* The design provides appropriate size and space for approach, reach, manipulation, and use regardless of user's body size, posture, or mobility. It provides a clear line of sight to important elements for any seated or standing user; makes

reach to all components comfortable for any seated or standing user; accommodates variations in hand and grip size; and provides adequate space for the use of assistive devices or personal assistance.

The implications of these principles in higher education range widely in respect to student veterans, but Table 8.2 provides some examples. Some of these implications are discussed more fully in the following two chapters.

TABLE 8.2 Universal Design Applications for Student Veterans		
Principle	*Higher Education Application for Student Veterans*	*Chapter of Emphasis*
Equitable Use	Statements on the syllabi that recognize military- and VA-related absences as excused.	8
Perceptible Information	Class materials are presented in multiple formats to be accessible to students with a broad range of abilities.	8
Tolerance for Error	Courses are designed so that students are able to actively assess and revise their work.	8
Flexibility in Use	Courses are designed so that students can demonstrate knowledge in a variety of ways.	9
Simple and Intuitive Use	Homework assignments are clearly described in the syllabus, and longer assignments for first- and second-year students are broken up into discrete assignments that lead to the culmination of the project.	9
Low Physical Effort	Course software doesn't require fine movements with the mouse or tracking pad.	10
Size and Space for Approach and Use	Recognition that some types of spaces (open classrooms with many windows and multiple doors, for example) can be extremely uncomfortable for veterans returning from ground operations in the Middle East.	10

These principles touch almost every aspect of a course, including the class climate, physical access, content delivery methods, information resources, assessment, classroom interaction, and direct accommodation. UD does not, however, lower quality or standards. In the end, the students must be responsible for achieving the learning objectives for the course. It is also important to note that applying UD reduces, but does not eliminate, the need for accommodations for students with disabilities.

Equitable Use

Courses that feature equitable use are accessible for students with diverse abilities. These classes provide the means for all students to succeed using identical or equivalent resources and do not segregate or stigmatize any student or group of students. One of the easiest ways to describe the application of equitable use within a course is related to course attendance. Most instructors have an attendance policy of some sort. Even the strictest policies give varsity athletes and other campus groups exceptions for missing class because of university-related events. Instructors should think seriously about what allowances should be given to student veterans and how these policies are communicated. Faculty members should understand that student veterans have a number of military-related commitments that may take them out of class, from weekend training activities (which can start on Fridays) to Veterans Affairs (VA) medical appointments. Faculty don't need to know exactly how the VA medical process works, for example, but they should be aware that the system is monolithic—and that making a VA appointment is not at all like scheduling an appointment with a family physician. VA appointments, if canceled, often cannot be rescheduled until months later. Faculty should develop attendance and class participation policies, therefore, that do not penalize student veterans who have to miss class because of VA appointments. Likewise, military obligations (such as weekend training or emergency deployment for National Guard units) are commitments that supersede the importance of any single class and should be regarded as the same type of excused absence that faculty would extend to varsity athletes. Presidential Executive Order 13607, signed on April 27, 2012, mandates that educational institutions receiving federal funding must "take additional steps to accommodate short absences due to service obligations, provided that satisfactory academic progress is being made by the service members and reservists" (Obama, 2012). Explicitly stating these revised attendance policies on a syllabus is one small but visible way to make a course more veteran-friendly. Instituting department-wide attendance policies would demonstrate even greater support.

Institutional policies regarding students with disabilities should also be referenced in the syllabus, and it is helpful to include the contact information for the institution's Disabilities Services Office. Many universities also require a standard Americans with Disabilities Act (ADA) statement such as this on every syllabus:

> If you have a disability for which you are or may be requesting an accommodation, you are encouraged to contact both your instructor and the Director of the Office of Disability Services, [location, phone number], as early as possible in the semester.

If there are external resources related to the class (such as peer mentoring or extra study sessions), these should also be clearly stated in the syllabus. The goal of these statements is to provide information without identifying or stigmatizing students. Those students who struggle with asking for help—whether veterans or not—will at least have the contact information available to them.

Perceptible Information

One of the most important tenets of UD is that information be presented in multiple formats that clearly communicate the desired content and tone of the message. This can include anything from turning on close-captioning when viewing video clips to recording all lectures and providing them as podcasts. At the very least, however, written materials should be provided in electronic formats that facilitate the use of assistive technology, and slide presentations should be converted to either physical or electronic handouts. Visual aids, if used, should be large or should be projected at high enough magnification that all can see them. Instructions for activities and assignments should be stated clearly and, if possible, in multiple ways. Faculty could provide written directions along with oral instructions, for example, or use graphics to enhance written guidelines.

Other strategies for applying the principle of perceptible information include:

- Write the course schedule in paragraph or table form on the syllabus and also include the schedule as a calendar within the course management system.
- List your office hours in the syllabus and also show them on a calendar within the course management system. Provide a map that indicates where your office is located and how to get from the classroom to your office.

- In addition to listing texts, provide information on where students might find the text, including electronic versions if available. Put articles on both physical and electronic reserve (subject to copyright restrictions).
- Provide electronic versions of anything you hand out in paper format and post videos and musical examples used in class to your course management system (subject to copyright restrictions).
- Try to include only basic information on your syllabus—move as much information as possible (rubrics, assignment descriptions) to separate documents. (adapted from Behling & Hart, 2008, p. 115)

Courses that are designed to implement the principle of perceptible information allow students to access information and materials in the formats that are easiest for them to comprehend. These techniques also allow students multiple ways to view the information, enhancing their ability to understand the material. As with all UD implementations, this helps not only student veterans, but many other types of students in the course.

Tolerance for Error

Courses designed using the principles of UD show tolerance for error in student work. Tolerating error does not require reducing standards on learning goals, but rather it promotes the structuring of activities and assessments so that the pace of learning accounts for individual learning styles and previous knowledge. Courses could be structured so that the students are given frequent, low-stakes assessments, for example, allowing them to discover how well they know the material before unit tests. Faculty may be able to break up large projects (such as term papers) into smaller components (such as an outline, rough draft, bibliography, and final product) that are each graded. One large, high-stakes learning activity thus becomes several activities that allow students to make errors initially but that still require them to achieve the final learning goal. Online simulations and practice tests could be provided so that students could self-assess their progress. This is especially important for student veterans who have recently entered or reentered higher education. The tolerance for error principle allows them to make mistakes as they get used to academic frames of inquiry and styles of discourse. It also gives them the time they need to refresh their understanding of concepts from prerequisite classes that they may have taken years before.

Universal Design and Online Education

Distance learning provides unique opportunities and challenges for service members and student veterans, and course designs need to recognize and allow for those opportunities and challenges. Online courses should also follow the principles of UD to maximize the opportunities for student learning. Best practices for UD in online courses include the following:

- The distance-learning home page is accessible to individuals with disabilities (in other words, it adheres to one of the following: the Section 508 amendment to the Rehabilitation Act of 1973, the World Wide Web Consortium standards, or institutional accessible-design guidelines or standards).
- A statement about the distance-learning program's commitment to accessible design for all potential students, including those with disabilities, is included prominently in appropriate publications and on websites. Contact information for reporting inaccessible design features is provided.
- Directions for requesting accommodations are included in appropriate publications and web pages.
- Directions for requesting alternate formats of printed materials are included in all publications.

UD increases the importance of selecting materials early, to enable faculty (and their students, if necessary) the time needed to convert materials.

Conclusion: Transforming Your Courses

Imagine your students five years from now. What do they remember about your course—specific names, terminology, and important dates? Or perhaps it's a broader understanding of how to critically review new information, how to communicate effectively, and how to be resilient in the face of change? At its heart, the course design process should be about transforming "learning as imagined"—that is, those long-term goals you have for your students—into "learning achieved" as evidenced by student accomplishments. It is a progression from the learning goals of the course to the learning outcomes of the students. In a strong course design, learning goals lead to learning and assessment activities that create opportunities for significant learning. These activities are mapped onto the academic calendar, and as students progress through the term they become engaged through significant learning. Student veterans benefit most from the design process when the principles of UD are infused into the course and when the steps between learning imagined and learning achieved are traversed with veterans' strengths and challenges in mind. The result of a well-designed course is a class of students who, despite individual abilities, have each accomplished the learning goals originally envisioned by the instructor (Fink & Fink, 2009, p. 5).

Chapter Summary

One of the most important facets of college life is the college classroom. Faculty should design courses that take advantage of the strengths of incoming student veterans and minimize the challenges they may face. Student veterans have already completed an incredibly formative educational experience through their military training, and this training can be both a benefit and a detriment to learning in a postsecondary setting. A well-designed course accounts for various situational factors, including the potential presence of student veterans. It establishes learning goals that go beyond content coverage and includes application, integration, caring, the human dimension, and learning how to learn. Learning goals should be assessed (but not all need to be graded), and these assessments should provide clear evidence that students have indeed achieved the learning goal. The principles of UD are an important component of the course design and enable students with many different abilities to succeed.

Key Points

- Student veterans have already undergone a formidable educational experience through their military training. Student veterans come to higher education with a broad range of knowledge and training, which may intersect powerfully (and unpredictably) with the course material.
- UD is a set of principles that can provide faculty with numerous ways to better serve all students with disabilities. Courses that incorporate UD are
  - equitable,
  - flexible,
  - intuitive,
  - varied in the ways they present information,
  - varied in the ways they assess information,
  - limited in the amount of sustained physical and mental effort that is required, as appropriate to the goals of the course, and
  - accessible to students with a variety of physical abilities.
- Courses that incorporate UD do not have lowered quality or standards.

- UD reduces, but does not eliminate, the need for accommodations for students with disabilities.
- Military- or VA-related absences should be given the same consideration as school-sponsored absences.
- Technology should be used to the fullest extent possible to enhance the accessibility of the course.

References

Asch, B. J., Kilburn, M. R., & Klerman, J. A. (1999). *Attracting college-bound youth into the military: Toward the development of new recruiting policy options.* Santa Monica, CA: RAND Distribution Services.

Assistive Technology Act of 1998, Public Law 105–394 Stat 2432, Section 3.a.17 (1998).

Behling, K., & Hart, D. (2008). Universal course design: A model for professional development. In S. Burgstahler & R. Cory (Eds.), *Universal Design in higher education: From principles to practice* (pp. 109–126). Cambridge, MA: Harvard Education Press.

Bloom, B. S. (Ed). (1956). *Taxonomy of educational objectives: The classification of educational goals—Handbook I: Cognitive domain.* New York: McKay.

Burgstahler, S., & Cory, R. (2008). *Universal Design in higher education: From principles to practice.* Cambridge, MA: Harvard Education Press.

Church, T. E. (2009). *Veterans with disabilities: Promoting success in higher education.* Huntersville, NC: Association on Higher Education and Disability.

Connell, B., Jones, M., Mace, R., Mueller, J., Mullick, A., Ostroff, E., Sanford, J., Steinfield, E., Story, M., & Vanderheiden, G. (1997). *The principles of Universal Design* [website]. Retrieved from http://www.ncsu.edu/project/design-projects/ udi/center-for-universal-design/the-principles-of-universal-design/

Covey, S. (2004). *The 7 habits of highly effective people: Powerful lessons in personal change.* New York: Free Press.

Dalton, K. S. (2010). *From combat to composition: Meeting the needs of military veterans through postsecondary writing pedagogy* (Master's thesis). Available from ProQuest Dissertations and Theses database. (UMI No. 1475346)

Fink, L. D. (2003). *Creating significant learning experiences.* San Francisco: Jossey-Bass.

Fink, L. D. (2005). *A self-directed guide to designing courses for significant learning.* Retrieved from http://www.deefinkandassociates.com/index.php/resources/

Fink, L. D., & Fink, A. K. (Eds.). (2009). *Designing courses for significant learning: Voices of experience.* San Francisco: Jossey-Bass.

GoArmy. (n.d.). *Advanced individual training: Preparing you for your Army job* [website]. Retrieved from http://www.goarmy.com/soldier-life/becoming-a-soldier/ advanced-individual-training.html

Obama, B. (2012). Establishing principles of excellence for educational institutions serving service members, veterans, spouses, and other family members. Presidential Executive Order 13607. Washington DC: White House Office of the Press Secretary. Retrieved from http://www.whitehouse.gov/the-press-office/2012/04/27/executive-order-establishing-principles-excellence-educational-instituti

U.S. Coast Guard. (2009). *Performance, training and education manual.* COMDTINST M1500.10C. Washington DC: U.S. Department of Homeland Security.

U.S. Department of the Army. (2002). *Training the force.* Field Manual 7-0 (FM 25-100). Washington DC: Headquarters, Department of the Army.

U.S. Department of the Army. (2005). *The Army.* Field Manual 1. Washington DC: Headquarters, Department of the Army.

U.S. Department of the Army. (2006). *Army leadership: Competent, confident, and agile.* Field Manual 6-22. Washington DC: Headquarters, Department of the Army.

U.S. Department of the Navy. (1999). *Navy military training policies and procedures.* CNETINST 1540.20. Pensacola, FL: Chief of Naval Education and Training.

Wheeler, H. A. (2011). *From soldier to student: A case study of veterans' transitions to first-time community college students* (Doctoral dissertation). Available from ProQuest Dissertations & Theses database. (UMI No. 3465899)

Wiggins, G. (1998). *Educative assessment: Designing assessments to inform and improve student performance.* San Francisco: Jossey-Bass.

9

TEACHING AND LEARNING ACTIVITIES

Critical Thinking: A deliberate process of thought whose purpose is to find truth in situations where direct observation is insufficient, impossible, or impractical.

—*Army Leadership* (U.S. Department of the Army, 2006, p. 6-1)

The military provides an educational experience unlike any other. It prepares its personnel to operate in complex and often dangerous environments and trains them to accomplish their mission regardless of personal cost. It also gives them specific frames for learning that colleges and universities must acknowledge if we are to create academic environments that are conducive to the education of our student veterans. The last chapter looked at three of the four basic elements of course design: situational factors, learning goals, and feedback and assessment. This chapter is dedicated to exploring the fourth element: teaching and learning activities (Fink, 2003, p. 82). Specific types of learning activities make use of student veterans' strengths, and others build up those areas in which student veterans may not be as well prepared. One of the great challenges all faculty face is to develop interesting and meaningful classroom activities for students with significant life experiences. This challenge is true for many nontraditionally aged students, but instructors must realize that no classroom simulation, debate, or service-learning project is likely to produce the same adrenaline-filled experience as working in a combat zone. Despite this, there are definitive ways to enhance the academic experience of student veterans.

Leveraging the Strengths of Our Student Veterans

Student veterans transition into higher education with tremendous strengths, including a "degree of maturity, experience with leadership, familiarity with diversity, and a mission-focused orientation" (American Council on

Education, 2010, p. 1). The life experiences of military students help them to clarify their academic goals:

> We have experienced life. You've got these 18- to 19-year-old kids still with mommy and daddy, and they don't have life experience, they don't know what it's like to live on their own, they don't know how to manage their own time, their own finances, their own, just their own being, because they have somebody to do that for them. We have. We've seen it, we've done it, and now it just kind of adds into this energy of actually being a student. (McDonald, 2011, p. 109)

Military students may have firsthand knowledge of the geography, politics, and sociology of strategic areas of the world. Depending on their advanced training, student veterans may come to higher education with specific, world-tested knowledge on topics ranging from government finance to law enforcement to engineering. Faculty should consider all these strengths as they design their courses. While much of this book is dedicated to helping faculty recognize the challenges that student veterans face, we must also understand that they can be tremendously valuable assets in an educational setting.

Teaching and Learning Activities

Teaching and learning activities must be fully integrated with the other components of the strategic course design and can be developed only after learning goals have been identified and assessment procedures solidified. Assignments and classroom activities should promote engaged, active learning that leads to critical thinking. Fink's taxonomy of significant learning, presented in the previous chapter, provides a basis for the development of critical thinking activities for any individual course. The key to understanding most topics is generally a sequence of activities that allows students to gain information about, to have experience with, and to reflect on the course topic (Fink, 2003, p. 108). Incidentally, as illustrated in Figure 9.1, the Army Training Execution Process models this.

Figure 9.1 U.S. Army Training Execution Process (U.S. Department of the Army, 2002, p. 5-2).

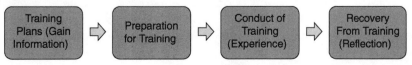

Students access the content of a course directly by analyzing original data, reading primary sources, applying the ideas being learned in real-world situations, and engaging in reflective dialogue. They access content indirectly when they use secondary data, read textbooks or stories, and participate in simulations and role-playing. Direct experience and analysis of material is generally most effective but may be impractical for some topics. The armed forces may use indirect exposure to information during the initial stages of training, but by the final stages of training service members are almost always fully engaged in exercises that are as lifelike as possible. Higher education, outside of a few experiences such as internships, lab sciences, and fine arts performances, rarely achieves that level of realism.

Reflection is equally important in the military and in higher education, but it plays a different role in each. Generally speaking, the military trains its personnel to act, with reflection as part of that process, whereas higher education trains its students to reflect, with action as part of that process. Instructors therefore need to emphasize the reflective nature of academic work for the benefit of all their students. Student veterans, who have been trained to make rapid decisions, "will benefit from experiences that help them in learning that rarely will they need to make such harrowing split second decisions and that when a decision needs to be made, they should spend the necessary time to do so" (Branker, 2009, p. 62). All students, including those with military backgrounds, will benefit from a course structure that encourages them to take their time with assignments and to be thoughtful in their academic activities. Asynchronous communication—the use of learning management discussion boards, wikis, blogs, or tweets—can help students build in time for this reflection (Grabinger, 2010).

Instructors can use many types of teaching and learning activities to help students learn new course material in significant ways. A few types of activities, however, are particularly relevant for student veterans. These activities build on the strengths of student veterans or bolster areas in which military training may diverge with the expectations of higher education. Specifically, this chapter examines activities related to communication and writing, team-based learning, service-learning, and cultural literacy.

Communication and Writing

The military trains its personnel to communicate in specific ways—a "precisely and formally standardized way of clearly transmitting essential information in a chaotic and noisy battlefield environment" (Dalton, 2010, p. 3). Students who transition from the military into higher education must not only adjust to a different culture but also change how they think about and use language:

Military language focuses on rapid, concise, direct communication that curtails the possibility of confusion or ambiguity about the message being sent. Part of this emphasis is due to the way military communication is shaped—and sometimes limited—by the technologies through which it is enabled. (Dalton, 2010, p. 15)

Effective communication is essential to the military. The Army's *Effective Writing for Army Leaders* states,

We must improve our communicating skills. An order that can be understood will be understood. When and if our soldiers are called upon to risk their lives in the accomplishment of their mission, there must be no mistaking exactly what we require of them. (U.S. Department of the Army, 1986, foreword)

The Air Force manual on communication, *The Tongue and Quill*, reflects the same attitude:

The military environment is unique, and much of its uniqueness requires extraordinary communication skills. We operate highly technical equipment in a lethal environment and we are held to very high standards by the country we serve. Miscommunication can cause expensive mistakes, embarrass our organization and in some cases causes accidents or even death. (McBride, 2004, p. 5)

Military communication can seem extremely terse and jargon-laden to civilians:

For example, a lengthy radio call such as "Squadron headquarters, this is helicopter number 614, I am currently ten minutes away from home base. When I land, I will have two and a half hours of fuel remaining, and I would like to fill up my tanks. Send out the next flight crew," is instead transmitted as "Indian base, 614. Ten mikes out, two plus three zero for a hot pump crew switch." (Dalton, 2010, p. 16)

Five minutes spent in a veterans' resource center or at an on-campus veterans meeting quickly reveals that student veterans maintain many of these communications habits when talking with each other. Some veterans find that "civilian" modes of discourse are inefficient and trivial:

One of the biggest changes I've undertaken has been relaxing my communication style. The Marine Corps values clear, direct, and accurate communication. Senior officers have little tolerance for meandering around your point, and they have zero tolerance for trivial or deceptive nonsense. Junior Marines are similar, except they can perceive this better than most field grade officers. I've learned that in civilian life many people want to banter about nothing for about 90 seconds before discussing anything of substance. I don't necessarily like it, but now I can handle it.

Before learning this I would initiate a conversation with a standard greeting and then jump right into my point. When the information transfer was complete I would say "thanks" and jet off to the next stop on my itinerary. I eventually learned that this offends and confuses many people, which was equally confusing to me, because I thought we were communicating about business, not knitting sweaters. (Barnett, 2009)

Sweaters aside, a student veteran who communicates to his or her classmates in such a direct manner may be perceived as gruff, rude, aggressive, or nonsocial.

The difference in communication styles is particularly pronounced in how the military and higher education each understand the writing process and product. The armed forces have explicit expectations: "The standard for Army writing is writing you can understand in a single rapid reading, and is generally free of errors in grammar, mechanics, and usage. . . . Good Army writing is clear, concise, organized, and right to the point" (U.S. Department of the Army, 1986, p. 1). The Army writing style guide is succinct:

a. Put the recommendation, conclusion, or reason for writing—the "bottom line"—in the first or second paragraph, not at the end.
b. Use the active voice.
c. Use short sentences (an average of 15 or fewer words).
d. Use short words (three syllables or fewer).
e. Write paragraphs that, with few exceptions, are no more than 1 inch deep.
f. Use correct spelling, grammar, and punctuation.
g. Use "I," "You," and "we" as subjects of sentences instead of "this office," "this headquarters," "all individuals," and so forth, for most kinds of writing. (U.S. Department of the Army, 1986, p. 1)

The Air Force stylistic conventions are similar, exhorting writers to "get to the point quickly" and to "cut through the jargon and passive voice, use the right word for the job and don't make [the readers] wade through an overgrown jungle of flowery words" (McBride, 2004, p. 12). The emphasis on directness does not always translate well into higher education:

[A] student-veteran's tendency to communicate in such clear and direct ways could certainly be an asset; however, habitual reliance on formulaic or standardized forms (or even words), or impatience with "meandering" around an idea might forestall or prevent altogether the kind of general curiosity, patient exploration, and interest in complicating an idea that is necessary for creative, insightful, complex writing. (Dalton, 2010, pp. 17–18)

At the same time, many college professors have wished that their students came preprogrammed with the following attitude toward writing espoused in the Air Force's communications guide:

Always edit! Editing is crucial to producing professional communication. Without solid editing your writing can be disjointed, your reader becomes confused, and your message may be lost. Does it take time? Absolutely! Budget time for editing—especially for time-critical assignments—and with practice the whole process will seem second nature. (McBride, 2004, p. 103)

Military training emphasizes language use that suits its needs. This communication style—especially when it comes to writing—does not, however, reflect current theories regarding academic composition (Dalton, 2010, p. 23).

Student veterans, especially those who have recently transitioned into higher education, may struggle with the format and rationale of academic writing. Academic writing has different purposes and goals than military writing:

There is no indication in the [military writing] guides that writing is a process of meaning-making; that form might somehow affect the meaning that can be made; that long sentences may sometimes be needed to convey complex or interrelated ideas; that there may be more than one acceptable way to say something; that the ideas a writer begins with may—and perhaps even should—change throughout the writing process. (Dalton, 2010, pp. 23–24)

This is especially important in English composition courses, but many (perhaps most) college courses require writing of some sort that is reflective in nature. Language conventions don't just convey information, they also provide a framework for how the members of a group think—a "habit of mind" (Bizzell, 1992, p. 227). The success of the military's work hinges on communication that is "unambiguous and undebateable" (Dalton, 2010, p. 31), and military students have established that communications trait as a habit of mind. Instructors should therefore emphasize that academic writing

should be understood as a nonlinear, sometimes messy process enroute to an eventual final product—that it's not as important to produce "clean" writing as it is to produce writing that *does* something to and with the way they (and their readers) think. (Dalton, 2010, p. 26)

Emphasizing this purpose for writing helps instructors develop a more reflective habit of mind in all their students, including student veterans. Instructors who are familiar with military writing styles will be better prepared to assist student veterans as they transition into accepted practices for communication in higher education.

Academic (and especially reflective) writing is different from what many of our student veterans have experienced, but there are specific techniques that instructors can use to enhance student veterans' success. All students benefit from clear writing instructions and evaluation criteria. Instructors should precisely define the goals of each writing assignment, in essence providing "mission objectives" that students can attempt to achieve (Dalton, 2010, p. 27). These objectives should be accompanied by the criterion that will define success for that particular assignment. Rubrics can provide these standards, regardless of whether or not the assignment is a term paper or a lab report. Faculty need to continually emphasize that college writing is a process, a working out of ideas through time. This process can be emphasized by dividing large writing assignments into a series of smaller projects that allow students to revise their work (Dalton, 2010, p. 49).

Student veterans may struggle to transition from military to academic communication styles, but they also bring powerful advantages to the composition process and to writing in general. As mentioned earlier, they are accustomed to receiving direct and honest feedback through the process of editing and revision. More than that, however, they have experienced life in ways that are beyond most beginning college writers. They have much to write about, if they will, and professors must understand and be prepared to read about experiences that are well outside the typical college student's life. Many student veterans have not experienced trauma, and some veterans who have experienced difficult circumstances have fully dealt with what they have experienced. For some student veterans, however, writing becomes an important component in restoring their lives.

Writing has a powerful ability to enable people to work through deeply meaningful, or deeply traumatic, experiences. Meaning-making occurs when thinking is shaped by the permanence of the written word, the explicitness required in writing, and the active nature of the process, which rewards rethinking and revising over time (Applebee, 1984, p. 577). One instructor who worked extensively with veterans noted,

> The veterans needed to write. They would write the unspeakable. Writing, they keep track of their thinking; they leave a permanent record. Processing chaos through story and poem, the writer shapes and forms experience, and thereby, I believe, changes the past and remakes the existing world. (Kingston, 2006, pp. 1–2)

Dalton (2010) expands on this theme:

> In this sense, a student-veteran's personal transition from the trauma and destruction of combat to the literal putting-together process of composition takes on another, more urgent significance than any concerns about academic development. For combat veterans suffering from psychological injuries such as post traumatic stress disorder, an understanding of writing as a way of making meaning, of shaping and reshaping experience, and of materializing realities in both the world and writer can be a productive source of self healing. (p. 4)

College instructors should never take on the role of professional counselors, but they should be prepared to see these issues come across in student writing. Furthermore, faculty should not assume that student veterans want to write about their military experiences—some will, and some won't, for a variety of reasons. As Leonhardy (2009) notes, "It is not my job to 'push' a veteran to relive his or her combat experiences or any other aspect of his or her military experience. The vets write about their military experiences if and when they are ready" (pp. 350–351).

Communication in the military differs substantially from the expected conventions of higher education. Student veterans will need to transition into a new communications style as they write and speak to classmates and teachers. Faculty who understand the military's writing processes and goals can facilitate this transition. They can guide student veterans toward successful modes of academic writing, an essential element of the collegiate experience. Readers who are interested in a deeper exploration of writing and the student veteran are urged to refer to Dalton (2010), *From Combat to Composition: Meeting the Needs of Military Veterans through Postsecondary Writing Pedagogy.*

Small Group Activities and Team-Based Learning

Small group activities, collaborative learning, and team-based learning are important pedagogical tools for college professors. These activities can range from simple "think-pair-share" techniques to instructional strategies that form long-term teams dedicated to learning and completing projects together. Collaboration is second nature to most student veterans. In the Army, "teams are formed to share information and lessons gained from experience" (U.S. Department of the Army, 2006, pp. 3–9). Small groups in the classroom serve much the same process, creating a learner-centered environment in which students share responsibility for their own learning. Leonhardy (2009) found in his work with student veterans that "small groups seem to facilitate class discussions, which allow vets to establish in-group relationships and non-veterans to ask questions—questions that some students deeply long to have answered" (p. 346). Small group activities require less planning and can be used with spontaneously formed student clusters. Techniques include the following:

- Think-pair-share: Students reflect on a question (usually in writing), then pair up with a classmate and share their answers. Pairs of students may be asked to share their ideas to the full class.
- Brainstorming or buzz groups: The class is divided into groups of four to six students. The groups develop answers to questions raised out of a lecture or presentation. One or more groups are chosen to present their thoughts to the entire class.
- Jigsaw activity: This technique is used for topics that have multiple concepts or perspectives. The class is divided into at least as many groups as there are concepts. Each group is then given one concept to master. After they have done so, new groups are then formed. The new groups must be composed of one member from each separate concept or perspective. Each student is then responsible for teaching their concept to the newly formed group.

These methods can be effective ways of moving beyond lecture to engage student veterans with course material, the instructor, and other students. The activities encourage learners to support each other, employ different skills and roles, and interact with each other (Burgstahler, 2011, p. 2).

While small group activities can be a highly useful pedagogical tool, there is a difference between the previously described techniques and team-based learning, which applies formal strategies to put students into high-achieving academic teams. These teams work together for a significant amount of time to accomplish a specific project. At its best, team-based learning offers two major advantages: students commit to a high level of effort in the activity, and the abilities of the team as a whole far exceed the capabilities of any individual student (Michaelsen, Knight, & Fink, 2004, p. 7). This type of activity requires a more significant time commitment from the instructor, who must fully develop and carefully organize each team project. The military's emphasis on team is highly structured, and roles and goals are clearly defined. Student veterans often have negative perceptions of team-based exercises that are unclear or have ambiguous goals. Well-designed team exercises, however, play into the strengths of student veterans and can be a highly positive educational experience for the entire class. Michaelsen, Knight, and Fink (2004) write, "Team-based learning creates conditions in which people who are very different from one another learn that they need to work together and that they can work together. They make their differences an asset rather than a liability" (p. 25). Student veterans, who often feel that they are set apart from their (especially traditionally aged) classmates, may find that this type of exercise connects them in positive ways to the other students in the class: "Last semester I had a group project and that helped. This semester I don't. So this semester's been real, like I don't really talk to anybody or anything" (Maurin, 2012, p. 68).

Team-based learning is effective because it "nurtures the development of high levels of group cohesiveness" (Michaelsen, Knight, & Fink, 2004, p. 27). Successful team-based learning exercises are based around four essential principles: (1) groups must be properly formed and managed; (2) students must be made accountable for their individual and group work; (3) group assignments must promote both learning and team development; and (4) students must have frequent and timely performance feedback (Michaelsen, Knight, & Fink, 2004, p. 28). As described in chapter 8, the military's educational experience models each of these principles. Well-designed team-based learning activities place student veterans in an environment with which they have experience and in which they are comfortable. It transforms the solitary learning experience into a collaborative environment where all students can connect with each other as they learn the material. As such, this type of learning activity can be an effective way to enhance the success of student veterans. Readers interested in a deeper discussion of team-based learning are urged to refer to Michaelsen, Knight, and Fink (2004), *Team-Based Learning: A Transformative Use of Small Groups in College Teaching.*

Service-Learning

Service-learning can be broadly defined as "a method under which students learn and develop through active participation in thoughtfully organized service experiences that meet actual community needs" (Furco, 1996, p. 9). Service activities are combined with reflective exercises to create opportunities for rich learning experiences. Student veterans can be of great value to service-learning projects. Many men and women join the military out of a sense of public responsibility, and data show that student veterans are much more likely to engage in service activities than the average college student. Student veterans volunteer more hours per month (22.9) than any other demographic and 7.6 hours more than nonveteran students (see Figure 9.2).

There is a reason that the armed forces are often called "the Service." Student veterans have an understanding of civic engagement, the leadership skills to successfully navigate between the institution and the community, the

Figure 9.2 Volunteerism and Student Veterans.

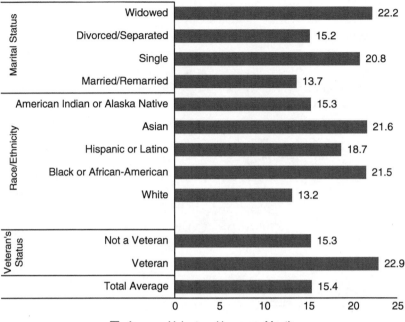

■ Average Volunteer Hours per Month

Note: Data compiled by the National Center for Education Statistics PowerStats Version 1.0 on May 6, 2011. 2004 Dataset. Variance estimation method: BRR.

organizational skills and work ethic that help them see projects through to full fruition, and life experience that engenders respect from the community. They are also often connected to community veteran organizations, which may themselves be involved in service activities. Faculty who use service-learning in their courses will find that student veterans are a tremendous asset and bring skills and community connections to the activity that few other students have.

Service-learning activities also benefit the student veteran. As noted in previous chapters, student veterans often perceive lower levels of campus support and interact less with faculty than other students (National Survey of Student Engagement, 2010). Service-learning contributes to stronger relationships with faculty, improves student satisfaction with the college, and has a positive correlation with student graduation (Astin & Sax, 1998). Service-learning projects allow student veterans to use their strengths as they connect with both their classmates and instructors. In addition, these projects are typically goal-oriented, are action-based, and have definable outcomes for the community—and in that respect, they come closest to the type of learning that student veterans experienced in the military. Finally, faculty may find that student veterans can help them develop tremendous synergy with external veteran organizations, both as service recipients and as service providers. Student veterans can serve as a force multiplier in service-learning, connecting the institution to the community in new ways that open up even more service opportunities.

Cultural Literacy

Student veterans represent both a resource and a challenge for faculty who teach courses related to cultures and policies in countries where the U.S. military is active. Higher education has become increasingly concerned with teaching students to understand diversity within the United States and our global society. The Association of American Colleges and Universities (AAC&U), for example, identifies

> diversity, global engagement, and social responsibility as compelling educational and institutional priorities that help students and campuses engage the social, civic, and economic challenges of a diverse and unequal world. AAC&U supports colleges and universities in their efforts to create settings that foster students' understanding of the intersection between their lives and global issues and their sense of responsibility as local and global citizens. (Association of American Colleges and Universities, 2012)

Student veterans understand in a uniquely personal manner how their lives intersect with global issues. The Army itself recognizes the importance of cultural awareness and diversity:

> In the new security environment, cultural awareness has become one of the most important knowledge areas for Army leaders. Army leaders develop their knowledge of major world cultures and learn how those cultures affect military operations. The Army's rich mix of Soldiers' backgrounds and cultures is a natural enabler of cultural awareness. Effective Army leaders get to know their Soldiers; in doing so, they increase their awareness of different perspectives. This knowledge helps them become more self-aware and adaptive. (U.S. Department of the Army, 2005, p. 1-19)

The Army emphasizes cultural literacy for a specific reason—to understand how cultures affect military operations—that some faculty may be uncomfortable with. Faculty must realize, however, that student veterans will likely have had cultural experiences and interactions that have shaped them significantly. Maurin (2012) quotes one veteran as saying, "It was probably the most impactful situation of my entire life. Impactful insofar as like seeing other cultures up close. I am obsessed with the Middle East now" (p. 62). Another veteran adds, "When you've experienced other cultures, you've seen it firsthand. You've seen the best and the worst of other cultures, if that makes sense" (Murphy, 2011, p. 170). Military students have lived the goals of the AAC&U: they have already developed a sense of the intersection between their lives and global issues. They have a global perspective and an understanding of diversity that most students lack.

Military students' personal experiences with the cultures of the Middle East may also create challenges in the classroom for both the student and the instructor. Student veterans may be resentful toward both faculty and students who speak of Middle Eastern cultures without having had firsthand knowledge of those peoples and places:

> And I feel I know a lot about the Middle East, being I was Special Forces and in 5th group, we studied the culture, their language, we learned a lot about the history of the area. I took, I tell you the only class I failed here was Middle Eastern politics. Like I totally disagreed with the professor with a lot of stuff. I feel like I had practical knowledge of . . . because I've been there, I've seen it, I've studied the language and the culture. I know the people. But, he knows what is in the books and he's heard from other people. He doesn't know what I felt like is really there and what I saw. I was . . . it was the only class where I had any kind of academic trouble. My other political science classes have all been A's. That was an interesting experience. (Murphy, 2011, pp. 106–107)

Instructors should differentiate their personal beliefs about current U.S. policy from their attitudes toward student veterans and should not assume that all veterans hold the same opinions about current political and military events. Although military students do tend to be more conservative, within the veteran population there are political and personal views that range from far left to far right.

Faculty should attempt to find a way to acknowledge the thoughts and ideas of student veterans as part of the overall learning experience for the class. Instructors who can develop ways to use student veterans' cultural experiences to enrich their course will find the experience hugely rewarding. Many students have personal anecdotes that can engage their classmates in ways that the traditional curriculum can't. There is a fine line to walk, however, as this student veteran relates:

> I had a professor in my journalism class. He kept pushing me for information and some sort of insight as to my experiences in the military and he was just annoying. I just wanted him to shut up because that was gone and that's a dif-

ferent life. For me that was really annoying. I just, I kind of got to the point of dreading going to that class. (DiRamio, Ackerman, & Mitchell, 2008, p. 88)

Faculty should also realize that some student veterans may not have served in the Middle East but instead have experience with cultures in Germany, the Philippines, South Korea, and other places where U.S. troops are stationed. Student veterans represent a ready resource of personal information on a wide array of world cultures and geography. Developing this resource takes care and sensitivity but in the end can improve the educational experiences for all students.

Universal Design of Learning Activities

This chapter concludes by examining how two principles of Universal Design (UD)—flexibility in use and simple and intuitive use—can be applied to learning activities. It also explores a few specific strategies that can be used in the classroom to enable students with posttraumatic stress disorder (PTSD), depression, and traumatic brain injury (TBI) to have a greater opportunity to succeed. All learning activities should allow flexibility in how students access and demonstrate knowledge. Furthermore, activities should follow the principle of being simple and intuitive, without jeopardizing the academic integrity of the course or hindering successful achievement of the learning objectives.

Flexibility in Use

Students generally have preferred methods of learning and demonstrating knowledge. Some learn best by reading, some by listening to an explanation, and some by solving a physical problem. In the same way, students have preferences for demonstrating knowledge—some do better on multiple-choice tests, whereas others do better on essays. The principle of "flexibility in use" allows students with different preferences to have the same opportunities for success in the classroom. Instructors who apply flexibility in use to their learning activities allow students to "learn and demonstrate knowledge through multiple channels, including reading, listening, viewing, manipulating, experimenting, discussing, responding to questions, each of which are available in formats accessible to all students" (Burgstahler & Cory, 2008, p. 24). Faculty should design courses that use multiple means of representation, expression, and engagement (Rose, Harbour, Johnston, Daley, & Abarbanell, 2008, 46). This is especially important for student veterans who have disabilities. A complex team-based project may be a highly positive experience for many student veterans because the military teaches the importance of personal responsibility within the context of team achievements. That type of project might be very difficult, however, for a student who has PTSD.

Burgstahler (2011, p. 4) recommends the following as ways to incorporate flexibility in use into courses:

- Provide multiple ways to demonstrate knowledge. Assess group and cooperative performance, as well as individual achievement. Consider using traditional tests with a variety of formats (e.g., multiple choice, essay, short answer), papers, group work, demonstrations, portfolios, and presentations as options for demonstrating knowledge. Provide students choices in assessment methods when appropriate. Allow students to use information technology to complete exams.
- Monitor and adjust. Regularly assess students' background knowledge and current learning informally (e.g., through class discussion) and formally (e.g., through frequent, short exams), and adjust instructional content and methods accordingly.
- Test in the same manner in which you teach. Ensure that a test measures what students have learned and not their ability to adapt to a new format or style of presentation.
- Plan for variety in students' ability to complete work by announcing assignments well in advance of due dates.

Faculty who are designing courses should vary the types of learning and assessment activities that are used in a class. A course that consists of nothing more than disinterested lectures punctuated with multiple-choice tests rarely engages any type of student, let alone students who have been steeped in the military's culture of action. One way to implement a variety of activities is to use the "cafeteria of assignments" strategy described in Weimer (2002, p. 2). This course design style allows students to choose from a variety of activities, each worth a certain amount of points. The final class grade is determined by the accumulated point total from all completed projects (see Weimer, 2002, pp. 203–212). A course design such as this is not practical in all cases, but flexibility in the use of learning activities and assessment methods can help student veterans build on their strengths to achieve academic success. Flexibility in use is more than just a principle of UD, it is a component of learner-centered teaching (Weimer, 2002, p. 2).

Simple and Intuitive Use

Students must cover highly complex topics through the course of their academic programs, so simplicity may seem misplaced here. In UD terms, however, it refers to how students are able to access and process the information in class. Almost every instructor knows the mayhem that can result from a poorly worded assignment or syllabus error. Assignments should be clearly described in course materials, and assessment methods should be clearly delineated. This is true of all courses but is crucial in online sections because distance-learning instructors rely more heavily on written policies. Course materials and grading policies should also be as intuitive as possible, allowing students to quickly understand the objectives of the assignments and the manner in which those objectives will be evaluated. Assignments that are simple to understand and intuitively designed enable students to focus on the course material and improve their ability to achieve course learning goals.

Posttraumatic Stress Disorder, Depression, and Traumatic Brain Injury in the Classroom

Students with PTSD, depression, and TBI face unique challenges in the classroom. Instructors can implement a number of instructional strategies to offset these challenges. The American Council on Education (2010, p. 8) and Burgstahler and Cory (2008, p. 117) suggest the following:

- Provide an agenda or flowchart at the beginning of class, highlight the order of topics and connections, and state the goal for each class period.
- Design activities that sequence from and build on previous assignments.
- Integrate the personal experiences of students into the subject or topic area under study.
- Plan for student-owned course time, when students work in teams or give presentations.
- Permit flexibility in class session attendance schedules, as long as absences do not conflict with the core requirements of the class.
- Utilize electronic platforms to store lecture notes and handouts, so that students may access the information through alternative electronic formats as needed.
- Permit in-class use of laptop computers for note taking.
- Permit the in-class use of digital recorders as memory aids.
- Allow students to take a short break (5–10 minutes) during class sessions or testing environments when stressful situations arise.
- If exams are necessary,
  - administer tests on a computer;
  - allow students to use index cards, blank paper, or a ruler to help keep their place on exams;

- allow students to use an index card with faculty-approved notes on exams;
- build memory joggers into the exams; and
- eliminate timed tests in favor of other assessment methods that do not penalize students who require extra time, low-distraction testing accommodations, or attendance flexibility, regardless of whether a disability has been identified.

Some of these strategies are relatively subtle, some are significant, and the extent to which instructors use them will depend on the course and the content being taught. Incorporating these techniques will allow students with PTSD, depression, and TBI—even if undiagnosed—to have a better opportunity to pass the class.

Learning Activities for Other Disabilities

While this book has focused on PTSD, depression, and TBI, student veterans may have other types of disabilities. Numerous studies have shown that there are specific teaching strategies and styles that can have a positive impact on the learning experience of these students. Representative strategies include self-regulated learning (Bandura, 1993; Butler, 2003; Schunk, 1994), the working model (Borkowski & Muthukrishna, 1992), strategic learning (Butler, 1993, 1995, 1998), concrete-to-representational-to-abstract (CRA) instruction (Witzel, Riccomini, & Schneider, 2008), peer-review evaluation process (PREP) (Graham, Slocum, & Sanchez, 2007), creating laboratory access for science students (CLASS) (Lunsford & Bargerhuff, 2006), and supported education (Bellamy & Mowbray, 1998; Best, Still, & Cameron, 2008; Guitierrez, 1994; Mowbray, 1999). Other techniques have been specially developed for students who are hearing- or vision-impaired (Moriarty, 2007; Poon & Ovadia, 2008; Supalo, Mallouk, Rankel, Amorosi, & Graybill, 2008; Zimmerman, 2007).

Conclusion

Military students are trained to think critically—to "find truth" even in situations that are chaotic and in which information is incomplete. Faculty can develop learning activities that build on the strengths of military students and help them understand and value postsecondary modes of communication and thinking. This often requires redesigning a class so that it is learner-centered, rather than teacher-centered (Weimer, 2002). Instructional change is never easy, but the product of that effort might just be a course that engages and enlightens students far beyond their expectations.

Chapter Summary

Student veterans are assets in every educational setting. They bring organizational and leadership skills, an understanding and appreciation of team dynamics, cultural experiences, and a propensity toward service that can enhance learning opportunities for all students. They may struggle, however, to shift to reflective writing styles and may find it frustrating to communicate with nonmilitary students and faculty. PTSD, depression, and TBI often manifest themselves in ways that look like traditional learning disabilities. Faculty should implement the UD principles of flexibility in use and simple and intuitive use to allow students with a wide range of learning preferences the greatest opportunity to succeed. These principles should be implemented, however, without compromising the academic quality of the instruction. Faculty who take the time to design learning activities that create opportunities for significant learning will improve the educational experience for all their students, including student veterans.

Key Points

- Student veterans transition into higher education with tremendous strengths, and faculty can leverage particular types of learning activities to enhance their academic success.
- Faculty may need to emphasize the reflective nature of academic work, which contrasts with the military's emphasis on rapid, concise, and direct communication.
- Writing assignments should have precisely defined goals, clear assessment standards, and opportunities for revision. These structures can help student veterans adjust as they transition into academic writing styles.
- Informal group activities and team-based learning projects build on student veterans' strengths if the exercises have clearly defined roles and specific, achievable goals.
- Service-learning builds on student veterans' propensity toward service, provides opportunities for them to apply education in ways that have real-world outcomes, and makes use of their leadership and organizational skills.
- Student veterans have often had highly contextualized experiences with cultures and societies that most students and faculty have not had.
- Faculty should design courses that allow students to find, engage with, and exhibit knowledge in many different ways.

References

American Council on Education. (2010). *Accommodating student veterans with traumatic brain injury and post-traumatic stress disorder: Tips for campus faculty and staff.* Washington DC: Author. Retrieved from http://www.acenet.edu/news -room/Pages/Accommodating-Student-Veterans-with-Traumatic-Brain-Injury -and-Post-Traumatic-Stress-Disorder.aspx

Applebee, A. (1984). Writing and reasoning. *Review of Educational Research, 54*(4), 577–596.

Association of American Colleges and Universities. (2012). *Global learning* [website]. Retrieved from http://www.aacu.org/resources/globallearning/index.cfm

Astin, A. W., & Sax, L. J. (1998). How undergraduates are affected by service participation. *Journal of College Student Development, 39*(3), 251–263.

Bandura, A. (1993). Perceived self-efficacy in cognitive development and functioning. *Educational Psychologist, 28*, 117–148.

Barnett, J. D. (2009, October 7). Let me get right to the point [blog]. *New York Times.* Retrieved from http://opinionator.blogs.nytimes.com/2009/10/07/let-me-get-right -to-the-point/#

Bellamy, C. D., & Mowbray, C. T. (1998). Supported education as an empowerment intervention for people with mental illness. *Journal of Community Psychology, 26*(5), 401–413.

Best, L. J., Still, M., & Cameron, G. (2008). Supported education: Enabling course completion for people experiencing mental illness. *Australian Occupational Therapy Journal, 55*(1), 65–68.

Bizzell, P. (1992). *Academic discourse and critical consciousness.* Pittsburgh, PA: University of Pittsburgh Press.

Borkowski, J. G., & Muthukrishna, N. (1992). Moving metacognition into the classroom: "Working models" and effective strategy teaching. In M. Pressley, K. R. Harris, & J. T. Guthrie (Eds.), *Promoting academic competence and literacy in school* (pp. 477–501). Toronto, ON: Academic.

Branker, C. (2009). Deserving design: The new generation of student veterans. *Journal of Postsecondary Education and Disability, 22*(1), 59–66.

Burgstahler, S. (2011). A checklist for inclusive teaching [brochure]. *Equal access: Universal Design of instruction.* Retrieved from http://www.washington.edu/doit/ Brochures/Academics/equal_access_udi.html

Burgstahler, S., & Cory, R. (2008). *Universal Design in higher education: From principles to practice.* Cambridge, MA: Harvard Education Press.

Butler, D. L. (1993). *Promoting strategic learning by adults with learning disabilities: An alternative approach* (Doctoral dissertation). Retrieved from summit.sfu.ca/ system/files/iritems1/5757/b15282806.pdf

Butler, D. L. (1995). Promoting strategic learning by post secondary students with learning disabilities. *Journal of Learning Disabilities, 28*, 170–190.

Butler, D. L. (1998). The strategic content learning approach to promoting self-regulated learning: A summary of three studies. *Journal of Educational Psychology, 90*, 682–697.

Butler, D. L. (2003). Structuring instruction to promote self-regulated learning by adolescents and adults with learning disabilities. *Exceptionality, 11*(1), 39–60.

Dalton, K. S. (2010). *From combat to composition: Meeting the needs of military veterans through postsecondary writing pedagogy* (Master's thesis). Available from ProQuest Dissertations and Theses database. (UMI No. 1475346)

DiRamio, D., Ackerman, R., & Mitchell, R. L. (2008). From combat to campus: Voices of student-veterans. *NASPA Journal, 45*(1), 73–102. doi:10.2202/1949–6605.1908

Fink, L. D. (2003). *Creating significant learning experiences.* San Francisco: Jossey-Bass.

Furco, A. (1996). Service-learning: A balanced approach to experiential education. In *Introduction to Service-Learning Toolkit: Readings and Resources for Faculty* (pp. 9–13). Providence, RI: Campus Compact.

Grabinger, S. (2010). A framework for supporting postsecondary learners with psychiatric disabilities in online environments. *Electronic Journal of e-Learning, 8*(2), 101–110.

Graham, M., Slocum, A., & Sanchez, R. M. (2007). Teaching high school students and college freshmen product development by deterministic design with PREP. *Journal of Mechanical Design, 129*(7), 677–681.

Guitierrez, L. (1994). Beyond coping: An empowerment perspective on stressful life events. *Journal of Sociology and Social Welfare, 21*, 201–219.

Kingston, M. H. (2006). Tell the truth, and so make peace. In M. Kingston (Ed.), *Veterans of war, veterans of peace* (pp. 1–3). Kihei, HI: Koa Books.

Leonhardy, G. (2009). Transformations: Working with veterans in the composition classroom. *Teaching English in the Two-Year College, 36*(4), 339–352.

Lunsford, S. K., & Bargerhuff, M. E. (2006). A project to make the laboratory more accessible to students with disabilities. *Journal of Chemical Education, 83*(3), 407–409.

Maurin, K. H. (2012). *Negotiating cultural transitions: Contemporary student veterans and Louisiana institutions of higher education* (Doctoral dissertation). Retrieved from http://etd.lsu.edu/docs/available/etd-01032012-155853/unrestricted/kayharrisonmaurin_diss.pdf

McBride, S. (2004). *The tongue and quill.* U.S. Air Force Handbook 33-337. Washington DC: Headquarters, Department of the Air Force

McDonald, M. A. (2011). *Engagement of community college student veterans: A mixed-methods study* (Doctoral dissertation). Available from ProQuest Dissertations & Theses database. (UMI No. 3486302)

Michaelsen, L., Knight, A. B., & Fink, L. D. (2004). *Team-based learning: A transformative use of small groups in college teaching.* Sterling, VA: Stylus Publishing.

Moriarty, M. A. (2007). Inclusive pedagogy: Teaching methodologies to reach diverse learners in science instruction. *Equity & Excellence in Education, 40*(3), 252–265.

Mowbray, C. (1999). Supported education for individuals with psychiatric disabilities: Long term outcomes from an experimental study. *Social Work Research, 23*(2), 89–101.

Murphy, M. P. (2011). *Military veterans and college success: A qualitative examination of veteran needs in higher education* (Doctoral dissertation). Available from Pro-Quest Dissertations & Theses database. (UMI No. 3490565)

National Survey of Student Engagement. (2010). *Major differences: Examining student engagement by field of study—Annual results 2010.* Bloomington: Indiana University Center for Postsecondary Research.

Poon, T., & Ovadia, R. (2008). Using tactile learning aids for students with visual impairments in a first-semester organic chemistry course. *Journal of Chemical Education, 85*(2), 240–242.

Rose, D. H., Harbour, W. S., Johnston, C. S., Daley, S. G., & Abarbanell, L. (2008). Universal Design for learning in postsecondary education: Reflections on principles and their application. In S. Burgstahler & R. Cory (Eds.), *Universal Design in higher education: From principles to practice* (pp. 45–60). Cambridge, MA: Harvard Education Press.

Schunk, D. H. (1994). Self-regulation of self-efficacy and attributions in academic settings. In D. H. Schunk & B. J. Zimmerman (Eds.), *Self-regulation of learning and performance: Issues and educational applications* (pp. 75–99). Hillsdale, NJ: Lawrence Erlbaum Associates, Inc.

Supalo, C. A., Mallouk, T. E., Rankel, L., Amorosi, C., & Graybill, C. M. (2008). Low-cost laboratory adaptations for precollege students who are blind or visually impaired. *Journal of Chemical Education, 85*(2), 243–247.

U.S. Department of the Army. (1986). *Effective writing for Army leaders.* Pamphlet 600-67. Washington DC: Headquarters, Department of the Army.

U.S. Department of the Army. (2002). *Training the force.* Field Manual 7-0 (FM 25–100). Washington DC: Headquarters, Department of the Army.

U.S. Department of the Army. (2005). *The Army.* Field Manual 1. Washington DC: Headquarters, Department of the Army.

U.S. Department of the Army. (2006). *Army leadership: Competent, confident, and agile.* Field Manual 6-22. Washington DC: Headquarters, Department of the Army.

Weimer, M. (2002). *Learner-centered teaching.* San Francisco: Jossey-Bass.

Witzel, B. S., Riccomini, P. J., & Schneider, E. (2008). Implementing CRA with secondary students with learning disabilities in mathematics. *Intervention in School & Clinic, 43*(5), 270–276.

Zimmerman, C. E., Jr. (2007). There's a deaf student in your philosophy class—Now what? *Teaching Philosophy, 30*(4), 421–442.

10

PHYSICAL, EMOTIONAL, AND BEHAVIORAL ENVIRONMENTS

The Soldier's Creed
I am an American Soldier.
I am a Warrior and a member of a team.
I serve the people of the United States and live the Army values.
I will always place the mission first.
I will never accept defeat.
I will never quit.
I will never leave a fallen comrade.
I am disciplined, physically and mentally tough,
trained and proficient in my Warrior tasks and drills.
I will always maintain my arms, my equipment, and myself.
I am an expert and I am a professional.
I stand ready to deploy, engage, and destroy
the enemies of the United States of America in close combat.
I am a guardian of freedom and the American way of life.
I am an American soldier.

—*The Army* (U.S. Department of the Army, 2005, p. iv)

According to Parker Palmer (2007), "to teach is to create a space in which the community of truth is practiced" (p. 92). A space such as this respects the instructor, the student, and the subject matter. It establishes an environment of trust that "can express itself in endless varieties, depending on the identity and integrity of the teacher" (Palmer, 2007, p. 118). This space "becomes environment when it is stretched to include a broader sense of place, as well as the people who participate and the culture in which these elements are situated" (Warger, EduServe, & Dobbin, 2009, p. 6). The environment should be accessible to all students—physically, emotionally, and behaviorally. This book has described the intense personal

179

transformations that are cultivated by the military. Members of the armed forces are trained to overcome physical, emotional, and behavioral barriers to achieve their mission. Higher education must also consider these three aspects of environment in order to create a space in which student veterans can become fully engaged in the community of truth that Parker describes.

The Physical Environment

The physical environment of a class plays a crucial role in providing students access to an extraordinary education. This obviously applies to accessibility for students with disabilities, but it also includes special considerations for student veterans who may feel uncomfortable in some physical environments that are fully accessible.

All institutions of higher education must comply with the regulations provided through the Americans with Disabilities Act Amendments Act (ADAAA). The ADAAA applies only to new construction and renovation for state and local governments, however, and many campuses have buildings of older construction that have limited accessibility for students with disabilities. In such cases, educational institutions must "relocate programs or otherwise provide access in inaccessible older buildings. . . . They are required to make reasonable modifications to policies, practices, and procedures where necessary to avoid discrimination" (U.S. Department of Justice, 2005, p. 3). The law also stipulates that "courses and examinations related to professional, educational, or trade-related applications, licensing, certifications, or credentialing must be provided in a place and manner accessible to people with disabilities, or alternative accessible arrangements must be offered" (U.S. Department of Justice, 2005, p. 5). Finally, Section 504 of the original Americans with Disabilities Act (ADA) stipulates that "no qualified individual with a disability in the United States shall be excluded from, denied the benefits of, or be subjected to discrimination under any program or activity that . . . receives Federal financial assistance" (U.S. Department of Justice, 2005, pp. 17–18).

It is clear that higher education has a legal obligation to provide reasonable accommodations for students with disabilities. Renovating classrooms to incorporate Universal Design (UD) can help alleviate the need to make specific accommodations. The following list, while not exhaustive, provides some examples of what to consider in terms of physical accessibility:

- *Ensure physical access to all facilities.* Student veterans with wheelchairs or other assistive mobility devices should be able to enter and egress easily from all rooms. Student veterans who have a hearing impairment should be given an opportunity to hear all audio cues in the classroom, including the instructor and any audio aids. If a student has full hearing loss, he or she should have a clear line of sight to all visual outputs and have access to close-captioning or hard copies/transcripts of the material. Student veterans with visual impairments should be provided with alternative formats for anything they can't clearly see. Students should have full access to any manipulatives in the course, including technology and lab equipment.

- *Ensure that everyone can safely use equipment and materials.* All students should be able to clearly read posted safety messages, and all students should be able to perceive hazard warnings, including students with hearing or vision loss. This often means the use of multiple alerts (both a flashing red light and an alarm bell, for example). Classroom facilities should be arranged to eliminate the possibility of injury due to hazards that are not perceivable by student veterans.

- *Arrange instructional spaces to maximize inclusion and comfort.* All students should be able to use the same entrance and egress routes. Furniture should be easily rearranged for different types of learning activities. Students should be able to reach all keyboards and other input devices. Controls, displays and instruction panels should be clearly legible, and controls and other input mechanisms should be easily manipulated (e.g., for students who have lost their dominant hand and are learning to manipulate objects with their nondominant hand). (Burgstahler, 2011, pp. 2–3)

These examples represent just some of the physical adaptations that institutions of higher education should consider. Classrooms that contain these features enhance the educational environment for a wide range of students, including student veterans. Military students, however, may face additional challenges in the physical environment that are not as obvious.

Physical spaces that are completely accessible may still pose challenges for student veterans owing to their training and the circumstances of their deployment. Students who are returning from ground operations in the Middle East have been trained to be hypervigilant in monitoring their immediate surroundings. Unknown people and unsearched items represent potential danger. Ground forces have been trained to "secure" locations, meaning that everything in the area is searched and all exits are closed or watched. Public areas where crowds of people congregate can be especially dangerous. For this reason, certain learning spaces can be distracting at best and overwhelming at worst for student veterans. Consider the following examples:

Figure 10.1 Active Learning Classroom, University of South Dakota. (Photo courtesy of University of South Dakota, © 2010)

- *A large room with multiple entrances and exits.* Military personnel are trained to stand and sit where they can watch every single person enter or leave a room. A large room with multiple doors may make this impossible and heighten a student veteran's sense of unease (perhaps unconsciously).
- *Rooms that force students to place their backs to others.* Active learning classrooms are becoming more prevalent, but these rooms (like the one pictured in Figure 10.1) force students to sit with their backs to one another. This can be a disconcerting experience for a student veteran who has recently transitioned out of the military.
- *Courses with large numbers of students.* Veterans may find that classes with large numbers of students—most of whom are carrying unsearched (and to a military mind unsecured) backpacks—are stressful.
- *Rooms with large numbers of windows.* Windows are dangerous, for they allow observation of one's activities and provide no cover. Student veterans in a classroom with many windows may find themselves constantly monitoring the activity outside as a training reflex and may find it difficult to pay attention to the lecture or to activities inside the classroom.
- *Rooms near construction or external sources of loud sounds.* The rumble of heavy trucks, the sounds of construction work, or even the popping of balloons can disrupt the attention of a student veteran.

The general hubbub and commotion of a typical campus may be distracting for student veterans, especially those with neurological disorders.

Instructors can improve the physical environment for their student veterans by following these general guidelines:

- Allow student veterans to sit in a location (such as the back row of the room) where they can easily watch everyone and where their "back" is secure.
- Consider the arrangement of your office—when student veterans come in to see you, are they forced to sit with their back to the door?
- Provide course sections that are veteran-only or that have reserved spaces for student veterans. When student veterans know they are around their peers, they can relax and not worry about what has or has not been searched and secured.
- Provide sections of courses in rooms that have few windows and only one door.

Faculty may need to work with their Disabilities Services Office to find ways of best serving student veterans who are struggling with the physical environment of a class. In many cases the challenges and the solutions are uniquely personal.

The Emotional Environment

All instructors should establish an emotional environment in the classroom that is conducive to student learning. Instructors should provide an atmosphere that welcomes every student and avoids stereotyping. Faculty should be approachable and available to students of every ability and background. This is especially important for student veterans, who may be experiencing culture shock as they transition into higher education. This inclusiveness is one of the guiding principles of UD.

Faculty can begin to establish a welcoming environment simply by incorporating some of the syllabus changes outlined in chapter 8. Syllabi might also include information about student veteran organizations (SVOs), especially if these organizations might serve as a resource for class topics such as leadership, Middle Eastern culture or geography, diversity issues, or public service. Prior to the start of the course, instructors need to determine how (or if) they wish to gather information about their students' military history. If instructors do want to collect this information, it should be done in a nonintrusive way—perhaps by gathering data from each student on a note card or through an online survey. The information should be treated as confidential, and an instructor should not publicly identify a student as a veteran without his or her permission. Many student veterans are quietly proud of their service—they believe that they have participated in events that are life-changing and significant, but they generally do not appreciate being put on the spot as "the veteran."

Faculty should foster an environment that encourages student veterans to interact with both the instructor and the other students. Compared to their peers, student veterans are more likely to be the following:

- male
- older
- enrolled part-time
- first-generation students
- transfer students
- distance learners (National Survey of Student Engagement, 2010, p. 18)

Each of these traits is even more pronounced among combat veterans. The 2010 National Survey of Student Engagement (NSSE) found that first-year noncombat veterans reported that they were less engaged with faculty than their peers and that first-year combat veterans perceived less campus support. Senior combat and noncombat veterans alike reported significantly lower student-faculty interaction and less support from their campus environment than did nonveteran students (National Survey of Student Engagement, 2010, pp. 9, 18). The NSSE (2010) report suggests that "baccalaureate-granting institutions should seek ways to more effectively engage student veterans in effective educational practices and provide them with the supportive environments that promote success" (p. 18). In light of the NSSE results, faculty should make concentrated efforts to interact with their student veteran population, both in and outside the classroom.

Faculty should thoughtfully consider on how they handle in-class issues related to the global war on terrorism in general and the Middle East in particular. Veterans often choose a strategy of blending in with other students and may be hesitant to acknowledge their military service in class:

> If you feel like you want to announce to the world and make it a central point of who you are as a student, that, you know, I'm a veteran, I served, I'm different than you, then you can do that certainly. . . but I think for the most part, all the guys I know . . . [put a] normal back pack on the shoulder, go to class, go to the library, eat at Chick-fil-A, and . . . blend, blend in I guess for lack of another word. We don't really try to stick out on purpose. (Murphy, 2011, p. 93)

At other times military students may react strongly to nonmilitary students or teachers who voice opinions about but who have not actually been to the Middle East:

The individual in the class was talking about . . . "leave the Iraqis alone, let them deal with their own problems, why do we have to keep invading their privacy. . . let them be free." This was absolutely idiotic considering the situation because that's not how it was working at that point in time. . . . So these people didn't understand how much of a presence Al-Qaeda and Iraqi nationalists and stuff like that there still was. This was one of the instances where I really got angry in class. (Wheeler, 2011, p. 119)

It is difficult to balance the two extremes. Faculty should be prepared to stimulate discussion on topics in this area with a variety of active learning techniques and at the same time have an exit strategy planned should discussion become uncivil.

Faculty should find ways of discussing current events and Middle Eastern policies in a way that is respectful to all students, including student veterans. This can be accomplished by keeping the following principles in mind:

- Don't downplay the need for national defense. Resource allocation is a legitimate topic for discussion, but don't be dismissive or "clever" in your discussions about the role of—or need for—the military.
- Don't underestimate the cost of even "easy" military victories. The United States fields the most powerful military in the world, but operations that have few casualties or that are quickly over can still have a significant personal cost and impact.
- Don't depict foreign policy choices as easy, and don't portray civilian leaders as liars or stupid. Political rhetoric can become heated and decidedly uncivil. While passionate debate belongs within—and enlivens immeasurably—the educational experience of our students, incivility should not be a part of the educational environment.
- Don't presume that all student veterans are Republicans/conservatives. Student veterans have opinions about foreign policy, our leaders, and the conflicts in which we are engaged that range from the far right to far left. What they share is a commitment to service and a can-do attitude toward mission accomplishment—important qualities from any political point of view.
- Don't treat your student veterans like charity cases. The military trains its personnel to be self-reliant and goal-oriented. Offers of help that come across as patronizing will quickly alienate your student veterans.
- Don't ask your student veterans to speak for all veterans, and don't pressure them to speak about issues or events that may single them out or make them feel unnecessarily uncomfortable.
- Don't assume that a student joined the military because he or she is militaristic. Members of the armed forces join for a variety of reasons, not the least of which is a core value of service to one's country.

- Don't assume that a student has seen combat, and don't make assumptions about how easy or difficult a deployment may have been.
- Understand some basics about the military and its structure. While this entire book is aimed at enlightening faculty with limited military knowledge or experience, Appendix C in particular provides a quick introduction to the military, its structure, and its organization. (adapted from Truman National Security Project, n.d.)

Finally, faculty members need to understand that certain questions should never be asked of a student veteran. No veteran should ever be asked intrusively personal questions, including, "Did you kill anyone?" or "Did you see anyone die?" If students ask such questions in class, the instructor should step in to immediately redirect the question, as one would with any patently offensive statement made in the classroom environment. One of the goals of education is to provide cognitive dissonance and discomfort, but not at the expense of the students themselves. Civility in the classroom goes a long way toward improving the educational environment for all students.

Student veterans have experienced the world in ways that most students have not. Faculty who understand and respect this fact can establish an environment in which student veterans are given the emotional space they need to succeed. This will allow student veterans, as well as the other students in the course, to be fully engaged in the learning experience.

Behavioral Environment

The behavioral environment—that is, the way that students and faculty interact in the classroom—can have a significant impact on the academic success of student veterans. Military students may expect instructors and students to behave in a certain manner and may be distracted when they do not. Instructors who are aware of these expectations can establish course policies that minimize distracting behavior. Instructors should also be aware of student behaviors that may indicate a need for referral to Disabilities Services or the Student Health and Counseling Center.

Military classrooms and briefings are in some ways similar to postsecondary classrooms. A person in charge walks in and delivers information, while the people who are not in charge take mental or written notes. Generally speaking, however, military presentations and classrooms are more formal than the typical postsecondary classroom. Military personnel may be asked to hold all questions until the information is presented, and questioners may be required to stand before speaking. Student veterans may initially hesitate to interrupt a college lecturer with a question because of these past experiences. Faculty members should take time during the first day of class to clearly explain their expectations in terms of interruptions and questions. This type of clarification can establish baselines for student behavior and can encourage students to contribute to the class discussion.

The behavior of other (nonveteran) students can be extremely off-putting for student veterans. Military instructors are listened to with respect and attention. In a briefing all cell phones are turned off, and food and beverages are prohibited. Depending on the formality of the briefing, personnel may be expected to sit up straight with feet together flat on the floor. Students who are whispering to one another, sending texts, surfing the web, or falling asleep can be distracting to student veterans, who may wonder why the teacher tolerates such behavior. This difference in expected behavior is magnified by the fact that most student veterans are older than the typical student, and it is not uncommon to hear student veterans complain vociferously about students who do not seem to take their education seriously:

> It makes me hate almost everybody in my classes. All these spoon-fed little punks are concerned with hitting on each other and what car their daddy is gonna buy them. They talk during class, their opinions are only as deep as what they can remember from the Fox news segment they watched, and they all act smart by puking up the words of their professors without an ounce of personal thought on the matter. (Doenges, 2011, p. 56)

Another veteran noted,

> I get irritated at people a lot because they do ridiculous things in class, like people will be talking on their phones, or their phone will ring in class, or they will show up late. I get so sick of people being late. You know, in the military, when you are in training and stuff, for example when the instructor speaks to you, you stand up before you speak back to them. And everyone is in their seat 15 minutes before the class starts. There is a whole lot of really rigid structure that you, you know it's not really necessary in the civilian setting, but it gets you thinking about like, you know, don't show up 20 minutes late every day for class in your pajamas. It just gets old. (Murphy, 2011, p. 91)

Instructors may want to try to lessen the "undirected" behavior of nonveteran students through a combination of stricter classroom policies and the implementation of learning activities that keep the students more heavily engaged.

One final guideline should be mentioned: Faculty should be careful about using red laser pointers. They are used in the military to indicate a weapon's aiming point, and their use in the classroom can be highly distracting for some student veterans.

Student veterans often view faculty as part of a chain of command. The chain of command in the military provides structure and order, and there is rarely doubt in a service member's mind about who should be seen about what issue. The same is emphatically not true in higher education. Large classes in which the instructor lectures and graduate teaching assistants (GTAs) lead recitation sections can be especially confusing. Who does a student veteran see about a homework question? Who do they tell about absences? Where should they go if they wish to question a test grade? Instructors should develop a repository of commonly asked questions regarding course processes and procedures, including some sort of guide to the academic chain of command. This repository can be kept online and shared with students at the beginning of each course.

Faculty should have a basic knowledge of behaviors that may indicate that a student should seek professional counseling. A faculty member should never take on the role of a professional counselor or attempt to diagnose stress-related behaviors, but awareness of this issue may allow an instructor to connect a struggling student with the appropriate campus or Veteras Affairs (VA) resource. Evidence of the following behaviors, especially if multiple reactions occur over time, may indicate that there is a problem for which a student should seek professional help:

- trembling
- jumpiness
- dizziness
- fatigue
- "thousand-yard" stare
- difficulty thinking, speaking, and communicating
- difficulty staying seated
- crying
- memory loss
- rapid emotional shifts
- social withdrawal
- apathy (U.S. Marine Corps, 2000, pp. 4–5)

Stress makes it difficult for students to make decisions, sort out priorities, and start routine tasks (U.S. Marine Corps, 2000, p. 6). The preceding behaviors can also signal that a student is a potential suicide risk. Students who are contemplating suicide often

- believe that they are in a hopeless situation
- appear depressed, sad, tearful
- have changes in patterns of sleep or appetite
- talk about or threaten suicide, or talk about death and dying in a way that strikes the listener as odd
- show changes in behavior, appearance, or mood
- increase or start drug or alcohol use
- injure themselves or engage in risky behavior
- abandon planning for the future
- withdraw from others, including family and close friends
- give away possessions
- appear apathetic, unmotivated, and indifferent (U.S. Marine Corps, 2000, p. 76)

A troubling number of veterans commit suicide each day. If any student exhibits these behaviors, then refer them to the appropriate campus or VA resources. To reiterate, faculty should not attempt to diagnose or resolve behavioral issues—leave this to the experts.

Online Environments

Online education has become increasingly popular. Higher fuel costs, student demand for flexible learning environments, greater choice, and a growing acceptance of this delivery method has increased the market for online education. Adult learners (and, thus, most student veterans) enjoy the flexibility that online learning offers as they attempt to juggle work and family (Capra, 2011, p. 289). Distance education also helps mitigate the challenges of physical or psychological conditions that student veterans sometimes face (American Council on Education, 2010b, p. 14). Online courses broaden the definition of what a *learning space* may be:

> The learning space remains the heart of the educational enterprise, but the time has come for educators to widen the scope of inquiry about effectiveness in learning to include a fuller list of factors. The term learning environment encompasses learning resources and technology, means of teaching, modes of learning, and connections to societal and global contexts. The term also includes human behavioral and cultural dimensions, including the vital role of emotion in learning, and it requires us to examine and sometimes rethink the roles of teachers and students because the ways in which they make use of space and bring wider societal influences into play animates the educational enterprise. (Warger, EduServe, & Dobbin, 2009, p. 3)

Technology does not remove the need to consider the physical, emotional, and behavioral elements of the online class. Online instructors must account for these factors as they design their courses. Technology does, however, create learning spaces that circumvent geography and time.

Online instructor should consider the possibility that some students may be overseas active-duty military personnel. These students may experience disruptions that are completely different from those of nonmilitary students:

> The active duty student must be military ready at all times. Frequent deployments and duty assignments that take the student away from educational resources, including internet access, often result in interruptions of the student's academic progress. Access to supplemental instructional materials, the inability to respond in a timely manner, and difficulties with group work due to access issues all create instructional challenges. (Brown & Gross, 2011, p. 46)

Online faculty should review their courses to check for flexibility in participation policies and course deadlines (American Council on Education, 2010a, p. 7). Student disruptions will often be unique, however, and many will require individual solutions.

Online teaching is an art. An ability to teach well in a face-to-face class does not necessarily translate into the ability to teach proficiently online. In general, quality online education exhibits the following characteristics:

- encourages student-faculty contact
- encourages cooperation among students
- encourages active learning
- provides prompt feedback
- emphasizes time on-task
- communicates high expectations
- respects diversity (Ritter & Lemke, 2000)

Each of these characteristics enhances the educational experience for student veterans. Prompt feedback, time on-task activities, and high expectations are foundational to the types of educational experiences they had in the military. As noted earlier, student veterans report less engagement with faculty and students than do nonveteran students. This can be a problem for all online students, who rate faculty responsiveness as very important to their level of satisfaction (Herbert, 2006). Faculty can implement a more responsive instructional posture by communicating daily, responding to inquiries expeditiously, and providing frequent feedback (Capra, 2011, pp. 290–291). These strategies positively affect students' attitudes toward the course and can influence their decision to persist or withdraw from an online class (Tello, 2007, p. 59).

Online courses typically reward self-directed behavior and disciplined work habits and therefore play into the strengths of many student veterans. This delivery method is an attractive educational option for many military students, especially those who may be hesitant or unable to enroll in a more traditional educational environment. In addition, online education reaches worldwide, allowing military students in remote locations to connect to higher education's learning spaces.

Conclusion

Higher education must create spaces for learning where student veterans are welcomed. Instructors need to be aware of the special environmental challenges that may affect student veterans, physically, emotionally, and behaviorally. Purposeful attempts to improve the learning environment for our student veterans inevitably leads to an improved learning environment for all students.

Chapter Summary

The classroom environment establishes a climate for learning. This climate can positively or negatively impact learning and can be broken down into three broad areas: physical, emotional, and behavioral. There are best practices regarding student veterans for each of these areas. Courses that establish welcoming physical, emotional, and behavioral environments will enhance student veterans' success. Online learning environments present their own unique challenges but can be a positive alternative for some student veterans.

Key Points

Physical environment:

- The learning experience should be physically accessible to student veterans. Colleges and universities must (under the provisions of the ADAAA) provide accommodations to individuals with disabilities.
- Student veterans may experience discomfort in some classroom environments that are ADAAA-compliant. Rooms with many windows, multiple doors, and large numbers of students may be distracting to student veterans.

- Allow student veterans to sit next to walls or in locations that will allow them to survey the classroom if that makes them feel more comfortable.
- Provide course sections that are made up solely of student veterans or that are held in smaller rooms with fewer distractions.
- In many cases student veterans' physical challenges and their solutions are unique. Faculty should always work in close cooperation with the Disabilities Services Office to address these challenges.

Emotional environment:

- Faculty should provide an atmosphere that welcomes every student and avoids stereotyping.
- Faculty should foster an atmosphere that encourages direct communication with their students and should seek ways to interact with their student veteran population, both in and outside the classroom.
- Faculty should thoughtfully consider how they handle in-class issues and discussion related to the global war on terrorism in general and the Middle East in particular. Military strategies and political policies should be distinguished from those individuals who have to carry out those strategies and policies.
- Faculty should understand which questions are unacceptable to pose to student veterans and step in if and when other students ask those questions.

Behavioral environment:

- Student veterans often find common student classroom (mis)behaviors—reading newspapers, checking social media, whispering, eating, or drinking—disrespectful and distracting. Student veterans may also be distracted by an instructor's tolerance of such behavior.
- Faculty should be aware of behaviors that may indicate that a student is under extreme stress or contemplating suicide. Faculty should not step into the role of professional counselor but should be ready to refer students to professional campus resources.

Online learning spaces:

- Faculty should incorporate flexible attendance and deadline policies to accommodate students who are taking online courses while on active duty.

- Online courses typically reward self-directed behavior and disciplined work habits and therefore play into the strengths of many student veterans.
- Faculty responsiveness is important to student satisfaction in online courses and can positively or negatively influence decisions to persist in or withdraw from such courses.

References

American Council on Education. (2010a). *Accommodating student veterans with traumatic brain injury and post-traumatic stress disorder: Tips for campus faculty and staff.* Washington DC: Author. Retrieved from http://www.acenet.edu/news-room/Pages/Accommodating-Student-Veterans-with-Traumatic-Brain-Injury-and-Post-Traumatic-Stress-Disorder.aspx

American Council on Education. (2010b). *Veteran Success Jam: Ensuring success for returning veterans.* Washington DC: Author. Retrieved from http://www.acenet.edu/news-room/Pages/Veterans-Jam-2010.aspx

Brown, P., & Gross, C. (2011). Serving those who have served—Managing veteran and military student best practices. *Journal of Continuing Higher Education, 59,* 45–49.

Burgstahler, S. (2011). An approach to ensure that educational programs serve all students [brochure]. *Universal Design in education: Principles and applications.* Retrieved from http://www.washington.edu/doit/Brochures/Academics/ud_edu.html

Capra, T. (2011). Online education: Promise and problems. *MERLOT Journal of Online Learning and Teaching, 7*(2), 288–293.

Doenges, T. (2011). *Calling and meaningful work among student military veterans: Impact on well-being and experiences on campus* (Doctoral dissertation). Available from ProQuest Dissertations and Theses database. (UMI No. 3468765)

Herbert, M. (2006). Staying the course: A study in online student satisfaction and retention. *Online Journal of Distance Learning Administration, 9*(4). Retrieved from http://www.westga.edu/~distance/ojdla/winter94/herbert94.htm

Murphy, M. P. (2011). *Military veterans and college success: A qualitative examination of veteran needs in higher education* (Doctoral dissertation). Available from ProQuest Dissertations & Theses database. (UMI No. 3490565)

National Survey of Student Engagement. (2010). *Major differences: Examining student engagement by field of study—Annual results 2010.* Bloomington: Indiana University Center for Postsecondary Research.

Palmer, P. (2007). *The courage to teach.* San Francisco: Jossey-Bass.

Ritter, M. E., & Lemke, K. A. (2000). Addressing the seven principles for good practice in undergraduate education with Internet-enhanced education. *Journal of Geography in Higher Education, 24*(1), 100–108.

Tello, S. F. (2007). An analysis of student persistence in online education. *International Journal of Information and Communication Technology Education, 3*(3), 47–69.

Truman National Security Project. (n.d.) *Message gone AWOL: The top ten mistakes civilians make when talking to the military.* Retrieved from http://www.trumaninstitute.org/training/materials

U.S. Department of Justice. (2005). *A guide to disabilities rights laws.* Washington DC: U.S. Department of Justice Civil Rights Division, Disabilities Rights Section. Retrieved from www.ada.gov/cguide.htm

U.S. Department of the Army. (2005). *The Army.* Field Manual 1. Washington DC: Headquarters, Department of the Army.

U.S. Marine Corps. (2000). *Combat stress.* MCRP 6-11C. Washington DC: U.S. Department of the Navy.

Warger, T., EduServe, & Dobbin, G. (2009). Learning environments: Where space, technology, and culture converge. ELI White Papers. Retrieved from http://www.educause.edu/Resources/LearningEnvironmentsWhereSpace/188507

Wheeler, H. A. (2011). *From soldier to student: A case study of veterans' transitions to first-time community college students* (Doctoral dissertation). Available from ProQuest Dissertations & Theses database. (UMI No. 3465899)

11

DEVELOPING FACULTY
AND STAFF

The biggest thing was probably the fact that people didn't understand what we had been through, and didn't understand how to approach us. . . . It takes work on both sides to get everything figured out.

—Bob, Army reservist (Rumann & Hamrick, 2010, p. 446)

T his book has identified numerous pedagogical and programmatic strategies to enhance the academic success of student veterans. These strategies work best, however, when faculty and staff are trained to understand student veterans' strengths and needs. In their comprehensive survey of 690 institutions, McBain, Kim, Cook, and Snead (2012) state that

> the top two actions responding institutions are considering are increasing the number of programs and services for veterans and service members . . . and providing professional development for staff on dealing with the issues facing many service members and veterans. . . . It is encouraging to see that both expanding programs and services and educating faculty and staff on the needs of military personnel and veterans continue to be top priorities. (p. 15)

Faculty and staff development is an integral part of any strategy to better serve student veterans. This chapter describes how to create an effective development team and provides a framework for how to organize faculty and staff training programs.

Creating a Development Team

Faculty and staff training should be led by a team of individuals who are committed to student veteran success and who understand the strengths of and challenges faced by these students. The personnel that make up this team will vary, but the following are often involved:

- Student veteran leadership. Student veterans often form networks (both formal and informal) within their institutions. It is vital to include individuals from this community who have taken on leadership roles. This might include officers from a student veteran club, local members of Student Veterans of America (SVA), or military students who may be in other leadership roles (such as student body president).
- The school certifying official (SCO). This person, usually located in either the Registrar's or Financial Aid Office, is one of the most important officials who serve student veterans. The SCO is an expert on Veterans Affairs (VA) educational benefits and can help the development team understand the intricacies of the bureaucratic requirements for both students and the institution. Because this individual works so closely with student veterans, he or she is an essential component of the development team.
- Staff from the Faculty Development Center or Center for Teaching and Learning. Some campuses have an individual who is in charge of faculty development, and some institutions have full-blown centers employing many staff that help faculty improve teaching and student learning. This group of people is experienced in reaching out to faculty through development programs and can significantly enhance the quality of any training initiative.
- Disabilities services professional. Faculty members often have a general sense of how to work with students who have disabilities. Student veterans may be discovering newly acquired disabilities while in the classroom and present a unique challenge to instructional staff. A strong disabilities services coordinator can be a tremendous asset to the development team.
- Human resources (HR) training specialists. Some HR Departments have a training specialist or team that provides development opportunities for the staff. This person or team can provide programming expertise in a manner similar to that of the staff from the Faculty Development Center. This position can be a key component in shaping the educational experiences that student veterans have outside the classroom.
- Faculty and staff who are veterans. Almost every campus has veterans who are serving as faculty and staff. These personnel can speak with authority about the transition experience and can establish a closer bond of trust with the current student veterans. These individuals

provide an important link between the students and the institution and can serve as role models for the student veterans themselves.

These personnel represent just a few of the potential members of a development team. Representatives from Admissions, Financial Aid, and the Counseling Center would also be logical choices. Regardless of its makeup, the development team should have the resources to offer meaningful programming and should be fully supported by upper administration.

Establishing a Developmental Program

Successful development programs for faculty and staff can take a variety of forms but should minimally accomplish four goals:

- Teach participants about the academic strengths of student veterans and how these strengths might be used to enhance the academic experiences of the entire campus community.
- Help participants become aware of the challenges that student veterans face both in and out of the classroom.
- Connect the participants personally with student veterans on their campus.
- Provide specific strategies and techniques that will enhance student veterans' educational experiences.

Successful development programs combine resources such as this text, web seminars, and online tools with institution-specific training that makes use of the expertise available at each college and university. Workshops can vary in length but a minimum of two hours is needed to accomplish the goals listed previously. Full-day workshops (or a series of workshops) provide time for deeper learning and are more effective at promoting change. Regardless of the format, each discrete training session should allow participants to gain information, work with that information through an activity or two, and reflect on what they have learned. Faculty Development Centers and HR training specialists can help tremendously in constructing workshops that use best practices in faculty and staff training.

Teaching Participants About the Academic Strengths of Student Veterans

Student veterans enter into higher education with a number of strengths, and military training brings certain advantages to students' academic pursuits. If we do not recognize these strengths, we risk slipping into a "deficit" model of training that focuses solely on the challenges veterans face as they transition into higher education. This type of training not only provides an inaccurate representation of student veterans' academic abilities but also risks alienating the students themselves. Faculty and staff developers should work closely with the student veterans at their institution to keep a balanced perspective.

Helping Participants Become Aware of Student Veterans' Challenges

Faculty and staff (who are not veterans themselves) often have a poor understanding of the challenges that student veterans face and are unsure of how to develop programs and procedures that can enhance student veteran success. A training program should identify those challenges and help faculty and staff develop the tools and understanding they need to best assist student veterans. Exercises like those presented in chapter 3 are excellent tools to help faculty and staff begin to understand—at a uniquely personal level—how students with disabilities process information in ways that are different from other students. Checklists such as the one in Figure 11.1 can guide discussion, serve as an assessment tool, and promote reflection for faculty and staff during a training event.

Faculty and staff need to understand the challenges of transition, the difficulties in identifying and overcoming recently diagnosed learning disabilities, and the many strategies that can enable student veterans to navigate through these barriers to achieve academic success.

Connecting With Student Veterans

Strong development programs provide faculty and staff with the opportunity to interact with student veterans. This can happen in a number of ways:

- Start the workshop with a student veteran–led flag presentation.
- Have student veterans serve as hosts for the workshop.
- Have student veterans participate in small group activities with faculty and staff.
- Incorporate student panels into the training program.

Student panels are uniquely helpful in providing a human dimension to the issues student veterans face. Faculty and staff who have attended workshops directed by the authors consistently rate student panels as one of the most interesting and informative parts of the training, and this type of event is strongly suggested if practical. If student panels are used, then care must be taken in the selection and moderation of the event. Student panelists should represent as many different services as possible, and gender diversity is

Figure 11.1 Veteran-Friendly Checklist.

Developing the Academic Promise of Student Veterans: Are you a veteran-friendly instructor?

- ❏ I use multiple delivery methods in the classroom and alternative media for reviewing classroom assignments.
- ❏ I provide the syllabus and PowerPoint presentations in advance.
- ❏ I provide opportunities for students to submit assignments for feedback prior to the final grade.
- ❏ I schedule time to interact with the student veteran population, both in and outside the classroom.
- ❏ I quietly ascertain if there are student veterans in my class by asking all students to provide certain information on note cards or through an online survey.
- ❏ I give useful, immediate feedback on all assignments.
- ❏ I develop a course packet to avoid expensive textbooks.
- ❏ I include contact information about counseling and disabilities services in my syllabus.
- ❏ I include an ADA statement in my syllabus.
- ❏ I have clearly defined all assignments in my syllabus.
- ❏ I foster an atmosphere that encourages direct communication with all students.
- ❏ I separate political policies from the individuals who have had to carry out those policies.
- ❏ I modified the attendance policy in my syllabus to provide flexibility for VA appointments and military-related course absences.
- ❏ I include visible signs of support for our troops in my office (an American flag, for example).
- ❏ I seek to minimize classroom behaviors (both my own and my students') that may be distracting for student veterans.
- ❏ I state clear learning objectives for the course.
- ❏ I include practical and hands-on types of learning activities.
- ❏ I scaffold longer assignments, breaking them up into smaller tasks with specific deadlines.
- ❏ I clearly define team projects and provide unambiguous goals.

Total the number of checked boxes: _____
1–9   Somewhat Veteran-Friendly
10–16 Veteran-Friendly
17–19 Veteran Ally

especially important. The moderator should be someone the students know and trust in order to facilitate an honest exchange. Moderators should be fully versed in what questions are and are not appropriate to ask of student veterans (see chapter 10), and it may be helpful if he or she is also a veteran. One word of caution when using student veteran panels: the presence of a military authority figure can subconsciously (or consciously) change the dialogue, especially if the students are not fully retired. Military students may be hesitant to give anything but formal military responses when answering questions in the presence of a commanding officer. This is a tricky area to negotiate because senior officers can also be a wonderful resource for faculty and staff training. In the end, however, student veterans are quite capable of telling their own stories of struggle and triumph, and their voices should be heard.

The development team should be aware that some elements of their training program (such as how to help student veterans with newly acquired disabilities) may not be embraced by the military community. Discussion of the negative consequences of military life, for example, runs counter to the goals of on-campus military recruiting programs such as ROTC. Development teams should work closely with formal military programs that may be on campus so that they understand the purpose and intent of your training.

The development team should also be aware of the political and cultural tensions within the military itself. College personnel often view "the military" as a monolithic entity, but there are rivalries and tensions within and between the services that can derail productive training. Members of the Regular Army may think that Navy personnel get off easy or believe that National Guard units aren't part of the "real army":

> If you want a cushy job, there's no water in Iraq so you just join the Navy. We had Navy guys there, but they were few and far between. The Air Force did like three month rotations and that was it. They weren't really in the combat zone, they were just far enough away to fly in if needed. They could drink and wear civilian clothes. Yeah, there was a little bit of tension between the services because they would complain about their ninety day deployments and here we were there for fifteen months. (Darren, Army veteran, quoted in Maurin, 2012, pp. 59–60)

Within the National Guard, there can be strain between the full-time staff and the on-call soldiers. Personnel who have been in combat may separate themselves from those who have not, rank and file may hold a grudge against all officers, and graduates of the academies may look down on officers promoted out of the ranks. Most of the time these rivalries are expressed in good-natured ways that will not hinder the training process. Development teams shouldn't necessarily look for trouble in this area, but they should be aware of and prepared for these tensions just in case they spring up.

Providing Specific Strategies and Techniques

The primary goal of faculty and staff training is to initiate change that will enhance the educational experiences of our student veterans. Development teams should present strategies and techniques that can facilitate this change. While the needs of each institution will dictate the specific strategies that are pursued, this book will hopefully provide many options for faculty and staff trainers. If faculty and staff leave a training workshop with specific plans to implement strategies and techniques that will enhance student veterans' success, then the goals of the workshop have been achieved.

Faculty and Staff Development: Two Models

Successful development programs set specific learning goals, contain measures of feedback and assessment, and include activities that create the opportunity for significant learning to occur (Fink, 2003). Two program models are provided in the following: a one-day training session and a two-hour workshop. An infinite variety of changes could be made to either to customize them for specific institutional resources and needs.

Just as faculty need to develop learning goals for each course they teach, faculty and staff developers should set learning goals for each workshop they conduct. It would be impossible to cover the breadth of issues related to veterans' education through even a series of full-day workshops, so development teams need to decide what needs are greatest on their campus. Questions such as those in the following Reader Reflection can help identify learning goals for the workshops.

Reader Reflection: Setting Learning Goals for Faculty Development Events

Think about one workshop you will soon be developing. Consider the overall goals you have for this workshop:

1. What do you want the participants to learn, beyond the content?
2. What distinguishes a person who has taken your workshop from one who has not?
3. What do you want participants to remember one year after they have taken the workshop? (adapted from Fink, 2005, p. 8)

Once learning goals have been established, learning activities can be developed that will give participants an opportunity to receive information, engage the information through active learning exercises, and reflect on their experience (Fink, 2003, p. 108).

The one-day program provides ample time for a variety of active learning and reflective exercises (see Figure 11.2). It provides an immersive experience that can be used as a starting point for a series of events on serving student veterans.

The culminating activity in the full-day workshop has faculty and staff working first individually and then in teams to identify specific changes that they can make in their courses or offices to enhance the experience of student veterans. The final event is a presentation by each group of their best ideas—an activity that generates much discussion and collaboration.

A two-hour workshop will have a narrower focus and should still include active audience participation and time for reflection. A sample schedule is provided in Figure 11.3.

Shorter workshops are generally not as effective as the more immersive experiences, but a series of such events can emphasize that service to student veterans is an ongoing, and not a onetime, concern for the university.

Figure 11.2 One-Day Workshop Schedule.

9:00–9:10	Introduction and pre-workshop assessment (see Figure 11.4).
9:10–9:30	Overview of national statistics regarding student veterans.
9:30–10:15	Veterans' transition stories (a student veteran and a faculty member who is a veteran each talk about returning to higher education after being deployed).
10:15–10:30	Break.
10:30–11:30	"In their shoes": Experiencing common disabilities (exercises from chapter 3).
11:30–12:00	The military's educational experience (see chapter 8).
12:00–12:45	Lunch.
12:45–1:45	Student veteran panel.
1:45–2:15	Establishing environments that enhance learning (see chapter 10).
2:15–2:30	Break.
2:30–4:15	Culminating learning activity.
4:15–4:30	Conclusion and post-workshop assessment and wrap-up.

Figure 11.3 Two-Hour Workshop Schedule.

9:00–9:10	Introduction and pre-workshop assessment (see Figure 11.4).
9:10–9:30	Brief overview of the topic of focus.
9:30–9:45	Veteran's point of view (a student veteran presents his or her experiences with the topic of focus).
9:45–10:00	Further description and information about the topic of focus.
10:00–10:30	Significant learning activity.
10:30–10:40	Reflection activity.
10:40–10:50	Group discussion.
10:50–11:00	Post-workshop assessment and wrap-up.

Assessment

Outcomes-based assessment is a crucial element of a strong faculty and staff development program. The effectiveness of a program must be measured by its impact. There can be a tendency to rely on assessments that measure outputs—tracking how many faculty attend a certain event, for example—and although this provides an important metric of how well the program is reaching out to its constituents, it provides little information about whether or not the program catalyzed change in its participants. Unfortunately, there is no quick and easy way to directly evaluate this change, and developers often feel overwhelmed trying to establish authentic measures of outcomes-based assessment. The following guidelines provide direction, but more research in this area is needed.

First, it is better to assess small than not at all—something is better than nothing. Momentum should not be slowed because the perfect assessment piece could not be found (it doesn't exist, anyway!). A simple pre- and post-workshop assessment, for example, can help determine changes in knowledge about veterans' issues or plans to implement future change (see Figure 11.4).

The fourth question in Figure 11.4 asks participants to be specific in identifying areas they plan to change. Participants who are able to name the changes they plan to make are more likely to actually do so. Follow-up surveys administered either by phone or through an online survey creator could determine whether or not the identified changes were implemented. Other assessment tools might include student veteran satisfaction surveys, an analysis of student veteran success in specific courses, or analysis of student veterans' use of specific resources, like financial aid counseling. None of these measures directly link success to faculty and staff training, but multiple measures can be used to determine the approximate effectiveness of training programs.

Figure 11.4 Pre-/Post-Workshop Assessment.

Circle the score that best represents your answer:

1. How familiar are you with the challenges that student veterans face?

1	2	3	4	5
Not familiar				Very familiar

2. How familiar are you with the resources available to help student veterans, both on this campus and off?

1	2	3	4	5
Not familiar				Very familiar

3. How willing are you to change your instructional techniques to enhance learning opportunities for student veterans?

1	2	3	4	5
Not willing				Very willing

4. If you marked scores 3, 4, or 5 for question 3, what specifically do you plan to change?

Second, find ways to collect data that conform to what Weimer (2006) refers to as "wisdom-of-practice" scholarship. These include personal accounts of change and experience-based pedagogical scholarship. This type of scholarship is often intuitive, but "with systematic review and reflective analysis can be made explicit and beneficially shared with others" (Weimer, 2006, p. 40). Examples of this type of scholarship include the following:

- American Council on Education (2010)
- Brown and Gross (2011)
- Ryan, Carlstrom, Hughey, and Harris (2011)

Wisdom-of-practice scholarship is valuable, but to truly advance our understanding of best practices related to student veterans, assessment must go further.

Colleges and universities need to institute formal research projects (both qualitative and quantitative) that examine the effectiveness of service to student veterans. This is a difficult undertaking and will likely require collaboration between members of the faculty, institutional researchers, and others within the university community. The result of such collaboration, however, will be data that can improve the educational opportunities for student veterans nationwide. Examples of this type of scholarship include the following:

- Dalton (2010)
- Loughran, Martorell, Miller, and Klerman (2011)
- Shea (2010)
- Wheeler (2011)

Development teams that formally assess service to student veterans will assume a central role in determining what truly works for these students. It is that research that will help higher education more fully understand the needs and strengths of military students.

Developing the Developer

The programs described here will not be effective unless the development team is itself given the opportunity to learn and grow. Sustained support is essential. Faculty and staff leaders should be given resources to go to relevant conferences, such as those listed in Table 11.1.

Professional associations within higher education, such as the Professional and Organizational Developers (POD) Network, the Student Affairs Administrators in Higher Education (NASPA), and the National Academic Advising Association (NACADA), often feature individual sessions at their national conferences at which best practices in serving student veterans are examined, and online training materials are also readily available. Institutions that are able to effectively train key individuals will find their investment well repaid.

Conclusion

Change is the primary goal of faculty and staff development, and it will take a coordinated effort between the development team, the administration, the faculty, and support services to ensure that meaningful change occurs. The developmental team should meet regularly and provide a steady stream of events and activities that raise awareness of best practices in serving student veterans. Development events and workshops should be provided as a component of an overall strategy of faculty and staff preparedness—they should never constitute the entire developmental program by themselves. A combination of on-campus (or internally provided distance) workshops, professional web seminars, speakers, student veteran events, and collaborative

TABLE 11.1	
Conferences Where Support of Military Students Is Emphasized	
Conference	*Description*
Military Veteran Symposium for Higher Education	This symposium focuses on issues relating to academic advising, admissions, counseling and student health, disability resources, financial aid, residence life, registration, and student affairs. The symposium is normally hosted in Louisville, KY. See http://stuaff.org/veterans/
Student Veterans of America National Conference	This is the official conference of the SVA, whose goal is to "provide military veterans with resources, support, and advocacy needed to succeed in higher education and post-graduation." The national conference supports that goal through seminars, workshops, and networking sessions. See www.student veterans.org
Certificate for Veteran Service Providers Training Program	This program is a component of Operation College Promise, which "supports the transition and postsecondary advancement of our nation's veterans." The program enhances dialogue between a variety of veterans' service providers and national experts to develop strategies to support student veterans' transition into higher education. See www.operationpromiseforservice members.com/ CVSP_Program.html

links with off-campus veterans' resources (such as the VA) can work to build momentum toward significant institutional change.

Chapter Summary

A highly successful development program involves collaboration between faculty, students, and administrative offices. A development team should be formed to provide leadership in faculty and staff training. Programs should set specific learning goals, contain measures of feedback and assessment, and include activities that create the opportunity for significant learning to occur.

Developmental activities are an essential element of fostering change and are an important component of an institution's strategy to enhance student veteran success. Sustained support for a variety of programs and events is necessary to ensure meaningful and lasting change.

Key Points

- Faculty and staff members who are familiar with student veterans' strengths and challenges are essential to establishing a veteran-friendly campus.
- A development team should be established at each institution to lead initiatives for change. Student veterans and faculty who are veterans can enhance the development team and can play a key role in developmental events.
- The development team should receive sustained support from upper administration.
- Successful development program for faculty and staff can take a variety of forms but should minimally accomplish four goals:
  - Teach participants about the academic strengths of student veterans and how these strengths might be used to enhance the academic experiences of the entire campus community.
  - Help participants become aware of the challenges that student veterans face, both in and out of the classroom.
  - Connect participants personally with student veterans on campus.
  - Provide specific strategies and techniques that will enhance student veterans' educational experiences.
- Successful workshops and training sessions set specific learning goals, contain measures of feedback and assessment, and include activities that create the opportunity for significant learning to occur.
- Elements of faculty and staff training are sometimes seen as counter-productive to some on-campus military constituencies.
- Development programs should develop outcomes-based objectives and assessments to help build a body of best practices that is grounded in research.

References

American Council on Education. (2010). *Accommodating student veterans with traumatic brain injury and post-traumatic stress disorder: Tips for campus faculty and staff.* Washington DC: Author. Retrieved from http://www.acenet.edu/news -room/Pages/Accommodating-Student-Veterans-with-Traumatic-Brain-Injury -and-Post-Traumatic-Stress-Disorder.aspx

Brown, P., & Gross, C. (2011). Serving those who have served—Managing veteran and military student best practices. *Journal of Continuing Higher Education, 59*, 45–49.

Dalton, K. S. (2010). *From combat to composition: Meeting the needs of military veterans through postsecondary writing pedagogy* (Master's thesis). Available from Pro-Quest Dissertations and Theses database. (UMI No. 1475346)

Fink, L. D. (2003). *Creating significant learning experiences.* San Francisco: Jossey-Bass.

Fink, L. D. (2005). *A self-directed guide to designing courses for significant learning.* Retrieved from http://www.deefinkandassociates.com/GuidetoCourseDesign Aug05.pdf

Loughran, D., Martorell, P., Miller, T., & Klerman, J. A. (2011). *The effect of military enlistment on earnings and education.* Santa Monica, CA: RAND Corporation.

Maurin, K. H. (2012). *Negotiating cultural transitions: Contemporary student veterans and Louisiana institutions of higher education* (Doctoral dissertation). Retrieved from http://etd.lsu.edu/docs/available/etd-01032012-155853/unrestricted/kayharrisonmaurin_diss.pdf

McBain, L., Kim, Y., Cook, B., & Snead, K. (2012). *From soldier to student II: Assessing campus programs for veterans and service members.* Washington DC: American Council on Education. Retrieved from http://www.acenet.edu/news-room/Pages/From-Soldier-to-Student-II.aspx

Rumann, C. B., & Hamrick, F. A. (2010). Student veterans in transition: Re-enrolling after war zone deployments. *Journal of Higher Education, 81*(4), 431–458. doi:10.1353/jhe.0.0103

Ryan, S. W., Carlstrom, A. H., Hughey, K. F., & Harris, B. S. (2011). From boots to books: Applying Schlossberg's model to transitioning American veterans. *NACADA Journal, 31*(1), 55–63.

Shea, K. P. (2010). *The effects of combat related stress on learning in an academic environment: A qualitative case study* (Doctoral dissertation). Available from ProQuest Dissertations & Theses database. (UMI No. 3438652)

Weimer, M. (2006). *Enhancing scholarly work on teaching and learning: Professional literature that makes a difference.* San Francisco: Jossey-Bass.

Wheeler, H. A. (2011). *From soldier to student: A case study of veterans' transitions to first-time community college students* (Doctoral dissertation). Available from Pro-Quest Dissertations & Theses database. (UMI No. 3465899)

12

CONCLUSION

Student Veterans and Academic Success

Let my spear lie idle for spiders to weave
their web around it.
May I live in peace in white old age.
May I sing with garlands around my white head,
Having hung up my shield on the pillared house
of the goddess.
May I unfold the voice of books,
which the wise honor.

—Euripides, *Erechtheus* (Trypanis, 1971, p. 256)

Two million veterans are poised to enter higher education. They bring with them tremendous energy, discipline, and an understanding of this world that few students can match. It is said that there is no greater love than to lay down one's life for his or her friends. The men and women of the armed forces have demonstrated sacrifice through the loss of time with loved ones and spent physical and mental health. Some have given their very lives. In doing so, they simply live up to the standards set by our military: "I am an American, fighting in the forces which guard my country and our way of life. I am prepared to give my life in their defense" (U.S. Department of the Army, 1988, p. 3). These men and women enroll in our educational institutions with the same seriousness of intent.

Higher education must be prepared to better serve these students. Their numbers have already increased to an extent unimaginable ten years ago. They come with tremendous potential but sometimes experience challenging transitions that hinder their academic progress. Service to these students cannot be relegated to a single office or person but should encompass the entire campus—faculty, staff, and administration. It is a collaborative effort involving almost every office and department, including those veterans already enrolled at or employed by the institution.

This book has explored many approaches to understanding and improving the educational experiences of student veterans. Each college and university should adapt and modify these approaches as needed to meet the unique needs of that institution. Successful initiatives require a great deal of listening, both to faculty and staff, who implement new changes, and to the student veterans themselves. They also require the collection and analysis of outcomes-based data, for too much of current practice is based on anecdotal evidence.

Colleges and universities have been offered a tremendous opportunity. This is a unique period in the history of higher education. The student veterans in today's college classes are already affecting the world in which we live. Like their predecessors from World War II, the Korean War, and the Vietnam War, they will be future politicians, business leaders, and the pillars of our communities. Considering this, higher education faces a choice: do we bother to change or not? Change is difficult, is expensive in both time and fiscal resources, and comes with no guarantee. The alternative, however, is to ignore and alienate a generation of veterans. As President Obama has said, "Change will not come if we wait for some other person or some other time. We are the ones we've been waiting for. We are the change that we seek" (Obama, 2008). It is time for all postsecondary institutions to carefully consider how well they are serving the men and women who have sacrificed so much.

Ideally, institutions will recognize their opportunity and obligation in serving military students and will implement some of the ideas proposed in this book. Individual instructors, however, should not underestimate their impact on the educational experiences of student veterans. Alumni rarely rave about the wonderful provost or dean that served while they were students—but they wax eloquently about faculty members who touched their lives. Faculty can reach out to students in ways that few others can:

> *It goes on one at a time,*
> *it starts when you care*
> *to act, it starts when you do*
> *it again after they said no,*
> *it starts when you say We*
> *and know who you mean, and each*
> *day you mean one more.* (Piercy, 1980, p. 45)

The process of helping our veterans to succeed is individual and it is institutional. Some policies will affect a few students, some many, yet all are an important part of the fabric that weaves together the educational experiences of student veterans. The ultimate goal of this book is to duplicate the success of the following student for every one of the 2 million student veterans who are entering or reentering higher education:

> No two experiences Veterans have are the same, but we share many things in common when returning to school. In my case the Ed S[chool] graduate program I started in 2001 was interrupted for two years for OEF/OIF [Operation Enduring Freedom/Operation Iraqi Freedom] from 2003–2005. When I returned home to South Dakota I no longer had the finances to complete the program as I had two of my own children in college. Four long years later a GI Bill for Reservists was passed and in 2009 I resumed taking classes to complete the program I had started in 2001. The School of Education faculty had changed, and my advisor and entire committee had either retired or left in those intervening years. I applied/appealed for an extension to complete my program. My situation is not unique and only because of an understanding School of Ed Department head and tenacity and commitment on my part was I able to [continue my program]. (Terry quoted in Kelley, Fox, Smith, & Wittenhagen, 2011, p. 183)

With the proper support, our student veterans can thrive. Terry graduated last year, one of the thousands of veterans who have successfully pursued their academic dreams. As we work to provide our student veterans with an extraordinary education, we will find that they add immeasurably to the educational experiences of us all. Now is the time for all institutions to prepare their campus for veterans' success.

References

Kelley, B. C., Fox, E. L., Smith, J. M., & Wittenhagen, L. (2011). Forty percent of 2 million: Preparing to serve our veterans with disabilities. *To Improve the Academy, 30,* 173–185.

Obama, B. (2008, February 5). Speech given on the night of Super Tuesday [transcript]. Retrieved from http://obamaspeeches.com/E02-Barack-Obama-Super-Tuesday-Chicago-IL-February-5-2008.htm

Piercy, M. (1980). The low road. In *The moon is always female* (pp. 44–45). New York: Knopf.

Trypanis, C. A. (1971). *The Penguin Book of Greek Verse.* New York: Penguin.

U.S. Department of the Army. (1988). *Code of the U.S. fighting force.* Army Pamphlet 360-512. Washington DC: Headquarters, Departments of the Army, Defense, the Navy, the Air Force, the Marine Corps, and the Coast Guard.

APPENDICES

APPENDIX A

COMMON MILITARY AND EDUCATIONAL ABBREVIATIONS

AACC: American Association of Community Colleges
AAC&U: Association of American Colleges and Universities
AARTS: Army/American Council on Education Registry Transcript System
AAS: associate's degree in applied sciences
ACE: American Council on Education
AD: active duty
ADA: Americans with Disabilities Act
ADAAA: Americans with Disabilities Act Amendments Act
AIT: advanced individual training
APD: auditory processing disorder
ARNG: Army National Guard
ASD: acute stress disorder
ASVAB: Armed Services Vocational Aptitude Battery
BDN: Benefits Delivery Network
BMT: basic military training
CBOC: community-based outpatient clinic
CCAF: Community College of the Air Force
CELO: chief education liaison officer
Chapter 30: Montgomery GI Bill (VA educational benefit)
Chapter 31: Vocational Rehabilitation & Employment (VA educational benefit)
Chapter 33: Post-9/11 GI Bill (VA educational benefit)
Chapter 35: Survivors' and Dependents' Educational Assistance Program (VA educational benefit)
Chapter 1606: Montgomery GI Bill Selected Reserve (VA educational benefit)
Chapter 1607: Reserve Educational Assistance Program (VA educational benefit)
CLEP: College-Level Examination Program

DANTES: Defense Activity for Non-Traditional Education Support
DEA: Dependents Educational Assistance Program (see **Chapter 35**)
DOD: Department of Defense
DODDS: Department of Defense Dependent Schools
DTAP: Disabled Transition Assistance Program
DVOP: Disabled Veterans Outreach Program
ELR: education liaison representative
ESO: educational services officer
FAFSA: Free Application for Federal Student Aid
FIPSE: Fund for the Improvement of Post-Secondary Education
FM: field manual
FTA: Federal Tuition Assistance
IED: improvised explosive device
IHL: institution of higher learning
LVER: local veterans' employment representative
M4L: Marine for Life
MCI: mild cognitive impairment
MEB: Medical Evaluation Board
MIVER: Military Installation Voluntary Education Review
MOS: military occupational specialty
MOSSP: Marine Operational Stress & Surveillance Program
MP: Military Police
MST: military sexual trauma
mTBI: mild traumatic brain injury
MTF: military treatment facility
NCD: noncollege degree
NCO: noncommissioned officer
NCP: Navy College Program
NSSE: National Survey of Student Engagement
OEF: Operation Enduring Freedom
OIF: Operation Iraqi Freedom
OND: Operation New Dawn
OSCAR: Operational Stress Control and Restoration Program
Palace HART: Palace Helping Airmen Recover Together
PEB: Physical Evaluation Board
PDHA: postdeployment health assessment
PDHRA: postdeployment health reassessment
PME: Professional Military Education
PTSD: posttraumatic stress disorder
ROTC: Reserve Officers Training Corps
SAA: state approving agency

SCO: VA school certifying official
SERV: Supportive Education for Returning Veterans
SMART: Sailor/Marine American Council on Education Registry Transcript
SMOLAA: Sailor/Marine Online Academic Advisor
SOC: Servicemembers Opportunity Colleges
SOP: standard operating procedures
STARS: Supporting Transitioning and Returning Service Members
SVA: Student Veterans of America
SVO: student veteran organization
TA: tuition assistance
TAP: Transition Assistance Program
TBI: traumatic brain injury
ToE: transfer of entitlement
TTT: Troops to Teachers
UD: Universal Design
USERRA: Uniformed Services Employment and Reemployment Rights Act
USMC: U.S. Marine Corps
VA: U.S. Department of Veterans Affairs
VAMC: VA medical center
VBA: Veterans Benefits Administration
VEAP: Veterans Educational Assistance Program
VHA: Veterans Health Administration
VONAPP: veterans online application
WAVE: web-automated verification of enrollment
WOT: war on terrorism

APPENDIX B

GLOSSARY OF IMPORTANT MILITARY AND EDUCATIONAL TERMS

Activation: Order to commence active duty.

Active duty: "Full time duty in the active service of a Uniformed Service including active duty training (full-time training duty, annual training duty and full-time attendance at a school designated as a military Service School, e.g., United States Military Academy)" (U.S. Department of Defense, 2007, p. A-17).

American Council on Education (ACE): ACE serves as a link between the U.S. Department of Defense and higher education to ensure that military veterans have full access to higher education. ACE credit recommendations are found on the AARTS and SMART transcripts that provide guidance to colleges and universities in the awarding of credit for military education, training, and experience.

Army/American Council on Education Registry Transcript System (AARTS): AARTS is a computerized transcript system that produces official transcripts for soldiers upon request by combining their military education, training, and experience with descriptions and credit recommendations developed by the American Council on Education (ACE). The other branches offer similar services to their members. (U.S. Department of Defense, 2007, p. A-17)

Army National Guard: "The Army National Guard has a dual mission that includes federal and state roles. In its federal role, the National Guard provides trained units able to mobilize quickly for war, national emergencies, and other missions. In its state role, it prepares for domestic emergencies and other missions as required by state law. National Guard Soldiers serve as the first military responders within states during emergencies. National Guard units are commanded by their state executive (usually the governor) unless they are mobilized for a federal mission. Members of the National Guard exemplify the state militia traditions of citizens answering the call to duty" (U.S. Department of the Army, 2005, pp. 2–10).

Army Reserve: "The Army Reserve is the Army's primary federal reserve force. It is a complementary force consisting of highly trained Soldiers and units able to perform a vast range of missions worldwide. Their primary role is to provide the specialized units, capabilities, and resources needed to deploy and sustain Army forces at home and overseas. The Army Reserve is also the Army's major source of trained individual Soldiers for augmenting headquarters staffs and filling vacancies in Regular Army units. The Army Reserve provides a wide range of specialized skills required for consequence management, foreign army training, and stability and reconstruction operations. Many of its Soldiers are civilian professionals" (U.S. Department of the Army, 2005, pp. 2-11 to 2-12).

Army Wounded Warrior Program: "This program provides support and coordination of care to the soldier and his/her family through all phases of recovery and rehabilitation from injury" (U.S. Department of Defense, 2007, p. A-17).

Battlemind Training: "Army program utilizing resiliency training that assists the soldiers transitioning from the combat-zone to the 'home-zone.' War-fighting skills and the 'battle' frame of reference sustain the soldier in the operational setting. It is critical to transition successfully as effectiveness at home is as important as effectiveness in combat" (U.S. Department of Defense, 2007, p. A-17).

Beneficiary: An "individual [who is] eligible to receive medical care provided by military medical facilities and the TRICARE network, and can include Active Duty personnel, active duty dependents, military retirees and their dependents, and survivors of deceased service members" (U.S. Department of Defense, 2007, p. A-17).

Chain of command: The structural hierarchy that determines levels of command.

Community College of the Air Force (CCAF): The CCAF is a federally chartered degree-granting institution that serves the enlisted personnel of the U.S. Air Force. Because it partners with more than 1,500 civilian academic institutions, it is the world's largest community college system. See www.au.af.mil/au/ccaf/

Defense Activity for Non-Traditional Education Support (DANTES): DANTES is a program that supports the off-duty, voluntary education programs of the Department of Defense and conducts special projects and development activities in support of education-related functions of the department. See www.dantes.doded.mil/DANTES_Homepage.html

Dependent/immediate family: "A service member's spouse, children who are unmarried and under 21 years of age or who, regardless of age, are physically or mentally incapable of self-support; dependent parents; including step and legally adoptive parents of the Service members spouse; and dependent brothers and sisters including step and legally adoptive brothers and sisters" (U.S. Department of Defense, 2007, p. A-17).

Disability: With respect to an individual disability means (1) a physical or mental impairment that substantially limits one or more major life activities of such individual, (2) a record of such an impairment, or (3) being regarded as having such an impairment (Americans with Disabilities Act Amendments Act of 2008).

eArmyU: This programs provides soldiers with extensive access to more than 100 degrees that are offered online through regionally accredited colleges and universities. Degree options range from certifications to master's degrees.

Educational services officer (ESO): The ESO directs the educational programs for a single military installation or for a command. He or she advises military members about the availability of voluntary education programs and encourages them to take part in these programs. The ESO also helps service members obtain vocational/technical certifications, high school diplomas, and college degrees.

GI Bill: A series of educational benefits bills that have been approved by Congress and the president since 1944. They offer a variety of benefits to veterans and their dependents. The most recent version is the Post-9/11 Veterans Educational Assistance Act, known informally as the "Post-9/11 GI Bill."

GoArmyEd: This website is a "virtual gateway for all eligible Active Duty, National Guard and Army Reserve Soldiers to request Tuition Assistance online, anytime, anywhere for classroom and distance learning" (GoArmyEd, n.d.).

Installation: A grouping of facilities located in the same vicinity that support particular functions. Installations may be elements of a base (U.S. Department of Defense, 2007, p. A-18).

Marine for Life (M4L): A program that provides transition assistance to Marines who honorably leave active service and return to civilian life. The program also supports injured Marines and their families (U.S. Department of Defense, 2007, p. A-18).

Marine Operational Stress & Surveillance Program (MOSSP): This program is "an integrated progression of deployment cycle-specific educational briefs, health assessments and leadership tolls designed to prevent, identify early and effectively manage combat/operational stress injuries at all levels" (U.S. Department of Defense, 2007, p. A-18).

Medical Evaluation Board (MEB): "The MEB is a process designed to determine whether a Soldier's long-term medical condition allows him or her to continue to meet medical retention standards, as established by the Army regulations. The process gives military physicians an opportunity to document Soldiers' medical conditions, and any limitations those conditions might place on a Soldier's duties" (Warrior Transition Command, n.d.).

Medical holdovers: "Demobilized Reserve Component soldiers with medical conditions and/or injuries sustained in the line of duty that render them non-deployable but volunteer to remain on active duty as they are treated medically" (U.S. Department of Defense, 2007, p. A-18).

Mild traumatic brain injury (mTBI): This injury to the brain is thought to be caused by concussive shock waves from explosions, as well as from direct impacts to the head. It has been labeled the "signature injury" of the wars in Iraq and Afghanistan. Identification and treatment of mTBIs have become a focus of the military health care community. See also **Traumatic brain injury**.

Military Installation Voluntary Education Review (MIVER): The MIVER program provides external reviewers who assess the quality of voluntary education programs at selected military installations and make sure all service members have access to quality educational programs.

Military occupational specialty (MOS): An MOS is a grouping of occupations that require similar qualifications and the performance of similar duties. The army has about 190 separate occupations groupings, from field artillery meteorological crew member (13W) to paralegal specialist (27D). The Navy calls its occupational groups Navy enlisted classifications (NECs) and the Air Force Air Force specialty codes (AFSCs). See http://usmilitary.about.com/od/enlistedjobs/tp/armyenlistedjobs.htm

Military One Source: This comprehensive resource is a toll-free, 24/7 in-person and online clearinghouse that provides information and resources to service members, family members, service providers, and command. Information is available on a wide range of counseling options and military life topics. See www.militaryonesource.mil/

Military sexual trauma (MST): The Department of Veterans Affairs uses this term to refer to "sexual assault or repeated, threatening sexual harassment that occurred while the Veteran was in the military. It includes any sexual activity where someone is involved against his or her will—he or she may have been pressured into sexual activities (for example, with threats of negative consequences for refusing to be sexually cooperative or with implied faster promotions or better treatment in exchange for sex), may have been unable to consent to sexual activities (for example, when intoxicated), or may have been physically forced into sexual activities. Other experiences that fall into the category of MST include unwanted sexual touching or grabbing; threatening, offensive remarks about a person's body or sexual activities; and/or threatening or unwelcome sexual advances" (U.S. Department of Veterans Affairs, 2012).

Military treatment facility (MTF): "A military hospital or clinic on or near a military base" (U.S. Department of Defense, 2007, p. A-18).

Navy College Program (NCP): "The NCP provides opportunities to Sailors to earn college degrees by providing academic credit for Navy training, work experience, and off-duty education. The NCP mission is to enable Sailors to obtain a college degree while on active duty. In support of the four R's—Recruiting, Readiness, Retention, and Respect, the NCP signals Navy's commitment to education by improving enlistment appeal, demonstrating [that] Navy service and achieving a college degree are compatible, helping Sailors apply themselves to new situations and challenges and better preparing them for advancement, building up Sailors' self-image, and producing higher quality Sailors. . . . The Navy College Program integrates all components of Voluntary Education. While the NCP is primarily geared toward enlisted Sailors, some NCP components are also available to officers" (Navy College Program, n.d., *Navy college programs*).

Operational Stress Control and Restoration Program (OSCAR): "Program where Navy behavioral health personnel are embedded with Marine Corps personnel involved in direct operational combat settings" (U.S. Department of Defense, 2007, p. A-18).

Palace Helping Airmen Recover Together (HART): A "U.S. Air Force program that provides resources and support for severely injured active airmen and officers and their families" (U.S. Department of Defense, 2007, p. A-18).

Physical Evaluation Board (PEB): If a soldier is unable to return to his or her current duties, as determined by the Medical Evaluation Board, then the soldier's file is analyzed by the Physical Evaluation Board, which determines whether the individual's injury precludes him or her from serving in any capacity in the Army. The board also determines eligibility for disability compensation, disability codes and percentage rating, and whether or not the restricting injury was combat-related. See http://wtc .army.mil/soldier/medical_boards.html

Postdeployment health assessment (PDHA): This assessment comprises two phases and is mandatory for service members redeploying from combat operations. For the first phase, service members must fill out a form that asks questions about their health. The second phase consists of a face-to-face interview with a trained health care provider (U.S. Department of Defense, 2007, p. A-19).

Postdeployment health reassessment (PDHRA): "A mandatory program designed to identify and address health concerns with a specific emphasis on mental health issues that may have emerged over time since deployment and redeployment. The PDHRA form is also web-based and can be filled out online, [and] provides a second health assessment for the three to six month period after redeployment. These forms must be reviewed by a health care provider and any follow-up with the service member must be undertaken" (U.S. Department of Defense, 2007, p. A-19).

Posttraumatic stress disorder (PTSD): PTSD is an anxiety disorder that can develop in response to exposure to an extreme traumatic or dangerous event. These traumatic events may include military combat, terrorist attacks, violent personal assaults, or serious accidents that a person responds to with fear or helplessness (American Council on Education, 2010, p. 3).

Predeployment health assessment: "A required form that allows military personnel to record information about their general health and share concerns they may have prior to deployment. It also assists health care providers identify issues and provide medical care before, during and after deployments. It is mandatory for all deploying military personnel to fill out the form" (U.S. Department of Defense, 2007, p. A-19).

Professional Military Education (PME): PME is a series of educational courses that progressively prepares officers for higher levels of leadership.

Redeployment: "The withdrawal and redistribution of forces; to transfer to another place or job" (U.S. Department of Defense, 2007, p. A-19).

Sailor/Marine American Council on Education Registry Transcript (SMART): SMART is a computerized transcript system that produces official transcripts for Sailors and Marines upon request by combining their military education, training, and experience with descriptions and credit recommendations developed by the American Council on Education (ACE).

Sailor/Marine Online Academic Advisor (SMOLAA): "The Navy College Program has added a 'Virtual Counseling' tool to the Sailor/Marine American Council on Education Registry Transcript. This degree-shopping feature allows Sailors and Marines to watch their SMART credits transfer into a degree program offered by accredited colleges" (Navy College Program, n.d., *SMOLAA*).

Service member: "A person appointed, enlisted or inducted into a branch of the military Services including Reserve Components (includes National Guard), cadets, or midshipmen of the Military Service Academies" (U.S. Department of Defense, 2007, p. A-19).

Servicemembers Opportunity Colleges (SOC): SOC is a consortium of approximately 1,900 institutions that provides educational opportunities to service members who, because of frequent redeployments, have had trouble completing college degrees. See www.soc.aascu.org/

Traumatic brain injury (TBI): "A blow or jolt to the head or a penetrating head injury. The injury may be caused by falls, motor vehicle accidents, assaults and/or other incidents. Blast and concussive events are a leading cause of TBI for active duty military personnel involved in war zones. TBI can temporarily or permanently impair a person's cognitive skills, interfere with emotional well-being and diminish physical abilities. Persons with TBI also remain at high risk for the development of delayed symptoms" (U.S. Department of Defense, 2007, p. A-19). See also **Mild traumatic brain injury**.

Tricare: The Department of Defense's "health care plan for active duty, active duty beneficiaries, retirees and their beneficiaries" (U.S. Department of Defense, 2007, p. A-19).

Troops to Teachers (TTT): The Troops to Teachers Program provides referral assistance and placement services to military personnel interested in beginning a second career in public education as a teacher. See www .proudtoserveagain.com/

Tuition assistance (TA): The armed forces offers soldiers, sailors, Marines, guardsmen, and airmen programs that will support their educational goals with up to 100% tuition assistance. Each service has its own criteria for eligibility, obligated service, application process, and restrictions. See www.military.com/education/money-for-school/tuition-assistance-ta -program-overview.html

Veterans Educational Assistance Program (VEAP): VEAP is a voluntary educational assistance program made available to those military members who entered the service for the first time between January 1, 1977, and June 30, 1985. Members of the armed forces who participate make contributions from their military paychecks, and those contributions are matched 2:1 by the government. VEAP may be used to obtain degree, certificate, correspondence, apprenticeship/on-the-job training programs, and vocational flight training programs. See www.gibill.va.gov/ benefits/other_programs/veap.html

References

American Council on Education. (2010). *Accommodating student veterans with traumatic brain injury and post-traumatic stress disorder: Tips for campus faculty and staff.* Washington DC: Author. Retrieved from http://www.acenet.edu/news -room/Pages/Accommodating-Student-Veterans-with-Traumatic-Brain-Injury -and-Post-Traumatic-Stress-Disorder.aspx

Americans with Disabilities Act Amendments Act of 2008, Public Law No. 110– 325, §3 (2008).

GoArmyEd. (n.d.). *Welcome to GoArmyEd!* [website]. Retrieved from https://www .goarmyed.com/

Navy College Program. (n.d.). *Navy college programs* [website]. Retrieved from www
.navycollege.navy.mil/dsp_ncp.aspx

Navy College Program. (n.d.). *Sailor/Marine Online Academic Advisor (SMOLAA)*
[website]. Retrieved from www.navycollege.navy.mil/smolaa.aspx

U.S. Department of Defense. (2007). *An achievable vision: Report of the Department
of Defense Task Force on Mental Health.* Falls Church, VA: Defense Health Board.
Retrieved from www.health.mil/dhb/mhtf/mhtf-report-final.pdf

U.S. Department of the Army. (2005). *The Army.* Field Manual 1. Washington DC:
Headquarters, Department of the Army.

U.S. Department of Veterans Affairs. (2012). *Military sexual trauma* [website].
Retrieved from http://www.mentalhealth.va.gov/msthome.asp

Warrior Transition Command. (n.d.). *Medical Evaluation Boards and Physical
Evaluation Boards* [website]. Retrieved from http://wtc.army.mil/soldier/
medical_boards.html

APPENDIX C

AN EDUCATOR'S GUIDE TO THE MILITARY

The military is a large organization with its own set of structures and organizations, many of which are unfamiliar to the average person in higher education. This appendix provides a brief overview of the military and describes the roles for each branch of the service. It also provides information on the size of ground units, describes military ranks comparatively with both business and higher education, and lists the options Army personnel have for advanced individual training.

General Structure

The U.S. military comprises five services: the Army, Navy, Air Force, Marine Corps, and Coast Guard. They play the following roles:

- The Army projects military force on land. It is composed of active-duty soldiers and Reserves (which include both U.S. Army Reserves and the Army National Guard). (www.army.mil)
- The Navy projects military force at sea. It is composed of active-duty sailors and the Navy Reserve. The Marine Corps and, at times, the Coast Guard fall under the jurisdiction of the Navy, but in some respects both are separate entities. (www.navy.mil)
- The Air Force projects military force in the air and in space. It is composed of active-duty personnel, as well as the Air National Guard and the Air Force Reserve. (www.af.mil)
- The Marine Corps works closely with the Navy and serves as an expeditionary force in being. As such, it conducts land operations that support naval activities and is responsible for the prosecution of amphibious landings. (www.marines.mil)
- The Coast Guard is officially housed within the Department of Homeland Security and is both a military force and a federal law enforcement agency. In times of war it may be activated by the Navy. It is responsible for search and rescue, maritime law enforcement, environmental protection, port security, and military readiness. (www.uscg.mil)

Size of Military Ground Units
(adapted from Truman National Security Project, n.d., p. 2)

Army fields units of various sizes contain more subordinate elements (such as a supply or medical unit) as they get larger. Units of the same size are sometimes given different names depending on their role. A company of infantry, for example, is roughly comparable in size to a battery (for artillery units) or a troop (for armored or air cavalry formations). While the exact composition of a unit will vary according to circumstances, Table C.1 provides a general guideline.

Personnel Classifications

Each branch of the service identifies its personnel differently.

Army = Soldier
Air Force = Airman
Navy = Sailor
Marine Corps = Marine
Coast Guard = Coast Guardsman

All terms refer to both male and female members of the military branch.

TABLE C.1 Size and Leadership of Military Ground Units			
Unit	*Approximate Number of Personnel*	*Composition*	*Commander*
Corps	45,000	2–5 divisions	Lieutenant General
Division	15,000	3 brigades	Major General
Brigade	5,000	2–5 battalions	Colonel
Battalion	1,000	4–6 companies	Lieutenant Colonel
Company	190	3–5 platoons	Captain
Platoon	44	4 squads	Lieutenant
Squad	10		Staff Sergeant

Military Ranks

Military classifications are divided into two major divisions: officers and enlisted. There is a sharp distinction between the groups. It would be similar in some ways to the distinction between general staff and management or faculty and administration. Officers provide leadership, whereas enlisted ranks engage in tactical execution and the management of leadership decisions.

Officers

Officers typically have college degrees and are responsible for leading units that range in size from 10 to 50,000 personnel. Officer titles vary according to service, but the Army ranks are described here as an example:

- Generals are the equivalent of a chief executive officer. They are responsible for a wide array of resources both in terms of personal and equipment. They set the strategic direction for their force and make major policy decisions. They also navigate the politics both within and outside the organization.
- Colonels are the equivalent of a vice president or other senior executive positions.
- Lieutenant colonels are similar to senior management and responsible for about a third of the resources of a full colonel.
- Majors are the equivalent of middle management, and it is difficult to move beyond this rank in the military. They coordinate staff operations from logistics to combat operations.
- Captains function as junior middle-level management. They execute the battle plans on the ground, often in combat situations.
- First Lieutenants are junior-level employees with typically 1 to 4 years of service.
- Second Lieutenant is the entry-level position for officers. (Adapted from Truman National Security Project, n.d., p. 2)

Enlisted

Enlisted service members fall into two categories: junior enlisted and non-commissioned officers (NCOs)

Junior enlisted personnel (privates) are given a rank from E-1 to E-4 (private first class to private third class; E-4s are called specialists). They serve as technicians and analysts and make up the majority of combat troops (and casualties). NCOs are any rank between E-4 to E-9.

- E-4: Corporal (note the distinction between and NCO E-4 and an enlisted·E-4)
- E-5: Sergeant

- E-6: Staff sergeant
- E-7: Sergeant first class (platoon sergeant)
- E-8: Master sergeant/first sergeant
- E-9: Sergeant major

The primary responsibility of NCOs is to train and provide direct supervision for junior enlisted troops.

Table C.2 compares military ranks with business and academic positions. It is difficult to draw direct analogs between the military's structure and that of higher education and business, however, so all comparisons are approximate.

TABLE C.2 Comparison of Military Ranks With Business and Higher Education		
Military	*Business*	*Higher Education*
General	Chief Executive Officer	President
Colonel	Senior Executive	Vice Presidents (Academic Affairs, Student Affairs, etc.)
Lieutenant Colonel	Senior Management	Deans/Assistant Vice Presidents
Major	Entry-Level Executive	Directors of Support Units
Captain	Middle-Level Management	Assistant and Associate Deans/Higher-Level Managers
First Lieutenant	Junior-Level Management	Chairs/Mid-Level Managers
Second Lieutenant	Entry-level Management	Assistant Chairs
Noncommissioned Officers	First Line Supervisors	Tenured Faculty
Junior Enlisted (E1–E3)	Associates	Specialists/Maintenance/Budget/Various Trade Skills, Nontenured, and Nontenure Track Faculty

Military Training

As mentioned in the text, military personnel have a variety of training options after basic training has finished. In the Army, personnel proceed to AIT schools in a wide variety of areas (GoArmy, n.d.). The following examples represent a sample of the wide range of training options that are open to members of the armed forces:

- **Adjutant General Corps School**: Human resource specialists
- **Infantry School:** Combat experts
- **Air Defense Artillery School:** Experts in antiair defense, including antiair missile systems
- **Military Intelligence School:** Specialists in gathering and analyzing military intelligence
- **U.S. Army Armor Center:** Experts in armored warfare
- **Military Police School:** Specialists in military law enforcement
- **Aviation Logistics School:** Specialists in servicing Army helicopters
- **Ordnance Mechanical Maintenance School:** Experts in the mechanical maintenance of a variety of Army weapon systems and equipment
- **Chemical School:** Specialists who detect and defend against nuclear, biological, and chemical agents
- **Ordnance Munitions and Electronics Maintenance School:** Specialists in handling, storing, and disposing of hazardous devices
- **Department of Defense Fire Academy:** Experts in military fire protection
- **Quartermaster School:** Specialists in providing food, water, petroleum, repair parts, ammunition, and other field services
- **Engineer School:** Experts in military engineering
- **Signal Corps School:** Specialists in military communications technology
- **Field Artillery Center:** Trains personnel to operate the electronics, communications, and weapons platforms related to the field artillery
- **Transportation School:** Personnel are trained to operate and maintain Army trucks, material handling equipment, and watercraft
- **Finance Corps School:** Specialists in finance and accounting

References

GoArmy. (n.d.). *Advanced individual training: Preparing you for your Army job* [web-site]. Retrieved from http://www.goarmy.com/soldier-life/becoming-a-soldier/advanced-individual-training.html

Truman National Security Project. (n.d.) *A 10-minute guide to America's military* [brochure]. Retrieved from trumaninstitute.org/files/training/ten-minute-guide-to-military.pdf

ABOUT THE AUTHORS

Bruce C. Kelley, PhD, is the director of the Center for Teaching and Learning at the University of South Dakota and an associate professor in the Department of Music. He received his bachelor of music degree in trombone performance from Nebraska Wesleyan University and his graduate degrees in music theory from the Ohio State University. His research is centered on pedagogy in higher education, as well as on the music of the American Civil War. He is the author of numerous articles and coeditor of *Bugle Resounding: Music and Musicians of the Civil War Era* (University of Missouri Press, 2004). In 2010 he led a team that received a $500,000 FIPSE grant to create faculty and staff development programs that would enable the university community to better serve student veterans. Materials developed out of this grant are now being used nationwide and form the basis for this book.

Justin M. Smith, PhD, serves as a faculty developer for the University of South Dakota's Center for Teaching and Learning. He received his PhD in human sciences with a specialization in leadership studies from the University of Nebraska–Lincoln. He developed and teaches the Veterans Success Seminar for the University of South Dakota and has created and implemented programming for faculty and staff within the South Dakota Regental system that has enabled them to better serve that state's student veterans. He has also served as a catalyst for implementing statewide changes in organizational systems that have improved the climate for student veteran success. Smith worked collaboratively with many talented and motivated student veterans, faculty, and staff to establish the Student Veteran Resource Center at the University of South Dakota, which now provides a place on campus that student veterans can call their own.

Ernetta L. Fox, MFA, MLS, is director of Disability Services at the University of South Dakota. She holds an MA and MFA in theater from the University of South Dakota and an MLS from Southern Connecticut State University. She has 27 years experience in higher education as an instructor, assistant professor, and librarian and has held multiple positions with the University of South Dakota's Center for Disabilities. Her academic interests are in the areas of disabilities, disability studies, and consumer health.

Holly Wheeler, PhD, is an associate professor of English at Monroe Community College in Rochester, New York. She received a bachelor of arts degree in English from St. John Fisher College, a master of arts in English with concentrations in rhetoric/composition and literature from the State University of New York at Brockport, and a PhD in education with a concentration in leadership in higher education from Capella University. Her dissertation examined the experiences of veterans who were attending community college for the first time after returning from deployment in Iraq and Afghanistan. This research led to various publications for the League for Innovation and in *The Community College Journal of Research and Practice* as well as various internal programming initiatives. Dr. Wheeler created and currently facilitates the Supporting Transitioning and Returning Service Members (STARS) Project, which is a six-session workshop series designed to educate faculty, staff, and administration regarding the challenges and opportunities military students provide to an educational institution.

Also available from Stylus

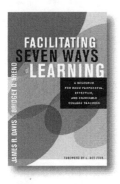

Facilitating Seven Ways of Learning
A Resource for More Purposeful, Effective, and Enjoyable College Teaching
James R. Davis and Bridget D. Arend
Foreword by L. Dee Fink

"Slam dunk, touchdown, goal, grand slam, ace!!! This book is fabulous. Davis and Arend have pulled together an exceptional resource for better understanding effective teaching strategies by demonstrating how to adjust teaching based on what students need to learn. As faculty, we expect students to learn a wide variety of concepts, processes, and applications. To accomplish this, research clearly suggests using a variety of strategies. This book not only explains that research, but also gives concrete examples and a solid rationale for each learning approach."

"While the authors note this material is not intended for those brand new to teaching, and although I believe just about anyone teaching at the postsecondary level could learn from this book, the primary audience really is faculty who are looking to rethink what they are currently doing. This book will result in seriously reassessing how to best facilitate learning."

"This is the perfect book for groups and reading circles of experienced teachers. I will certainly add to my faculty development collection."

—Todd Zakrajsek,
Associate Professor,
School of Medicine, University of North Carolina at Chapel Hill

"The seven ways of learning identified by Davis and Arend will add a great deal of precision to the task of selecting the right set of learning activities for a rich, or in my language, significant set of learning goals."

"Another feature of this book that adds major value is the fact that the authors clearly understand the important relationships in learning-centered, integrated course design. Therefore for each of the seven ways of learning, i.e., the seven sets of learning activities, they comment on the learning goals and the assessment activities that are appropriate for that way of learning."

"For those of us who care about our students' learning – and I believe that is the attitude of the majority of teachers – this book offers valuable strategies for improving learning, and will be worth reading for years to come!"

— L. Dee Fink

Sty/us

22883 Quicksilver Drive
Sterling, VA 20166-2102

Subscribe to our e-mail alerts: www.Styluspub.com